WHO ARE WE UKRAINIANS?

Georgii Chornyi

Originally Published by Jaroslaviv Val, Kyiv, 2020

Translated from the Ukrainian by Stephen Komarnyckyj

ISBN: 978-0-9931972-9-1

*In honour of Ukrainians of all times,
hidden by different names of the same people*

A Note on the transliteration:
Place names are transliterated using the Ukrainian National Transliteration system. The International Scholarly System is used for other Ukrainian words.

Copyright note:
The copyright of the original text and book remains with the author and the original publisher: the translator retains the rights to the English translation.

Author's note:
The history of Ukrainians is presented in an unconventional fashion in this book: their genetic make up tells us about the most ancient period of their history and their language and that of those who knew their ancestors tells us about the medieval and most recent periods. Everything presented is confirmed by the material witnesses to their past life which have been discovered by archaeologists.

Contents

A Note on the transliteration: 4

Copyright note: 4

Author's note: 4

Foreword 10

**Chapter 1: Ancient and Modern
             Names for Different Peoples 13**

1.1 The French 13

1.2 The Romanians 14

1.3 The Russians 14

1.4 The Bulgarians 18

1.5 The Germans 19

1.6 The Hungarians 21

1.7 In the Depths of History 24

Chapter 2: What Genes Tell Us 28

2.1 Chromosomes and Mitochondria 28

2.2 Haplotypes 31

2.3 The Molecular Clock 34

2.4 Male Haplogroups 35

2.5 Female Haplogroups 41
2.6 Female Mobility 45
2.7 The Crisis in Males 47
2.8 The Ukrainian Ice-Age Refuge 48
2.9 The Primal Ancestor of Eastern Europeans 54
2.10 The Flooding of the Pontic Lake 58
2.11 The Origin of the Trypillians 60
2.12 Steppe-Folk 63
2.13 From the Black Sea Coast to Siberia 65
2.14 The Tarim Mummies 67
2.15 The Aryans in India 71
2.16 The Steppe-Folk in Europe 73
2.17 The Triumphal Progress of Haplogroup R1a1a 78
2.18 The End of Trypillian Civilisation 82
2.19 The Reverse Migrations of the Steppe-Folk 84
2.20 The Ancient Homeland of the Slavs 86
2.21 Ukrainians Through the Eyes of Archaeogenetics 89

Chapter 3: What Languages Tell Us 94
3.1 The Genealogical Tree of Indo-European Languages 94
3.2 The Primeval Homeland of Indo-European Languages 98
3.3 Languages as the Mirror of the Steppe-Folk's Migrations 100
3.4 Mykhailo Krasuskyi on the Ukrainian Language 111
3.5 When and Where Did the Ukrainian Language Originate? 115

3.6 The Trypillians and Their Language 135

3.7 The Aryans 139

3.8 The Cimmerians 147

3.9 The Scythians 157

3.10 The Sarmatians 165

3.11 From where does your name come, Kyiv? 168

3.12 How Kyiv was hidden beneath the name Metropolis 175

3.13 The Distorted translation of the Chronicle's
    Phrase Concerning Kyiv 178

3.14 The Huns, the Kuns, the Kyians, the Kuyavs, the Antes 182

3.15 The name Ukraine is older than the name Rus'! 194

3.16 Where was the Capital of the Huns? 199

3.17 Why has the truth concerning the Huns been silenced? 207

3.18 The Origin of the Name Rus' 212

3.19 The Kyiv Stronghold of Sambatas 224

3.20 The Early States of the Ruses 227

3.21 The Ruses - The Cossacks -The Ukrainians 237

Chapter 4: What the Artefacts Confirm 241

4.1 The Archaeological Heritage left by the People of Trypillia 242

4.2 An Aryan God on the Oril River 248

4.3 The Weird Mare Milkers 261

4.4 From the Antes and the Huns, to the Ruses and the Cossacks 273

Chapter 5: A System Analysis of the Witness Testimonies 279

5.1 The Antiquity of the Ukrainian Nation 279

5.2 What Language did the Scythians Speak? 287

5.3 When was Ukrainian Statehood Born? 289

5.4 How Old is Kyiv? 293

Epilogue 301

Works Cited 303

*"Everyone must know his people
And himself within his people"*
Hryhorij Skovoroda
Ukrainian Poet and Philosopher

*"And you thought that Ukraine was just so simple.
But it is marvellous and exclusive
All of history's steamrollers have passed over her
She has been tempered to the utmost
In the modern world she is priceless."*
Lina Kostenko
Ukrainian Poet

*"My brothers if you are not slaves
Of this empire that spits in you face,
Or a nation bought cheaply from flea markets
Then tell your true name and surname.
Tell of your thousand year old language
And song like a star spangled heaven
And through the manacles and whips of the foe
The salute of our triumphs will shine."*
Dmytro Pavlychko
Ukrainian Poet and Political Figure

Foreword

The official historiography in Ukraine asserts that the history of Ukrainians begins synchronously with that of other European nations in the middle ages and has a duration of no more than one to one and a half thousand years. It tells us not to look beyond that time frame. However, our professional historians make exceptions for some peoples by asserting, for example, that the national roots of Italians extend as far back as two and a half thousand years and those of the Greeks even extend as far back as three and a half thousand years. Why are Greeks and Italians permitted to have more ancient ancestors but Ukrainians not?

The fact is that our official historians, who defended their dissertations in the institutions of the former Soviet Union, look upon the history of Ukrainians with the eyes of Moscow. The Italians and Greeks are permitted an older history because they are remote from the sphere of Moscow's political interests. However, Ukrainians, to whose history Moscow is always trying to attach its own, are forbidden under fear of retribution not only to discuss but even to think or speak aloud about this theme. The history of Ukraine's period before independence was always written under the dictation of Moscow and immorally falsified. I will therefore refer to authoritative European and American sources in my work and ignore

Soviet and Russian sources, which are littered with great-power chauvinism.

On the basis of the results of scientific research undertaken by unbiased academics, I want to prove that, within the aphorisms above written by renowned Ukrainians, giving an account of their inner feelings, there lies a deep historical reality.

In order to compile a wealth of material on Ukrainian history in a small book that will be accessible to a large circle of readers of any age, I plan to include only fundamental, principally important facts and moments of their historical path. I will only go into details where my interpretations differ from that generally accepted by official historiography. Those who wish to do so may explore, to a greater extent and in more depth, the themes of each chapter.

The reader should not be surprised that the theme of this book is far removed from the theme of my main work, which is related to missile technology. Firstly, this book represents a consolidation and continuation of my many years of research on linguistic and historical themes, the results of which were published in Ukrainian newspapers and journals, and my previous books. Secondly, half a century's experience of working with complicated technical complexes has imbued me with a systematic causal approach to solving problematic issues, which can successfully be applied to both historical and technical research. This approach lies in a critical stance towards generally accepted conclusions and in the search for the logical, objective reasons behind the appearance of certain events and phenomena; these incorporate scientific achievements in various spheres of knowledge in the search for answers at the interstices of the sciences. In particular, the book uses scientific achievements in the sphere of genetics, linguistics, archaeology, geology, mathematics and other sciences to research the historical path of Ukrainians. This approach reveals a new perspective on the historical path of Ukrainians that can clearly be traced as far back as forty-five centuries.

We Ukrainians need to have our own just and objective history, not only for the recent past but also for those ancient times stretching back over millennia. The question arises, why do we need to know it in such depth? Is one and a half thousand years just a little period for us? The German philosopher Friedrich Nietzsche spoke very acutely and laconically in regard to this topic when he said that, "the future individual is the one with the longest memory." I want my people to have the longest memory so that Ukrainians are acutely conscious that they belong to a very ancient nation and they are original so that, ultimately, they have a future. I will be grateful to destiny if my work assists them at least a little with this endeavour.

Chapter 1: Ancient and Modern Names for Different Peoples

Every people who live at present on our planet has developed along its own historical path which is different from that of other people and stretches back for many thousands of years. They have been given different names during the course of their development by neighbouring peoples and have themselves repeatedly changed their designation under the influence of certain historical circumstances. These have most often arisen due to the conquest of one people by another and there are numerous historical examples of this phenomenon. Let us examine only a few such instances which concern the European peoples.

1.1 The French

The French were known historically as the Gauls and lived on the territory of modern France, Belgium and Northern Italy. They were conquered by the Germanic tribes of the Franks in the fifth century and as a result the Frankish Kingdom was formed and the Gauls became the French from that period onwards. However, in some languages, the traces of the old name, Gauls, are not lost. In Greek, for example, France is still called Gaul (Γαλλια). It is interesting that our renowned Ukrainian chronicler Nestor, in *The Tale of the Bygone Years*, when listing the peoples of

Europe who existed in his time (the eleventh to twelfth centuries), names the Galicians. (Note these are not the French nor the Gauls but the Galicians as we currently term our Carpathian Ukrainians.)[1]

1.2 The Romanians

A people named the Dacians lived on the western territory of what is now Romania in the first century BC and had their own state. Dacia was conquered by the Roman Empire and when the Dacians' state was ruined they became known as *the* Romani from the Latin name for the Roman Empire, the Imperium Romanum. Today the ancient state of the Dacians is recalled by the brand name *Dacia* on vehicles of Romanian manufacture. Recently, a movement to renew the old name of Dacia, instead of the current name of Romania, has increased in popularity and this is certainly because Romanians are conscious that they never had any kinship with the Romans nor the Italians and that this name was imposed by the conqueror. The sole thing they yearn for with this movement is rectifying a historical injustice which has lingered for over two thousand years.

1.3 The Russians

A similar situation has developed with regard to the Russians whose ancestors are Finno-Ugric peoples (the

---

[1] *Повість врем'яних літ: літопис (за Іпатським списком)* / пер. з давньоруської, післяслово, комент. В. В. Яременка. Київ: Рад. письменник, 1990. p. 8.

Chapter 1: Ancient and Modern Names for Different Peoples

Mordvin, Mera, Muroma, Meschera and Ves peoples and other Finno-Ugric groups). After their conquest by the Slavonic state of Rus' in the twelfth century they began calling themselves Ruskyj. This, among other things, is a rare instance when the name of a people became not a noun but an adjective. This adjective, this one little word, later became a "Trojan Horse" which was so indulgently and recklessly left by the Ruses[1], to the detriment of their inheritors, the Ukrainians. In the fifteenth century, when the state of Muscovy was established on the lands of the Finno-Ugric peoples, the rulers of Moscow utilised the temporary statelessness of Ruses and also its name; swapping it for their proper title, Muscovy. They conceived a false historical conception in place of Rus', the name they had stolen, Kievan Rus'. There has in fact never been a state named Kievan Rus', it was simply termed Rus'. A theft of history occurred within which the name of the Ruskyj was used as the pretext for encroaching on a neighbouring state whose name had the same etymological root. The purpose of this deceitful theft was to acquire seemingly legitimate rights to the history and territory of the Kyiv state which existed in the ninth and tenth centuries when Muscovy was

---

[1] In this book the word "Ruses" [rusiz] (Ukrainian - Руси) means the old former name of Ukrainians according to the famous nineteenth century work "Istoria Rusiv" ("The History of the Ruses"), written by an unknown author. In the ancient times which the book describes when the Ukrainians were named the Ruses the Russians were called the Ruskyj or the Muscovites.

not even an embryo. The prominent historian Mykhailo Hrushevsky was compelled to introduce a new more precise name for our state and territory, Ukraina-Rus', in order to distance himself from the thief and its attempt to tie the history of the Finno-Ugric peoples to the history of the Ruses. Modern historians, comprehending the essence of this historical theft, deploy, with increasing frequency, the names the Kyiv State and the Great Kyiv Princedom and Rus' for that medieval state. They simultaneously eschew the fake names of Kievan Rus' and Ancient Rus'. It is pertinent to note that folk memory is far more stable than any of these political re-namings. The modern Latvians, for example, call the Russians Krievs, which originates from the Krivichs, the ancient neighbours of the forebears of the Latvians. In the lexicon of the Finnish language the word Russia is translated as Venäjä, which originates from the general name of some peoples who were known as the Veneti. We see, therefore, that resilient folk memory does not accept any of the later names of the Russian state, neither Muscovy nor the name Rus' stolen from the Ukrainians nor the artificially conceived word Russia.

Apart from the similarity in the renaming of these two ancient peoples, the Dacians and the Finno-Ugric peoples, there is a great difference between them. The descendants of the Dacians never claimed the history and territory of their former conquerors and their descendants. This contrasts with those descendants of the Finno-Ugric peoples who are now the Russians and whose appropriation of history

Chapter 1: Ancient and Modern Names for Different Peoples

is an eternal and painful problem for their neighbours, the Ukrainians. It transpires, furthermore, that the same problem existed much earlier when the terrain of modern Ukraine was inhabited by the ancestors of the Ukrainians and the Ruses, the Aryans. At that time, several Finno-Ugric tribes lived to the north of the Aryans in the forest belt between the Vistula and the eastern Urals. We have discovered the nature of the difficult, unfriendly relations between the Aryans and their northern neighbours four thousand years later thanks to the linguistic witnesses of the past. Philologists have determined that the word *orja*, which references the name Aryan, means slave or servant in most Finno-Ugric languages.[1] This linguistic relic tells us of the capture of the Aryans and that their captivity by the Finno-Ugric peoples was sufficiently large scale that, for the Finno-Ugric people, the word Aryan became synonymous with slave.

The eternal confrontation between these two neighbouring peoples continues up until the present era. Its most recent manifestation is the capture of Crimea and part of the Donbas by the successors of the Finno-Ugric peoples in the first half of 2014. The capture occurred in the same criminal manner as the theft of the name Rus' and according to the established principles of an experienced marauder. While the neighbour's house was

---

1 Тищенко К. *Етномовна історія прадавньої України*. Київ: Аквілон-Плюс, 2008. pp. 36-37.

burning the "polite green men" were simultaneously abducting his cow.[1] In the words of Taras Shevchenko, "he will see your misfortune and sink his claws into you - do not plead for the tears of your wife and children will not move him."[2]

1.4 The Bulgarians

The history of the people who are now called Bulgarians is unique and not like that of any other people. It is now known that during the eleventh to the sixth centuries BC the territory of modern Bulgaria was inhabited by the Thracians who had their own state. However, they were conquered by the Roman Empire in the first century BC and, like the Dacians, Romanised. In the seventh century the Severians and other Slavic tribes relocated there from what is now the territory of modern Ukraine, the Black Sea region, along with the nomadic tribe of the Bulgars.[3] As a result of wars and the intermingling of the new settlers with Thracians, a new state called the Bulgarian Kingdom was formed in 681 and led by the Bulgari Khan Asparuh. Today the vast majority of people in Bulgaria are the Slavic population and the Slavic language is dominant, but the name of the people,

---

[1] The Russian President Vladimir Putin masked his troops, with whom he flooded Crimea prior to its seizure, while Ukrainians were distracted by the revolutionary events unfolding within their country.

[2] Шевченко Тарас. *Сон (Комедія).*

[3] Translator's note: The Bulgars spoke a now extinct Turkic language.

its language and state remains that of the Bulgars with the substitution of only a few letters (Bulgars has been changed to Bulgarians).

1.5 The Germans

A group of tribes called the Germanic tribes were known to exist from the first century BC. Initially they inhabited Southern Scandinavia and the Jutland Peninsula. Subsequently, they gradually expanded to the south and east and displaced the Celts and other ancient peoples. During their history they probably had the largest number of names of all the European peoples, being known variously as the Teutons, Goths, Franks, Burgundians, Alemanni, Theodiscus, Vandals, Cimbri, Nemets, Saxons, Germans and many other names. Philologists believe that the word for a German, Nimets, in Ukrainian and other similar words in the other Slavonic languages, derives from the language of the Celts, who called one of the tribes then living on the Rhine by the name *Nemetes*. The Slavs then used this name, modifying it according to their languages, so in Ukrainian it became німці, in Polish Niemiec, and in Czech Německy.[1] The other widespread version that the Ukrainian and similar Slavonic words for a German, німець, derives from the word німий, which means "dumb" in the sense of

---

1 Стрижак О. С. Про що розповідають географічні назви. Київ: Наукова думка, 1967. p. 47.

being unable to speak has no convincing arguments in its support.

One of the Germanic tribes, the Goths, whose name is associated with the island of Gotland in the Baltic Sea, migrated south from the shores of the Baltic in the third century AD and began the conquest of the north-western territory of what was then Sarmatia. However, they were compelled to bypass the Kyivan territories and head for its south-eastern regions on the lower reaches of the Dnipro. They apparently received a resolute response from the people of Kyiv and one and a half centuries later they were driven out by the united forces of the Antes and the Huns under the leadership of the Kyivan Prince Bolemyr whose name is known in other languages as Balamber.[1] The sojourn of the Goths in Ukraine and the great hostility towards them on the part of the local population is reflected in the unsympathetic names of two cities in Ukraine, Zmiiv and Hadiach, which were possibly the historical administrative centres of the Goths. Philologists believe that the word Goth was perceived by the hostilely disposed local population as being akin to the old Slavonic word *gad*, which means viper or snake and this determined the popular names of these cities which have been preserved by folk memory up to the present day.[2]

---

1 Вельтман Олександр. *Аттіла і Русь IV та V століть*. Основа. Київ, 1996. № 30 (8). pp 105, 106.

2 Тищенко К. *Мовні контакти: свідки формування українців*.Київ Аквілон-Плюс, 2006. p. 282.

1.6 The Hungarians

The name for the Hungarians in Ukrainian (*Uhortsi*) derives from the Old Rus' word *Ugre* and in most European languages their name derives from the Latin word *Hungari*. The word *Węgier*, which is derived from Polish, is also used to refer to a Hungarian. The Hungarian people call themselves the Magyarok and are still referred to as Magyars on occasion. The ancient homeland of the Hungarians is located between the Volga and the Urals on the lower stretches of the River Kama. Their linguistic relatives, the Khanty and Mansi peoples, live beyond the Urals. The Hungarians left their ancestral homeland in AD 893 and settled in the southern Steppes of what is now modern Ukraine where they established a state union, a union of seven Hungarian tribes. Their resettlement occurred, of course, due to conflicts and wars with the local population and the displacement of the local population to other territories. The Hungarians subsequently moved in a northerly direction towards Kyiv. Here is a description of their journey from an ancient chronicle:

"The Ugre passed Kyiv by the hill which is now called Uhorske. And, coming to the Dnipro, they set their wagons because they moved (thus) like the Polovtsians. And, coming from the east, they rushed through the great mountains that were called the Hungarian's mountains and began waging war against the Slavs and the Vlachs who lived there... and they sat with the Slavs, subduing them to themselves and from that time onwards the land has been called the Hungarian's land."[1]

We see that on this occasion, as on a similar occasion seven centuries earlier when the Goths descended on Kyiv from the north-west, the Kyivans, with Prince Oleh at their head, did not permit the Hungarians to conquer Kyiv but let them pass by. The Hungarians would certainly have known about Prince Oleh's military prowess; before this incident he had conquered the Drevlians, the Severians and the Radymychi. The issue of their further advance must have been resolved diplomatically without recourse to warfare.

The name of the tract of land, Uhorske, where Askold's grave now lies, bears witness to their stay on what was then the outskirts of Kyiv. It was there that they established their camp with "wagons" which were nomadic dwellings on wheels. Today the Hungarian's mountains are the Carpathians.

The Hungarians settled in their new homeland on the Central Danube Basin and mingled with the local population, among whom the Slavs were most numerous. This is illustrated by studies of the Y chromosome among modern Hungarians which shows that they differ little in genetic terms from modern Polish people and Ukrainians.[2]

---

[1] *Літопис руський* / пер. з давньорус. Л. Є. Махновця; відп. ред. О. В. Мишанич. Київ: Дніпро, 1989. p. 14.

[2] Passarino G. et al. The 49a, f haplotype 11 is a new marker of the EU19 lineage that traces migrations from northern regions of the Black Sea. Human Immunology, 62, 922–932 (2001). p. 927.

Chapter 1: Ancient and Modern Names for Different Peoples

However, the resolute measures adopted by the Hungarian authorities in the nineteenth century regarding the introduction of the Hungarian language as the sole state language have resulted in the current situation. Firstly, a linguistic island has been preserved in the heart of Europe and surrounded by Indo-European languages, even though it belongs to another language family, the Uralic. Secondly, the vast majority of the Hungarian population currently communicates exclusively in the state language and regard themselves as Hungarians by ethnicity. This latter consequence offers a suggestion to the present day Ukrainian authorities regarding the necessity of following their example in questions of state language policy. It simultaneously exposes the double standards of the Hungarian authorities who have succeeded in securing international pressure on Ukraine in response to the entirely legitimate introduction of education in the state language of Ukraine in schools in Zakarpattia.

There is a sensitive historical issue between Ukrainians and Hungarians. It concerns the fact that the Latin name for Hungarians, *Hungari*, half corresponds with the Latin name for the Huns, *Hunni*, and has tempted some Hungarian historians to regard them as a single people and view the Huns as their own ancestors who came to Ukraine from their ancestral homeland in the fourth century. In order to prevent this version contradicting the testimony of Ptolemy, they state that his text refers to the first wave of the Huns in the first and second centuries and that the main bulk of the supposed Hungarians fell upon the Goths in the fourth century. One circumstance in particular gives these historians confidence in their version, this being the fact that the king of the Huns, Attila, moved his capital on two occasions when he extended the boundaries of the state. On the first occasion he moved the capital from Kyiv to the River Tysa and on the second occasion to the Danube where the Hungarians settles 443 years after his death.[1] There is a direct mystification here, as if Attila, like a prophet, showed the place where the Hungarians had to settle a few centuries later. The descendants of those settlers believe so strongly in the myth of their descent from the Huns that today the name of Attila is ascribed en masse to their new-born baby boys. However, it is a myth and the truth is linked to Kyiv and the Kyivans. The Byzantine author Priscus of Panium, the sole witness to the life of the Huns, whose records are preserved to the present day, albeit partially, provides testimony to that truth. However, we will cover his account subsequently.

1.7 In the Depths of History

The examples of changes in the nomenclature of European peoples that we have examined here show that the emergence of a new name for a people during the course of its history does not mean that a particular people has

---

[1] Боргардт А. А. *Бич Божий (Аттила – 5-й каган гуннов и его время)*. Донецк : Изд-во Донецк. физ.-техн. ин-та им. А. П. Галкина НАН Украины, 1998. p. 225.

Chapter 1: Ancient and Modern Names for Different Peoples

disappeared and been replaced by another group. The Gauls did not vanish after they became designated the French: the Dacians remained on their lands although they became the Romanians: the Danube Slavs, who were conquered by the Hungarians, did not go anywhere although they adopted the language and name of their conquerors: the Slavonic tribe of the Severians, resettled from the banks of the Desna to the Balkans and retained their Slavonic customs and language under the Turkic name of the Bulgarians: the Volga-Oka Finno-Ugric peoples, conquered by the Ruses, are still enemies of their neighbours as they were previously and are occupied with "increasing their lands" under the Slavonic name of the Russians: the ancient Kyivans, who were named the Huns, did not disappear from their land whereon the medieval state called Rus' commenced. This is how changes in the nomenclature of any people occur during their historical path because no conquering army can ever fundamentally change the conquered people who outnumber them by hundreds/thousands of times.

The examples we have considered also show that changes in the name of a given people at a certain period on its historical path mask and render opaque previous periods of their history, giving rise to erroneous interpretations and often evoking historical speculation. In order to avoid this it is necessary for historical research not to rely solely on archaeological data but to take a holistic approach towards these issues and utilise elements from other spheres of knowledge that can shed light on the past.

WHO ARE WE UKRAINIANS? Georgii Chornyi

Modern scientific authorities assert that the history of any people is narrated by a triad of objective witnesses, which are language, genetics and culture. Each of these witnesses forms its own version of that history; a reflection of what happened earlier in the life of that people. Language in particular leaves traces in the vocabulary of the descendants of historical peoples, in the ancient names of rivers, mountains, lakes, settlements and other place names which are a kind of book about their life prior to the development of writing. Genes are continuously transmitted from generation to generation and secure a repetition of the characteristics of a people which distinguish it as a separate human population, a separate race. The culture of a given people which it created in antiquity is found in the remains excavated by archaeologists. Genes are the most durable of these three witnesses, their traces "live" for tens of thousands of years. Language is less stable but its traces exceed those of archaeology in terms of their duration. It is thanks to the durability of genes and language that we are permitted to look into depths of history which are unachievable for archaeology. This is why by utilising an integrated approach based on the parallel analysis of information, which emerges from all three witnesses, it is possible to achieve a reliable picture of the past of a people and to reconstruct a historical path that extends into the depths of history.

Insofar as there are no direct linguistic witnesses from the ancient period when the ancestors of the Ukrainians lived, the discovery by archaeologists of traces of ancient people living in Ukraine before the Trypillian period does not provide firm grounds for regarding them as the work of our ancestors' hands. There is, therefore, only one option - to ask the sole independent witness of those distant times, the genes of modern Ukrainians.

Chapter 2: What Genes Tell Us

The paradoxical phenomenon of our time is that the longer humanity lives, the deeper its understanding of its past becomes. At the end of the twentieth century, microbiologists studying molecular phenomena in the human body opened up the possibility of reading extremely valuable information from human genes. This would allow an individual's genetic links with their close relatives, as well as a long chain of previous generations of their kind, to be identified. The discovery of how to read human DNA found practical applications in criminology, genealogical research, diagnostics and, recently, the science of history. A new scientific discipline entitled archaeogenetics, which significantly deepens and expands our knowledge of human history, has emerged.

2.1 Chromosomes and Mitochondria

The informational basis of archaeogenetics is the result of the study of human chromosomes, particular molecular structures that contain genes which are responsible for the preservation and transmission of inherited characteristics. Every individual has two sex chromosomes within the cells of their body, one of which he receives from his father and one which he receives from his mother. Every young female receives one X chromosome each from her mother

Chapter 2: What Genes Tell Us

and father so she has two X chromosomes which form the XX combination. Every young male receives one X chromosome from his mother and one Y chromosome from his father which form the XY combination. Therefore, all women have two X chromosomes and all men have one X and one Y chromosome. In addition to the two sex chromosomes every individual also has 22 pairs of autosomal chromosomes (also known simply as autosomes) and this structure is alike in both men and women. Autosomal chromosomes are responsible for hereditary characteristics such as the colour of the eyes, skin, hair and also the character, temperament and other traits of the individual.

It is obvious that with regard to the sex chromosomes heredity can only be traced along the paternal line, this possibility is absent along the maternal line because the X chromosome can be received from either an individual's mother or father. However, it is possible to trace heredity along the maternal line, not only via chromosomes but also through other biological composites known as mitochondria which are transmitted exclusively via the mother.

When a new life is conceived, the autosomes and a part of the genes of both sex chromosomes, which are receive from the mother and father, mingle and transmit hereditary information from both parents; some attributes from the father, some from the mother. However, a part of the sex chromosomes remains in an unchanged state. The unchanged part of the Y chromosome is transferred as an integral whole from father to son, to grandson etc.

However, this unchanging portion does not contain those basic genes which form the exterior appearance; character, eye and skin colour and other attributes of the new born child. These attributes are mainly formed by the genes that recombine (mingle) during conception. In scientific literature the unchanging portion of the Y chromosome is known by the abbreviation NRY which stands for non-recombining region of the Y chromosome and the molecule of deoxyribonucleic acid (DNA), which is part of the mitochondria, is known as mtDNA.

However, the error-free copying of the NRY through generations of inheritors cannot continue indefinitely. Sooner or later within a particular generation a tiny change will occur, a failure of the coded information caused by nature itself independently of the person - a mutation. These mutations grant us the possibility to distinguish the genes of descendants from those of their ancestors and trace the hereditary line connecting them. The information is encoded in each segment of the NRY by certain numbers of short repetitions of sequences composed from chemical compounds of the human body. There are four of these in total: adenine (A), thymine, (T), guanine, (G) and cytosine (C). Nature has created a quadruple coding system from these compounds by contrast with the binary coding system subsequently created by the human intellect. Combinations of the letters signifying these compounds (G-C-A-T) and the number of repetitions of the same combinations function as signs by means of which it is possible to distinguish the

Chapter 2: What Genes Tell Us

portion of NRY and its code. If there is single change in the number of repetitions in one of the segments this means that a mutation has occurred. If this change occurs in a boy at birth, when he is mature he will pass his chromosome to the succeeding generations with a changed portion of NRY, while his brothers, whose chromosomes have not mutated, will transfer their NRY to their successors as it was transferred before, unchanged. In consequence, there is a split, a new branch, in the transmission of hereditary information. Subsequent generations of men born into this family will transfer two types of NRY along two lines of successors until a further mutation occurs in one of the lines, which will lead to a new branch, a new genetic line. Ultimately, and across the life of many generations, a genealogical tree of these NRY portions, a pedigree which begins with the ancestor from whom the genetic line commenced, is formed. Microbiologists refer to this individual as the most recent common ancestor (MRCA).

2.2 Haplotypes

Each new mutation, of course, engenders a new type of NRY, which is referred to as the haploid genotype or in brief the haplotype (the term is derived from the Greek word haplos, single, unpaired, because the reproductive cells, by contrast to the other cells in the body, have a single set of chromosomes). Scientists have assigned symbols known as markers to differentiate between separate segments of haplotype. The DYS19 marker, for example, refers to the number 19 segment of the NRY in which the TAGA sequence (Timine-Adenine-Guanine-Adenine) is repeated. The number of repetitions of the TAGA sequence is one of the elements of the coding of this haplotype. DYS19=14, for example, indicates that during the research of this marker in a given instance 14 repetitions of the TAGA sequence were identified and the number 14 is an element of its code. The complete code of a haplotype is formed as a set of the number of repetitions in each of the selected markers. When researching haplotypes 10 to 22 markers are usually selected and in some instances up to 67 are chosen. The greater the quantity of markers chosen, the more accurate the result but also the cost of the research increases accordingly.

Each man has his own haplotype which he obtained, like a biological passport, from his father. Similarly, every woman has her own haplotype which she obtained from her mother in the form of mitochondria. However, because Y-chromosomes and mitochondria differ greatly in their biological structures we will consider the haplotypes of men and women separately.

If at the moment of conception a relevant mutation occurs in a man's DNA, the newborn child will become the founder of a new haplotype which he will transmit to his son, who will in turn transmit it to his son. This father-son transference will occur over the span of approximately 500 generations until the appearance of the next mutation if, of course, the genetic line of this haplotype is not broken in a

Chapter 2: What Genes Tell Us

particular generation due to war, natural disaster, disease, unborn boys or for other reasons. If this occurs, this new haplotype, which has not had a prolonged existence in several generations and does not acquire a successor, disappears forever from the arena of life. These haplotypes, which have not disappeared and fortunately have prolonged their existence until the present and are in each of us, bear within themselves extremely valuable information. This concerns details of the era when a given mutation occurred, and in what genetic line, and the temporal period between us and our most recent common ancestor. This information allows us to determine the origin of haplotypes from each other and construct an according schematic of their connections known as the phylogenetic or pedigree tree of haplotypes. Furthermore, if this research is combined with the results of investigating the chromosomes extracted from the remains of ancient people whose age can be precisely established via isotopic methods, it is possible to identify a very important feature of genetic processes. This comprises the average rate of genetic mutations or the corresponding inverse value of the average number of generations per a single mutation. The mean average is utilised because the mutation rate in NRY DNA segments differ from each other. Subsequently, given the duration of the life of one generation (with adults reaching an average age of 25 to 27 years until they give birth), it is possible to approximately identify the time period that separates us from our most recent common ancestor.

2.3 The Molecular Clock

Everyone of us contains, in addition to our biological passport which we can never lose, a component part of the collective molecular clock whose measurements should be used in historical research. An ordinary clock, of course, measures time per units derived from one twenty-fourth of the duration of the complete rotation of the earth. A molecular clock measures time in units based on the average period for the appearance of genetic mutations to emerge. It indicates how many mutations separate us from our common ancestor. This molecular clock, which will live for as long as humanity itself lives, stores information about the time and events that occurred during the lifetimes of our remote ancestors. There is no man-made material receptacle of information (including cave paintings, earthenware, papyrus inscribed with hieroglyphics, clay tablets with cuneiform script, computer discs) that can compete for durability with human haplotypes; the biological receptacles of information. This information is stored within living people and the remains of those who died long ago: their bones, hair and other biological remnants. This is why archaeogenetic research can extend to depths of history unattainable to conventional archaeology. The failure of historians to take account of the findings of archaeogenetics leads to misconceptions of the past and distortions of historical truth; indeed, it generates all the negative effects caused by a deficit of information.

2.4 Male Haplogroups

Scientists combine the similar haplotypes that occur in neighbouring genetic lines and derive from a single common ancestor into distinct groups which are termed haplogroups. A haplogroup is a genetic trait belonging to a certain portion of humanity, a certain human population which commences from the time of the most recent common ancestor of that population. Research of the NRY segments, extracted from representatives of peoples across the world, has identified 20 major, large-scale haplogroups that began tens and hundreds of thousands of years ago with the emergence of primary mutations. These groups are also referred to by scientists as clades and are akin to the branches of a genealogical tree for the male half of humanity. They are signified by capital letters from *A* to *R* of the Latin alphabet in the temporal order of their origin. Subsidiary branches, which consist of smaller haplogroups formed by secondary mutations, sprouted from the main branches of the tree. These secondary haplogroups are denoted by the addition of numbers to the uppercase letters signifying the primary groups, there are, for example, secondary haplogroups referred to as R1 and R2. Those haplogroups formed from tertiary mutations are denoted by adding lowercase Latin letters to the signifiers for the secondary groups, creating designations such as R1a, R1b, etc. Quaternary mutations are designated by adding numbers to the signifiers for tertiary haplogroups e.g. R1a1, R1b1, etc.

WHO ARE WE UKRAINIANS? Georgii Chornyi

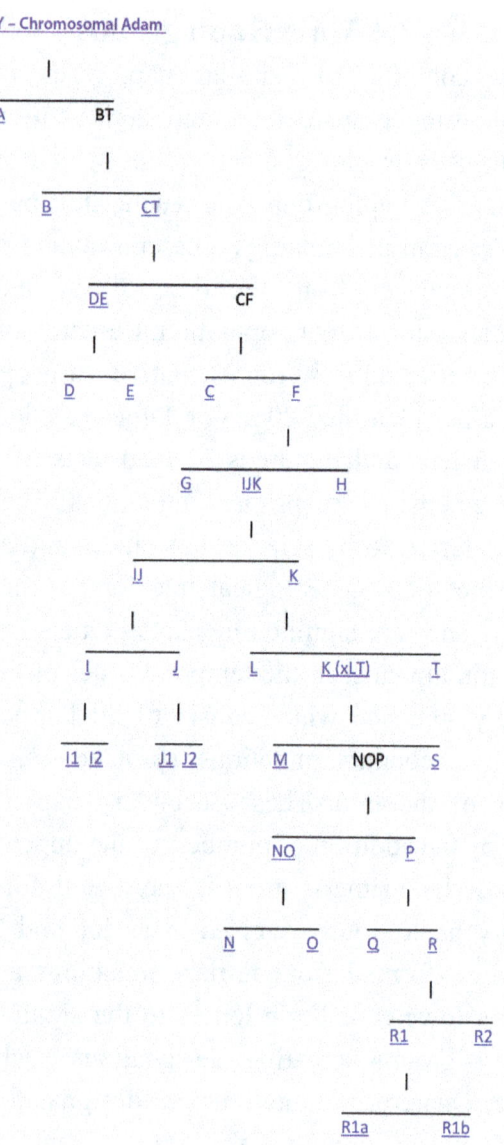

Figure 2.1: The family tree of the human Y DNA haplogroups

Chapter 2: What Genes Tell Us

The International Society of Genetic Genealogy (ISOGG) constantly updates the nomenclature and structure of NRY haplogroups and mtDNA trees as the Results Of New Biological Research Emerge. A sample NRY haplogroup tree is presented in figure 2.1.[1].

It demonstrates that the entire male population of the planet commences with a single common male ancestor who is referred to as Genetic Adam or Y-Chromosomal Adam. The oldest haplogroup, designated A, is depicted on this figure and its members still live in Africa, an indication that this continent is the place where Genetic Adam originated. He lived approximately 60,000 to 140,000 years ago according to calculations based on the number of mutations on this genealogical tree.[2] Other genetically primary males have claimed the honorary role of the ecumenical ancestor of the human race but the genetic lines have either not been fully investigated by geneticists or were broken before they reached the present day.

In 2013, for example, there were reports of the discovery of unknown haplotypes among the inhabitants of Africa that did not fit into the structure of haplogroups studied to date. These new groups might lead to the determination of a much more ancient Genetic Adam who would have lived

---

1 See link for original image: http://znaimo.com.ua/Гаплогрупа#link3.
2 Mendez F. L. et al. *An African American Paternal Lineage Adds an Extremely Ancient Root to the Human Y Chromosome Phylogenetic Tree*, Am. J. Genet. 2013, Mar 7; 92 (3). p. 454.

approximately 338,000 years ago.[1] Therefore, the question of the ecumenical ancestor of the human race will be more precisely determined by the scope of the results of new chromosomal research. When only certain haplogroups of the total volume of human haplogroups are examined then other Genetic Adams pertaining to them may emerge who lived later than the ecumenical ancestor and initiated those lower order haplogroups which subsequently emerged.

Every people who currently exists on this planet includes haplotypes from different haplogroups. However, there are many instances where one haplogroup becomes dominant over the others among representatives of a particular people. Among the European peoples, for example, haplogroup R1b, which is illustrated in figure 2.1, is significantly more common among the Basques, Irish, Welsh and Scots, with a predominance of 70-90%. The dominant distribution of this haplogroup, in the range of 50-65% is also observable among other Western European peoples: the Spaniards, Belgians, Danes, English, Portuguese, French, Germans. However, in Eastern Europe, by contrast, it is the sister haplogroup R1a which dominates and which, similarly to R1b, derives from a mutation of the older R1 haplogroup but does not reach such maximum values of predominance as R1b. Haplogroup J is dominant among Armenians and Ashkenazi Jews, accounting for 35- 40% of their genotypes. Haplogroup I is predominant

---

1 Ibid.

Chapter 2: What Genes Tell Us

among Bosnians, Croats, Swedes, Romanians and Serbs, between the range of 35-70%. Haplogroup E is predominant among Greeks and Albanians in the range of 30-40%.[1]

Among Ukrainians R1a1a, previously termed R1a1, is dominant. This haplogroup, which is also called Eastern European or Aryan, is one of the two branches of haplogroup R1a1 which in turn branched off from R1a, which is itself a branching off from haplogroup R1. Within this hierarchic structure each senior haplogroup unites not only the two that immediately branched off from it but the whole extended chain of further haplogroups which continue to proliferate. Therefore, the more senior the haplogroup, the more voluminous it is, the greater the quantity of haplotypes which have arisen during its existence, the longer the list of peoples who are its bearers.

Scientists find individual markers for each haplogroup in order to distinguish them within this extremely complex genetic "bouquet". There are currently many researchers working at genetic centres who have given their names to the markers they have found. As a result there are many markers which, while being identical in nature, have different names. The most common markers at present are those which originate from Stanford University and begin with the letter M. Haplogroup R1a, for example, is distinguished among the mutations derived from the senior

---

[1] Y-DNA haplogroups in populations of Europe. http://en.m.wikipedia.org.

haplogroup R1 with the assistance of a marker which has been ascribed the number M420. Its sister haplogroup R1b also derives from R1 by means of marker M343. The R1a1a haplogroup, which is dominant among Ukrainians, is distinguished by the M17 marker. Insofar as markers show the location on the genealogical tree where the mutations emerged which led to new haplogroups, the names of both markers and haplogroups are equally significant. Therefore, the genealogical tree is often illustrated with markers and the names of the haplogroups are omitted or have an abbreviation with a dual reference to their designation and that of the associated marker is utilised. Haplogroup R1, for example, is denoted R-M173, the more junior haplogroup R1a is designated R-M420 and the still more junior R1a1a is termed R-M17 or R1a1-M17. According to another classification system, haplogroup R1a1a is distinguished by the European index EU19. The genetic passport of this haplogroup, according to estimates from various sources, is borne by 44-54% of modern Ukrainian men.[1] We will look at when and how this became their main haplogroup subsequently, but we will now pay due attention to women by examining how to read events from the ancient history of humanity in their genes.

---

1 Kharkov V. N. et al. *Gene Pool Structure of Eastern Ukrainians as Inferred from the Y Chromosome Haplogroups. Rus J. of Genetics, 2004, vol.* 40. p. 328; Semino O. et al. *The Genetic Legacy of Palaeolithic Homo sapiens sapiens in Extant Europeans: A Y Chromosome Perspective. Science*, 2000, vol. 98. p. 1157.

2.5 Female Haplogroups

As previously stated, hereditary along the female line is determined via studies of mitochondria, those miniature biological formations are present in all the cells of the human bodies of both men and women. They are, however, passed on to children of both sexes exclusively by their biological mothers. The main function of the mitochondria is to produce energy in every cell by breaking down the nutrients ingested with food. The greater the need of a particular cell for energy, the larger the number of mitochondria it must have in its composition. These numerous "power plants" may range in number from a few dozens to several thousands in a cell. As an adult grows older, the quantity of mitochondria decreases, there is a corresponding reduction in their energy level, they grow weaker and their bodies age. Mitochondria are present in other living organisms including, for example, plants within which they also produce energy for cellular processes. The mitochondria have a similar structure to bacteria, so some scientists suggest that it evolved from an ancient bacterium which entered a living organism approximately two billion years ago. The bacterium acquired a comfortable, mutually beneficial existence with the organism; a symbiosis. However, it simultaneously preserved its gene system and adopted it for coordinated work within the "foreign economy" of the nuclear cell where it "settled". This mitochondrial gene system (or mtDNA genome) is the molecular clock which permits us to count the quantity of mutations in genetic lines of mtDNA and thereby determine the time when events which happened long ago occurred. A characteristic difference of the mtDNA genome by comparison with the Y chromosome is its significantly shorter genetic text, which greatly simplifies research. It is therefore unsurprising that the first results of archaeogenetics have been achieved via investigations of mtDNA rather than the Y chromosome. The emergence of mutations and hence new mtDNA haplotypes is identified by the substitution of one letter referring to the chemical compounds such as thymine or cytosine in the genetic text. The groups of haplotypes that have a common ancestor in the female line are also united in a haplogroup referred to as the mtDNA haplogroup. The set of the main haplogroups of mtDNA formed by primary mutations unite into a female family tree. One of the variations of the family tree of female haplogroups is illustrated in figure 2.2.[1]

Due to the adjustment of the initial informatically poor schematics of the female tree, its haplogroups have been assigned letters somewhat chaotically rather than in the order of their emergence, which is the case with the male tree. As a result of the emergence of more recent genetic research scientists have decided not to fundamentally change this tree but only to amend it and make the tree more accurate. They have, for example, introduced the haplogroup pre-JT (which precedes the JT haplogroup).

---

[1] Haplogroups. https://ru.wikipedia.org/wiki/Гаплогруппы.

Chapter 2: What Genes Tell Us

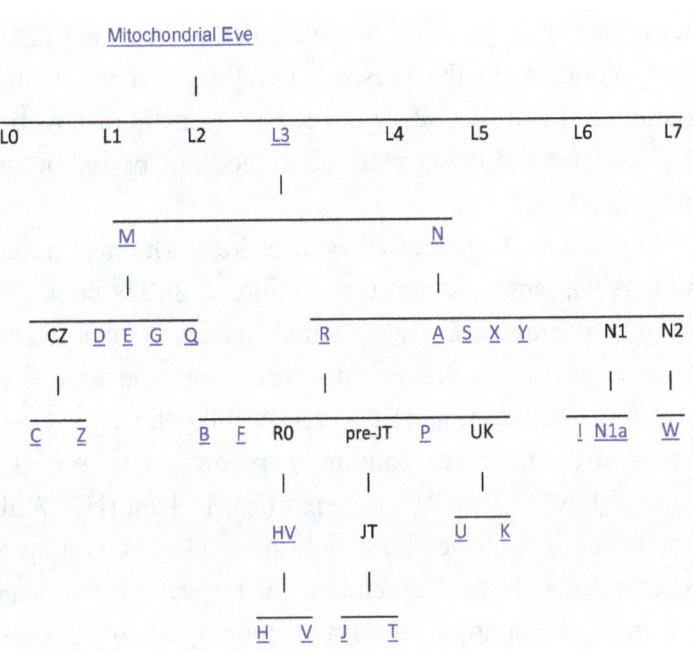

Fig. 2.2: The family tree of the mtDNA haplogroups of humanity

The oldest female haplogroups donated by the terms L0, L1, L2, L3 originate in Africa, which indicates where the primeval mother of all the people on the planet dwelled and whom we term mitochondrial Eve. According to recent mtDNA studies she lived approximately 150,000 years ago.[1] It is apparent that Y-chromosomal Adam and Mitochondrial Eve were not a couple. Their lifetimes do not coincide chronologically, on the contrary, there is a gap of tens of thousands of years. However, the most important

---

1 Mitochondrial Eve. http://en.m.wikipedia.org.

fact is that their genetic lines were not severed and fortunately continue to the present. The time that these lines commenced is a secondary issue. New genetic discoveries may lead to them being ascribed to the same period but no more than that.

The British Geneticist Bryan Sykes, who researched mtDNA haplogroups common in Europe, in his book *The Seven Daughters of Eve* gave female names to the founders of these groups in descending order from the time they were founded between 45,000 and 8,500 years ago. These names with the corresponding haplogroups in brackets are as follows: Ursula (U), Xenia (X), Helena (H), Velda (V), Tara (T), Katrine (K) and Jasmine (J).[1] According to Sykes's research, the descendants of Helena are dominant in Europe, accounting for 41% of the population, and are especially prevalent among the Basques where, as we have previously noted, the male haplogroup R1b is the most prevalent. The European population percentages of other haplogroup founders are much more modest, with Jasmine accounting for 12% of the population and Katrine and Tara 10%.[2] It is interesting that the author, without amending the title of his book, added "during the course of the action" an eighth daughter, Ulrika who, approximately 18,000 years ago, lived in the so called Ukrainian Ice-Age Refuge

---

1 Sykes Bryan. *The Seven Daughters of Eve.* London: Transworld Publishers Ltd, 2001. Chapter 16.

2 Distribution of European mitochondrial DNA (mtDNA) haplogroups by region in percentage. http://eupedia.com.

during the last Ice Age (or last Glacial Maximum). Her descendants may frequently be encountered in the Baltics and Scandinavia.

Helena's descendants are also dominant in Ukraine, accounting for 39% of the population, and second and third places are shared by Jasmine and Tara, who each account for 8%. This suggests that the nature of the distribution of female haplogroups in Ukraine differs little from the overall European pattern by contrast with male haplogroup R1a1a which is typically present in some European nations, including Ukrainians.

2.6 Female Mobility

A similar picture of the significantly wider geographic spread of the female sex compared with the male is typical and not only for Ukrainians. Scientists who have researched the genetic make up of different peoples estimate that the quantity of specimens of female haplotypes is two and a half times greater than for male haplotypes. They found that men are generally more attached to the territories where they reside by comparison with women.[1] It seems as if genetics has acquired an illogical result because men are inclined to travel to distant worlds, conquer new territories, embark on long quests and pursue their prey, etc. However, it transpires that all these chaotic male relocations fade to

---

1 Scielstad M. T. et al. Genetic evidence for a higher female migration rate in humans. Nature genetics, 1998, November. p. 278.

insignificance before the mass movement in one direction whereby a wife from another tribe or village moves to live in her husband's dwelling. Conquerors returning from their campaigns brought not only pillaged goods but also women taken to be their wives or concubines. It was thus that our girls/Roksolanas ended up in Turkey, the Crimean Khanate and other countries.[1] There was also a traditional practice to strengthen friendly relations between tribes and states by inter-marriages. The daughters of Kyivan Prince Yaroslav the Wise, for example, married European rulers at his instruction. Similarly, the daughters of Polovtsian Khans became the wives of the Siverskyi princes, including the grandfather and the father of Prince Ihor, whose campaign against the Polovtsians is sung of in the epic poem *The Tale of the Host of Ihor*.[2] In addition, people had long ago noted that marriage between close relatives harms their descendants. So, in order to ensure the health of the next generation, wives were chosen and brought from far away places.

All of the above factors have led to higher levels of migration amongst women and in consequence a greater geographic blurring of their genetic data, making it a less reliable source for reconstructing past events. The

---

[1] Translator's note: Roksolana (1533/4- 1558) was a Ukrainian woman taken captive by the Turks who rose to become one of the most powerful women in Ottoman history. See https://en.wikipedia.org/wiki/Hurrem_Sultan.

[2] The Novhorod-Siversk principality which existed from 1185-1240 was located in what is now the Chernihiv oblast of Ukraine. See https://en.wikipedia.org/wiki/Novhorod-Siverskyi#History.

genetic data of men secures us a more reliable source for researching the past and is closely related to the territories they inhabit. However, and contradictorily, mitochondria are more simply structured and are more thoroughly studied so it is worth combining research in both these areas. The British archaeologist Colin Renfrew has said in this regard that the study of mitochondria shows us the path and makes clearer how best to research the Y chromosome.[1]

2.7 The Crisis in Males

Scientists discovered an unusual phenomenon while researching the Y-chromosomes and and mitochondria of modern humans. The number of men in Europe, Asia and North Africa suddenly declined about 7,000 years ago, but there was no corresponding decrease in the number of women. Therefore, an unusual situation arose with women outnumbering men by 17 times. This fact was identified via the acute genetic impoverishment of the male sex revealed in the research. The lines of most haplotypes of the Y chromosome were severed, did not pass through the so called "bottleneck" and departed the arena of life. However, if women survived, this event was not due to an epidemic or natural disaster.[2] The most common hypothesis suggests

---

[1] Gibons A. *Europeans Trace Ancestry To Palaeolithic People.* Science, November, 2000, vol. 290. No. 5494. p. 1081.

[2] Karmin M. et al. *A resent bottleneck of Y chromosome diversity coincides with a global change in culture.* Genome Research, 2015, Mart; 25 (4). p. 459–466.

that this male population decline occurred as the result of prolonged wars between individual patriarchal clans for territory in connection with humanity's transition from hunter-gathering to agriculture and animal husbandry.[1] Let this event be a warning for those of us who are alive today regarding the possible consequences of nuclear confrontation and misconceptions in the minds of dictators who seemingly believe that everything in this world is decided by violence, because, as wise people say, the dinosaurs perished not because they had little brawn but because they had small brains.

2.8 The Ukrainian Ice-Age Refuge

Having described the general information available regarding archaeogenetics we will now focus on more specific issues regarding the hereditary lines of Ukrainians and, in particular, where and when their dominant haplogroup was created. In one of the works by globally authoritative geneticists Semino O. et al. (2000), who researched the Y chromosome in over one thousand men from different regions of Europe and the Middle East, it was demonstrated that approximately half of the individuals researched belonged to the two dominant haplogroups, EU18 and EU19 (these are currently more frequently referred to by their genetic marker names of R-M343 and

---

[1] Collins N. *Wars and clan structure may explain a strange biological event 7,000 years ago, Stanford researchers find.* Stanford News Service, May 30, 2018.

Chapter 2: What Genes Tell Us

R-M17 respectively).[1] Both these haplogroups originate from the more senior haplogroup R1 (or M173) which was started by tribes of homo-sapiens humans (homo-sapiens sapiens) in the upper Palaeolithic period 40,000 to 35,000 years ago. This startling fact, which reflects the uninterrupted longevity of the genetic links between modern human beings and primitive Stone Age hunter-gatherers, is embodied in the title of the article as the main, new result of this research: *The Genetic Legacy of Palaeolithic homo-sapiens sapiens in Extant Europeans*. The authors reveal a strange, asymmetrical distribution of these two sister haplogroups within Europe. The EU19 haplogroup is most commonly observed in Eastern Europe, but the further west you go the lower its percentage becomes, to the point where it is almost zero. The EU18 haplogroup on the contrary is most often observed in Western Europe with its percentage declining towards the east. This suggests that for an extended time period, over the course of several millennia, the bearers of these haplogroups were isolated from one another while their development followed parallel paths and created disparate lower-order haplogroups which are referred to as sub-clades. Scientists believe that the cause of this isolation was a further glaciation of the planet which commenced 110,000 years ago, reached its peak approximately 20,000 years ago and ended approximately 11,000

---

[1] Semino O. et al. *The Genetic Legacy of Palaeolithic Homo sapiens sapiens in Extant Europeans: A Y Chromosome Perspective*. Science, November, 2000, vol. 290. p. 1155–1159.

years ago. This kind of glaciation has occurred frequently in the history of the earth. Scientists find various "files" wherein nature has "recorded" the time and sequencing of vast glaciations. They unearth these records, for example, from the Antarctic ice which had been preserved from the last glaciation and whose layers reflect the changing temperatures in the planet's history. Drilling into glaciers and researching samples taken from deep within them has revealed a pattern: the higher the planet's temperature, the greater the concentration of the isotopes of oxygen, O-18, and carbon, C-13, contained within samples extracted from deep glacial layers. The concentration of the isotopes in the samples allows the cycles of average planetary temperatures to be determined.

There have been, in total, 10 periods of glaciation in the last one million years, each of which persisted for 90,000 to 100,000 years, with the periods between them lasting only 8,000 to 15,000 years. Given that the last such interval began, according to the most recent data, 11,600 to 11,700 years ago, humanity is at present living on the brink of another unfavourable period. It may be that we are under threat of a planetary loss not so much due to greenhouse gasses but a further decrease in solar activity and a further change in the movement of the giant gyroscope which is our planet.[1] However, completely reliable data that would

---

1 Заморка А. *Новий льодовиковий період – уже чекаємо*. http://naturalist.if.ua/?p=307.

Chapter 2: What Genes Tell Us

confirm the development of climatic conditions towards one direction or the other is not yet available; this is an issue for future research.

When the last Ice Age, which lasted nearly 7,000 years, between 20,000 and 13,000 years ago, began, people were compelled to leave the areas of Europe where they had previously settled because these were now covered in thick layers of ice. They gathered in natural refuges, which were less affected by the Ice Age and where conditions were more or less suitable for supporting their existence. The authors of the article distinguish two main climatic refuges in Europe wherein bearers of haplogroup R1 (M173) remained: the Iberian refuge on the Iberian peninsula and the Ukrainian refuge, situated to the north of a vast freshwater lake known as the Pontic Lake (figure 2.3).[1]

Subsequently, when the glaciers thawed and the level of the oceans rose by a few dozen metres as a result, water from the Mediterranean flooded into the Pontic Lake, it became overwhelmed and the Black Sea was created. However, we will discuss this extraordinary geological event subsequently and focus for now on the issue of haplogroups.

The prolonged existence of groups of people isolated from one another in climatic shelters resulted in the

---

[1] Великий потоп і виникнення Чорного моря – Аратта – Україна http://aratta-ukraine.com/text_ua.php?id=26.

Figure 2.3: The Pontic Lake

formation of new haplogroups, these being EU18 and EU19 in the Iberian and Ukrainian climatic refuges respectively. After the glaciers began to retreat and climatic and living conditions improved, people swiftly emerged from the climatic refuges as a result of rapid population growth. They began resettling and surrounded the previously abandoned areas. The prolonged Ice Age led to the dominance of the EU18 and EU19 haplogroups in Western Europe and Eastern Europe respectively.

The hypothesis that EU18 developed on the Iberian peninsula and was subsequently spread by humans who emerged from there is also in accord with a study of the mitochondrial DNA of 419 people from Eurasia by Torroni et al(1998)8.[1] The study in particular indicates that the female haplogroup V (Velda) spread about 10,000 years ago from the Iberian peninsula and to the then ice-free territories of Britain, Scandinavia, the Baltics, Central Europe, Northern Africa and others (figure 2.4).[2]

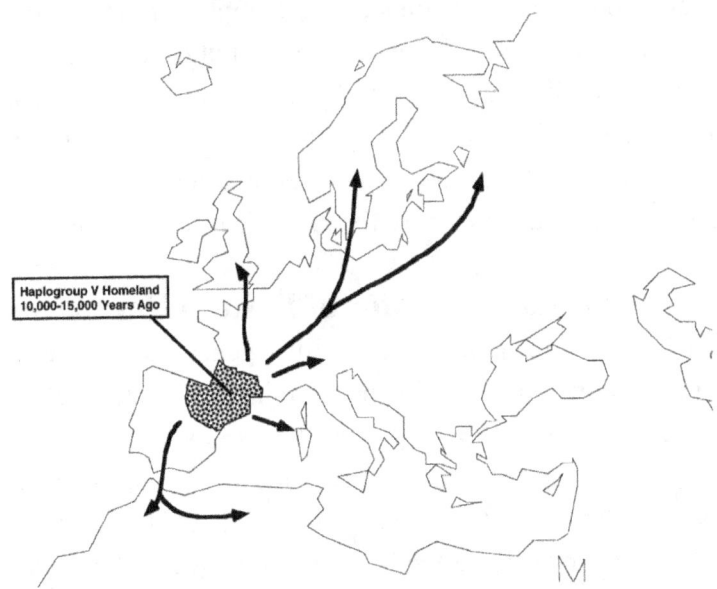

Figure 2.4: The emergence of bearers of the Velda haplogroup from the Iberian Peninsula

It is apparent that it was not solely the descendants of the Velda haplogroup's founder who settled there but also

---

1 Torroni A.et al. *mtDNA analysis reveals a major late Palaeolithic population expansion from South-Western to North-Eastern Europe. Am. J. Human Genetic*, May, 1998, vol. 62 (5). p. 1148.

2 Torroni A. et al. 1998. figure 4.

men who bore the same mtDNA haplotypes. These groups "sowed" Western and Northern Europe abundantly with the EU18 male haplogroup.

The existence of climate refuges in Europe is also confirmed by studies of the global plant and animal populations. So, for example, biogeographers have mapped Europe according to the areas of distribution of particular plants and animals, including beech trees, hedgehogs and brown bears. The map clearly indicates the link between each of the flora and fauna represented and certain geographic locations where the climatic refuge existed.[1]

2.9 The Primal Ancestor of Eastern Europeans

It is possible to understand how the genetic structures of humans developed within the Ukrainian Climate Refuge and how the EU19 haplogroup (also know as R1a1a and M17) developed by reading the work of a group of scientists in Passarino G. et al. (2001).[2] They utilised DNA probing to investigate the haplotypes of over 2,000 indigenous representatives of Eurasian peoples. Indigenous individuals were defined in this study as those whose ancestors (father, grandfather, great grandfather) had lived and who themselves lived in the same area. It transpired

---

[1] Willis K. and Whittaker R. *The Refugial Debate*. Science, February, 2000, vol. 287. p. 1406.

[2] Passarino G. et al. *The 49a, f Haplotype 11 is a New Marker of the EU19 Lineage that Traces Migrations from Northern Regions of the Black Sea*. Human Immunology, June, 2001, vol. 62. p. 922–932.

that, among the bearers of haplotypes who belonged to the EU19 haplogroup, over half originated in Eastern Europe. These included Polish, Ukrainians, Hungarians, Czechs and Slovaks. The researchers found 48 haplotypes of this group within their chromosomes and used computer modelling to map out their relationships (figure 2.5).[1]

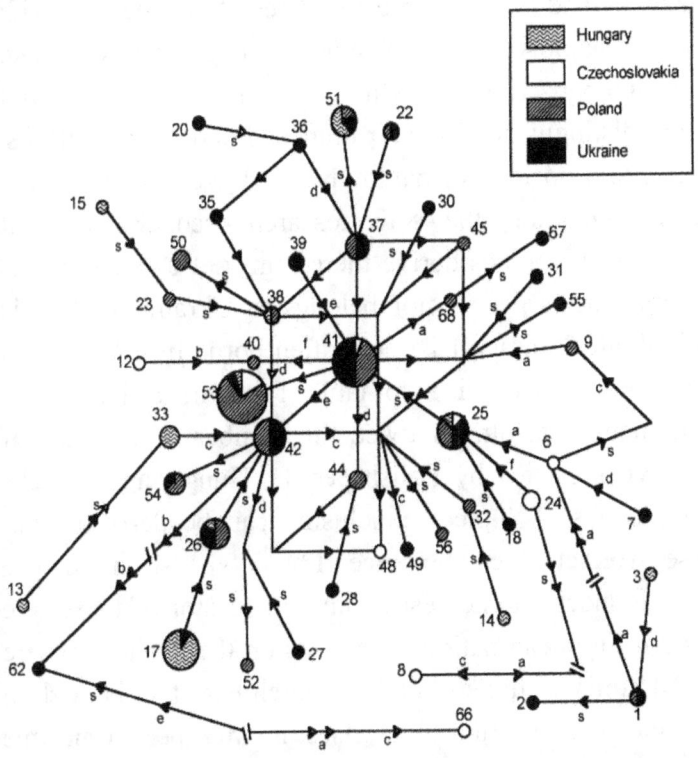

Figure 2.5: Schematic of the genealogical connections of Y haplotypes found in Eastern Europe

---

1 Passarino G. et al. 2001. Figure 3.

The schematic depicts each haplotype as a circle whose area is proportionate to the frequency with which it was detected among the four peoples. The area of each sector indicates the frequency with which each haplotype occurred among the four peoples.

A haplotype numbered 41 is indicated at the centre of the schematic and has the largest number of connections with the other haplotypes. The nine nearest haplotypes originate from number 41. Those which are numbered 42, 37, and 25 are distinguished by their branched hereditary patterns. The central position of haplotype 41 suggests that it is the oldest from among the 48 the research discovered and that the other haplotypes derive therefrom. Let us examine its sectors. The largest sector belongs to Ukrainians, that is its biological passport is most often borne by Ukrainians. Furthermore, according to table 1 of the article cited, Ukrainians bear almost twice the number of varieties of haplotypes carried by Polish people, Hungarians, Czechs and Slovaks. A logical conclusion can be derived from these two facts: the emergence of haplotype 41 and the life of its founder, the nearest common ancestor of these five Eastern European nations, occurred on the territory where the Ukrainians studied in this research live; that is modern Ukraine. The question then arises, in what period did this ancestor live? The authors assume that the lifetime of one generation is 27 years and utilise the known rate at which mutations in individual sectors of the haplotype occur to make calculations according to two methods which are distinguished from each other by the means according to which data is averaged. One method resulted in a figure of 7,654 years ago for the lifetime of the founder of haplogroup 41, while the other gave a figure of 13,031 years ago, and the average of both methods indicates he lived about 10,000 years ago.

The results demonstrate that haplogroup EU19 was founded on the territory of modern Ukraine when people dwelled in the Ukrainian Climate Refuge, or not long after they departed its boundaries. Insofar as this haplogroup did not perish but, fortunately, thrived to the present day, the man who founded it should be considered the primal ancestor of many Eastern Europeans whose biological passport belongs to the EU19 haplogroup. Over half of modern male Ukrainians bear the passport of this haplogroup and may be regarded as the four-hundredth generation descendants of that distant ancestor.

The schematic in figure 2.5 shows that two haplotypes, these being 53 and 17, which are prevalent among Polish and Hungarians respectively, derive from the central haplotype number 41. Therefore, both of them developed later during the distribution of EU19 haplogroup carriers from the Ukrainian Climate Refuge and towards the west. However, this is not the sole direction of this haplogroup's distribution. The subsequent large-scale climatic changes which followed the Ice Age contribute to the resettlement of its bearers in every direction, north, east, south and west. Figure 2.5 illustrates another interesting fact, this being that genes, in terms of longevity, are far more stable than language. After all, despite the fact that the Hungarian language is prevalent in Hungary and the name of the country itself, the dominant haplogroup among the population there is EU19. This haplogroup was typical of the Slavs who dwelled in these lands before the arrival of the Hungarians.

2.10 The Flooding of the Pontic Lake

The prolonged existence of people over several thousands of years in the extreme conditions of the Ukrainian Climate Refuge, adjacent to the glacier, hardened the bearers of haplogroup EU19. It imbued them with a steady character and the necessary skills to overcome the surprises and caprices of nature and a new problem which followed shortly after the retreat of the glacier. The melting ice caused the levels of the oceans globally to rise by several tens of metres. The inhabited areas around the Pontic Lake were under threat of flooding from the breakthrough of the Mediterranean Sea across the Bosphorus Isthmus. There are several hypotheses concerning this flood which, in turn, raise many questions. Was this a swift breakthrough or did the lake gradually fill with water and over what time period did the flood occur? The discussions are continuing but there are two extremely significant objective facts which add specific elements and shed some light on what happened. Firstly, a radio-carbon analysis of sediments from the Black Sea bed showed that the flooding occurred

Chapter 2: What Genes Tell Us

about 5,000 years BC[1] or, more precisely, 7,560 ± 50 years.[2] Secondly, there is a huge difference in the years between the ones chronology adapted in Byzantine times and modern chronology. The first mention of Kyiv, for example, in *The Tale of the Bygone Years* is dated 6,390 years from *"the creation of the world"* or, according to modern chronology, AD 882.[3] The difference in the dates of 5,508 years, as we see, makes the Byzantine system's year zero very close to the time at which the Pontic Lake flooded. This chronological correspondence is not coincidental. According to geologists, the lake's area increased one and a half times following its flooding and huge inhabited areas were submerged. The Ukrainian Climate Refuge, or most of its area, was also submerged. People were stunned by this dramatic event which radically changed their lives and compelled them to move from the territories they inhabited and embark on a new life in other conditions. This extraordinary event was engraved in the memory of the succeeding generations as the Great Flood, the boundary between the old and new modes of life as a reference point was designated "from the flood". Subsequently, due to the influence of religious tracts, including

---

1 Великий потоп і виникнення Чорного моря – Аратта – Україна. htpp://m.aratta-ukrai-ne.com/text_ua.php?id=26.
2 Shopov Y. et al. *Migrations caused by catastrophic flooding of the Black Sea during the Holocene.* Geologica Balcanica, September, 2010, vol. 39. p. 358–359.
3 Translator's note: a medieval chronicle compiled in Kyiv in approximately 1113: see https://en.wikipedia.org/wiki/Primary_Chronicle.

the biblical story of Noah's ark, the countdown changed and dates commenced not from the flood but from the "creation of the world". This system entered the chronicles although the world, of course, existed long before the flood.

2.11 The Origin of the Trypillians

Where did the inhabitants of the flooded areas move to? If you revisit the map (figure 2.3) you will realise that the northern shores of the Pontic Lake were for the most part flooded. These primarily comprised a huge area from the shores of Bulgaria to Crimea where the waves of the Black Sea now roam. The main flow of refugees was directed to the north and north-west of the lake. People abandoned their dwellings and struggled to the utmost to take their household items with them. In order to make transporting their possessions easier they loaded them on boats and rafts and headed in a north-west direction along the River Dniester which, at that time, flowed into the Pontic Lake. They did not know at what point the floodwaters would cease rising and so headed towards the source of the river and far from the lake which had become strange and dangerous to them. They settled in Middle-Transnistria in the exact location where archaeologists discovered the most ancient settlements of those people who created that renowned archaeological culture, Cucuteni-Trypillia. The year these Trypillian settlements were founded (in the vicinity of Bernashivka village, Vynnitsia oblast and Okopy village in Ternopil oblast) is estimated to be 5,400

Chapter 2: What Genes Tell Us

BC, two hundred years after the Pontic Lake flooded.[1] This suggests that the refugees from the Great Flood are those same Trypillians who subsequently, over two millennia, extended their presence eastwards to the Dnipro, north-east towards Kyiv, and southwards across Romania and Moldova to the Bosphorus. They had left cultivated fields and orchards that were now at the bottom of the Black Sea. Their longing for a forsaken paradise was passed on through their descendants and emerged in a surprising aphorism by the genius poet Taras Shevchenko:

"And insatiable will not plough
The field on the bottom of the sea" [2]

The antiquity of the Trypillian period means that a definitive answer regarding the descendants of the Trypillians could only be provided by archaeogenetics. However, unfortunately, the early Trypillians did not leave burial sites where their relatives were interred, which means they probably cremated them. There was, however, a single instance where geneticists were fortunate enough to find remains in the Verteb cave in the Ternopil region. The carbon dating of the remains, which were not a burial but individual human bone fragments interspersed with animal bones, indicated they were between fifty-six and forty-five

---

1 Відейко М. Ю. Трипільська цивілізація. Київ: Академперіодика, 2002. p. 30.

2 Шевченко Тарас. Кавказ.

centuries old. However, even this scant biological material was sufficient to conduct the first analysis of the mitochondrial DNA of the Trypillians. The research was undertaken at a US university under the direction of Dr. A. G. Nikitin.[1] The main finding was that, within the skeletal remnants of the Trypillians, the maternal haplogroup H was dominant in the variations of which were different from variations common in Central Europe and therefore had originated locally in what is now modern Ukraine after the Ice Age. Those locals, as we have noted, were the descendants of the people who had emerged from the Ukrainian Climate Refuge and were then compelled to move to Transnistria as they fled the Great Flood. The genetic research of the mitochondrial DNA of the human remains in the Verteb cave therefore confirms the autochthonous (local) origin of the Trypillians. It illustrates that their ancestors emerged from the Ukrainian Climate Refuge where the R1a1a haplogroup, which is dominant among modern Ukrainian males, commenced and where the H haplogroup, which is prevalent among modern Ukrainian women, appeared.

It should be noted that studies of the remains of people, who lived much later than the early Trypillians, from the Verteb cave also found they included less widespread maternal haplogroups. These included J, T2 and HV/V, which are characteristic of agrarians in Anatolia (which is

---

1 Никитин А. Г. *Генетические корни трипольцев: что мы узнали после восьми лет исследований*. Stratum Plus, № 2, 2014. №2: 303-307.

now modern Turkey). This may indicate that agrarian tribes, who crossed the Balkans and reached the lands where the Verteb cave is located, emerged among the Trypillians. Alternatively, prior to the flooding of the Pontic Lake, the Anatolians and Trypillians were close neighbours living on its opposite shores. It is also possible, therefore, that the maternal haplogroups referred to could have been acquired before the flood among wives the Anatolians might have taken from the opposite shore of the lake. In addition, it is not known who was most responsible for teaching the other agriculture between these peoples, the Trypillians, whose cultivated fields remained at the bottom of the Black Sea, or the Anatolians who, according to archaeologists, founded European agriculture. It was, most probably, a mutual exchange of knowledge.

2.12 Steppe-Folk

The Great Flood affected and changed the lifestyles of many peoples, including those who, upon leaving the Ukrainian Climate Refuge, began living on both banks of the River Don's lower reaches. The river, like the Dniester, then flowed into the Pontic Lake. After the Great Flood, the Sea of Azov flowed over their former habitation and submerged the vast lands which were once suitable for agrarian use and cultivating livestock. People were compelled to flee to the Black Sea and the Pryazovskyi Steppes where they developed their own lifestyle, quite different from the Trypillian one. If the Trypillians, who lived in the forested

Steppe zone, could combine agriculture and livestock cultivation and lead a settled existence, then their neighbours, similarly, had little alternative but to adopt to their surroundings. They developed livestock cultivation on the Steppe grasslands and led a primarily nomadic mode of life based around breeding livestock. Mothers and older people remained in temporary settlements while the younger, healthier members of the tribe grazed cattle in the surrounding steppes. When the pasture around the temporary settlements was no longer suitable for grazing they moved to a new location, to fresh grass. No one knows what name these neighbours of the Trypillians bore. We will, for convenience's sake, call them the Steppe-Folk to distinguish them from the Trypillians who also bear a name conditionally ascribed to them by archaeologists. However, these two groups were in fact one and the same people who emerged from the Ukrainian Climate Refuge with that same Y chromosome R1a1a haplogroup. However, fate and, most importantly, nature compelled them to adopt different ways of life.

The favourable climatic conditions swiftly led to an excessive increase in livestock, resulting in the emergence of rich tribal clans in the Steppe. These clans, in turn, developed combat units to protect their herds from marauders and conquer new territories suitable for grazing livestock. When new generations of Steppe-Folk emerged and increased, the population captured more and more territories and spread towards the west and east and the south

Chapter 2: What Genes Tell Us

and north. This expansion contributed to their invention of the wheeled cart and the domestication of bulls and horses used to pull them. When they had mastered wheeled transport, the Steppe-Folk acquired almost limitless opportunities for moving to new territories. Their military, now equipped with swift chariots and armed horsemen, swept aside any local resistance. Some conception of how this occurred and the despair of the locals in the face of this irresistible military force that descended upon them can be gleaned from an extract from the bible (the Old Testament) in which an eyewitness, the prophet Jeremiah, foretells their coming:

Behold, he shall come up as clouds, and his chariots shall be as a whirlwind: his horses are swifter than eagles. Woe unto us! for we are devastated.[1]

The large-scale conquests of new territory by the Steppe-Folk are illustrated by research of their remains. We will consider some of these studies.

2.13 From the Black Sea Coast to Siberia

In the work of Keyser C. et al (2009), DNA molecules from female and male skeletons that were found between 1964 and 2000 in burial mounds in the vicinity of Krasnoyarsk in Russia were studied.[2] The 32 skeletons discovered dated

---

[1] Jeremiah 4:13, King James Version. But with "devastated" replacing "spoiled".

[2] Keyser C. et al. *Ancient DNA provides new insights into the history of South Siberian Kurgan people. Human Genetics*, June 2009. p. 395–410.

from between the middle of the second millennium BC to the fourth century AD. Their fragments are preserved in specially cooled boxes in the Medical Academy of Russia at Krasnoyarsk University. Samples extracted from the skeletons were sent to a laboratory in Strasbourg, France and researched to establish which Y-chromosomal and mitochondrial haplogroups they belonged to. It transpired that nine Y-chromosomes out of the 10 male skeletons studied in Strasbourg belonged to the R1a1-M17 haplogroup; the same that belonged to the people who originated in the Ukrainian Climate Refuge. Furthermore, in addition to the analysis of Y-chromosomes and mtDNA, the authors of the study conducted autosomal research and examined the genes involved in the mingling of maternal and paternal DNA during conception. The scientists chose genes relating to the skin, eye and hair colour of the individual for their research. The results were extremely striking. It emerged that at the time the bearers of these genes lived, the southern part of Siberia was inhabited by people who originated from Europe; they had white skin, blonde hair and blue or green eyes. All these characteristics indicated a population whose haplotypes belonged to the haplogroup R1a1-M17. This haplogroup had been borne to Siberia from the distant northern coast of the Black Sea.

The mitochondrial analysis, as expected, revealed a completely different result when compared to the Y-chromosomes, giving a very diverse picture of mitochondrial haplogroups. Eleven of these haplogroups were of West-Eurasian origin and five were of East-Eurasian origin. This contrasts with the Y-chromosomal research which showed the presence of practically only one group to which nine out of the 10 individuals researched belonged. This indicates that on their path from the Black Sea to Siberia the men were not always accompanied by their native "Helens" (women belonging to haplogroup H) with whom they had emerged from the Ukrainian Climate Refuge. Instead, it was local young ladies who most often became the wives of these conquerors and together comprised such a marvellous bouquet of 16 mitochondrial haplogroups, adorning them with practically one single male one, R1a1a.

2.14 The Tarim Mummies

The expansion of haplogroup R1a1-M17 continued through Central Asia, the Tien Shan and the Pamir Mountains to Northern India and North-Western China. Archaeologists, as recently as last century, discovered the Tarim Mummies when excavating sand burial mounds in the Takla-Makan Desert in the Xinjiang-Uyghur Autonomous Region of China in the Tarim River Basin (figure 2.6).[1]

These mummies were the corpses of ancient people from the second millennium BC which had been very well preserved in the arid climate of the desert. It was not

---

1 Таримські мумії. https://uk.wikipedia.org/wiki/Тарим ські_му мії#media/Файл:Ta rimrivermap.png.

Figure 2.6: A map of the Tarim River Basin

only the bodies that had been well preserved, there were also clothes, made of red and blue woven fabric in which the dead had been buried, along with the leather shoes on their feet and dark plaited hair on the heads of the men and women. There was also a baby's dummy made from a goat's udder, a vessel made from cow horn for giving food and drink to the baby and many other things which had been well preserved for four thousand years. The bodies were buried in boats which probably bore them to the burial sites along the once overflowing tributaries of the Tarim River. At this time more than three hundred mummies were found in various parts of the river basin, which had gradually transformed into a desert with small, parched riverbeds that flowed into the Tarim.

Chapter 2: What Genes Tell Us

In one of these sites, which is known as the Xiaohe Cemetery and is located near Lake Lobnor, the well-preserved remains of several dozen people were discovered in 2004-2005. Twenty of these bodies, seven male and 13 female, were studied by Chinese geneticists to determine their mitochondrial and Y-chromosomal haplogroups.[1] The research showed that all seven males belonged to the Eastern European haplogroup R1a1a. However, among the women, in nine out of 13 instances, the C4 haplogroup was dominant. Various types of C4 are currently widespread among the Evenks, Yakuts, Tuvans, Buryats and others. In addition, C4 mitochondrial DNA was discovered in five of the male mummies, which indicates their mothers were Siberian locals. Only two of the 13 female mummies studied possessed haplogroups of European origin, these being H (Helen) and K (Katrine). This indicates that women of these groups did not have time to accompany the men in their unrestrained process of seizing and developing ever more new territories.

The mummy of one such woman, whose female ancestors did not lag behind the men in their prolonged migration from the Black Sea to Siberia over several generations, was discovered in 1980. She was unearthed near the ancient Uighur city of Kroraina, now known as Loulan. Her mummy is stored in a museum in the Chinese city of

---

[1] Chunxiang, Li et al. *Evidence that a West-East admixed population lived in the Tarim Basin as early as the early Bronze Age*. BMC Biology, 2010, 8:15.

Urumchi and is known by the name ascribed to her as the "Loulan Beauty".

The woman died when she was approximately 40 years of age and was quite tall, approximately 180 cm (according to other data 155cm), with long, light-brown hair protruding from under a tall felt cap decorated with birds' feathers. Her mummy, along with a facial reconstruction, is depicted in figure 2.7 and clearly has European facial features.[1]

Figure 2.7 - The "Loulan Beauty" mummy and her facial reconstruction

The Loulan Beauty is one of the oldest mummies found in the Tarim River Basin with an age, according to isotopic dating methods, of approximately 3,800 years.

---

1   Loulan Beauty closeup.jpg

Chapter 2: What Genes Tell Us

2.15 The Aryans in India

There is an opposing thesis with regard to how the Steppe-Folk spread the R1a1-M17 haplogroup to the territory of India which suggests that in fact the haplogroup was distributed from India to Europe. The reason this hypothesis emerged was probably because, according to the results of genetic tests, the sister haplogroups of R1 and R2 are both found in India, whereas R2 is practically absent in Europe. This fact may have impelled the authors of the hypothesis to believe that the branching of the senior *R* haplogroup into R1 and R2 occurred in India but only one, R1, developed and extended over territory with its subclade R1a1a spreading beyond India to Europe. So, two opposing hypotheses emerged which we can summarise as follows: "from India to Europe" and "from Europe to India". This contentious issue might be clarified by genetic studies of ancient Indians but no suitable specimens can be found. The country's hot climate and overcrowding necessitates the immediate cremation of the dead. A large-scale team of 92 geneticists from all over the world, including India, tried to resolve this difficult issue. The results of their work were published in 2018 under the title *The Genomic Formation of South and Central Asia*.[1]

The scientists utilised the fact that 612 ancient human remains were found on the periphery of Indian territory:

---

1 The Genomic Formation of South and Central Asia.
https://www.biorxiv.org/content/biorxiv/early/2018/03/31/292581.full.pdf.

in East Iran and South Asia and in Turan, a historic region whose territory is now occupied by Uzbekistan, Turkmenistan, Tajikistan, Kazakhstan and some other countries adjacent to India. The scientists utilised these remains as genetically identical substitutes for the remains of ancient Indians.

Genetic research was undertaken on the human remains of 362 individuals that were discovered and the results compared with the results of analogous studies of modern people from various Southern Asian population groups. One of the significant findings of the work was that the hypothesis we designated "from India to Europe" is not genetically confirmed. In fact the genetic flow of the R1a1a haplogroup runs from the north to the south of Asia, not in the opposite direction, and its bearers were the Aryans, a tribal branch of the Steppe-Folk. Indeed, the authors, recollecting the inexcusable misappropriation of the name "Aryan" by the German Nazis, suggest using softer terms such as "formerly known as the Aryans" or "the old term Aryans" and refer to them as "Steppe pastoralists" (Steppe-herdsmen, shepherds, horsemen). However, we will not slink away bashfully from the fiction created by the Nazis. Our task consists of debunking their baseless myths and preserving the purity, respectability and nobility of the "Aryans" who entered history with that name. It should be added that the high percentage of haplogroup R1a1a in the peoples of Central Asia is explained by the fact that on their way to India they gradually conquered new territories in the former Turan where the ancestors of these peoples live. Genetic research of the population of Afghanistan, for example, has shown that haplogroup R1a1a is common among Pashtuns (51%), Tajiks (30%), Uzbeks (18%) and other ethnic groups in Afghanistan.[1]

2.16 The Steppe-Folk in Europe

As we have already mentioned, the Steppe-Folk expanded their territory in all directions, including towards the west in Central Europe where many of their remains have been found. One example, found in 2005 in the vicinity of Eulau in Sachsen-Anhalt, Germany, consisted of the burial of a family of Steppe-Folk who died during battle. The group comprised a mother and father and their two sons aged five and nine. The boys were buried face to face with their parents, the younger facing his mother and the older facing his father. It is clear that this burial was arranged according to the custom of the Steppe (figure 2.8).[2]

A genetic analysis of the remains found that the father and sons belonged to haplogroup R1a, but the authors did not specify which subclade of the haplogroup. Isotopic dating was used to determine that the family had been buried approximately 4,600 years ago, which means that

---

[1] Haber M. et al. Afghanistan's Ethnic Groups Share a Y-Chromosomal Heritage Structured by Historical Events, J. Plosone, 2012, 7 (13).

[2] Haak W. et al. Ancient DNA, Strontium isotopes, and osteological analyses shed light on social and kinship organisation of the Later Stone Age. PNAS, November 2008, vol. 105, no. 47. Figure 2.

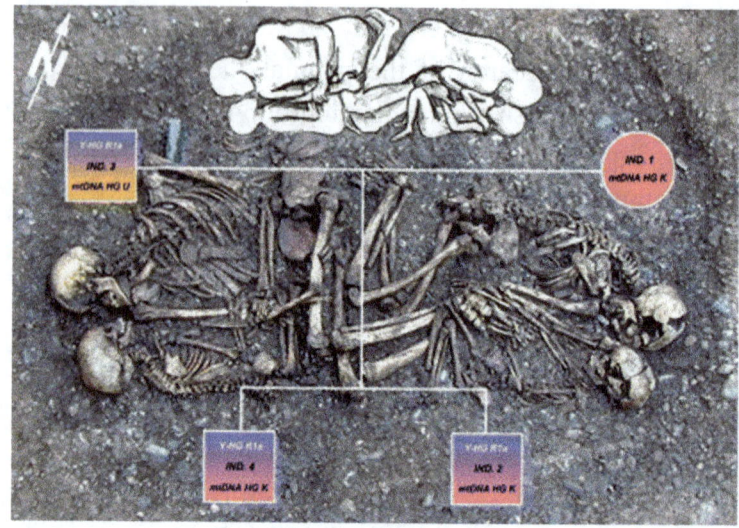

Figure 2.8 - The burial of a family of Steppe-Folk discovered near Eulau in Germany

the Steppe-Folk reached Central Europe long before they reached Siberia and China. This is explained by the large difference in the distances between the burial sites against the northern Black Sea coast. We can make some calculations relating to the spread of the Steppe-Folk, assuming that the lower stretches of the Dnipro were the starting point of their migration. The distance in a straight line on a map from the lower Dnipro to Loulan in China is approximately 4,200 kilometres, but the distance from there to Eulau is 1,800 kilometres so there is a difference of approximately 2,400 kilometres. If you divide the difference in the distance by the difference in the time of the arrival of the Steppe-Folk in these places (4,600-3,800=800 years), the average speed of their migration is three kilometres

Chapter 2: What Genes Tell Us

a year. The relatively slow pace of the expansion of the Steppe-Folk suggests that this was not a risky, rapid conquest of states akin to that of Alexander the Great who, having subdued half of the world, did not then know what to do with it. The expansion of the Steppe-Folk was driven by the vital need for new territories to continue their chosen nomadic way of life. We can obtain the approximate time that the Steppe-Folk took to reach Loulan from the Dnipro, 1,400 years, by dividing the distance between these two points by the average speed of their migration. During this time we can calculate how many generations they passed through by dividing 1,400 by the average lifespan of a generation, 25, to give a figure of 56 generations. Then by adding the figure of 1,400 to the time of the burial of the Loulan Beauty we acquire and extremely important historically significant date of 5,200 years ago. This was the point at which the Steppe-Folk began their triumphal progress from the banks of the Dnipro through the endless Eurasian lands, spreading haplogroup R1a1a and its subclades.

Scientists have recently achieved huge successes in the genetic study of ancient human remains due to the increase in the volume of genetic information that was recorded during the research and the speed with which it can now be read and processed. This has provided them with the ability to rapidly obtain data not only on Y-chromosomes and mitochondria but also on all, or almost all, of the human genome. The rapidity with which data has been obtained has allowed the processing over a certain period of more ancient DNA than was previously possible, resulting in more accurate and reliable results. There is now a possibility to compare the genomes of various human populations and determine from what prior sources they originate.

In one of the thorough studies of this area (Haak W. et al, 2015), a group of scientists studied the genomes of 69 Europeans who lived between 8,000 and 3,000 years ago and compared them to those of modern Europeans.[1] Their article confirmed the results of earlier research that today's Europeans are the descendants of three main ancestral groups who lived sequentially at different times in Europe. These were the hunter-gatherers of the Upper Palaeolithic (40,000 to 35,000 years ago), the first farmers who came from Anatolia during the Neolithic era (approximately 8,500 years ago) and finally the population that came from Eastern to Central Europe during the Bronze Age (approximately 4,500 years ago). The authors associate the last group of ancestors with the archaeological cultures of Corded-Ware and Yamna and refer to it as the "population with an eastern pedigree" or simply "the population of the Steppe". (We referred to this population as the Steppe-Folk in the present text.) The article demonstrates that after the defining boundary dates (4,500 years ago) significant changes occurred in

---

1 Haak W. et al. Massive Migration from the Steppe Was a Source for Indo-European Languages in Europe. Nature, 2015, vol. 522, no. 7555, p. 207–211.

Chapter 2: What Genes Tell Us

European genomes: genes which signified Steppe-Folk origins were found in each of the 69 individuals studied who lived after that date but were absent in all the individuals who lived prior to that date. This indicates a mass migration from the Steppe to Central and Northern Europe after 2,500 BC, i.e. seven centuries after the date we have determined when their multi-vector resettlement commenced. However, the work of Swedish geneticists from Uppsala University shows that these mass migrations were mainly undertaken by men: on average there was only one woman per 10 men in the migration.[1]. The traces of this migration are particularly noticeable in the northern regions of Europe. Among modern European nations the largest contributions of Steppe-Folk genes are possessed by the genomes of Norwegians, Lithuanians, Estonians, Icelanders and other northern peoples.[2] The lowest percentage of Steppe-Folk genes is found on the island of Sardinia which, obviously, was not part of the planned expansion of the Steppe-Folk. Ukrainians, on whose territory the dominant haplogroup of the Steppe-Folk originated, now occupy an average position with their genomes bearing about 50% of the joint contribution of Steppe-Folk and Trypillians; carriers of that same dominant haplogroup R1a1a.

---

1 Genetic data show mainly men migrated from the Pontic Steppe to Europe 5,000 years ago, PHYS.ORG, February 21, 2017.
2 Haak W. et al. 2015. Figure 3.

2.17 The Triumphal Progress of Haplogroup R1a1a

If we begin with the start date we have calculated for the Steppe-Folk's migration of 3,200 BC we see that they unceasingly conquered vast territories stretching from Western Europe to Western Siberia and Scandinavia to North Africa. They distributed their dominant haplogroup R1a1a to these territories and its new subclades formed during these migrations. It is understood that some of the Steppe-Folk did not depart with the others for new lands and remained among the subjugated peoples in the higher echelons. They imposed their rules, language, religions and customs upon the conquered. The enormous influence of the Steppe-Folk upon the destiny of European peoples is eloquently testified to by the title of a book written by the American scientist David Anthony: *The Horse, the Wheel, and Language: How Bronze-Age Riders from the Eurasian Steppe Shaped the Modern World.*[1] The result of the millennial activity of the Steppe-Folk on the territory of Eurasia is shown by a map of the distribution of haplogroup R1a1a (figure 2.9).[2]

The darker spots on the map, located on the territories of India, Afghanistan, Central Asia, Western Siberia and eastern and north-eastern parts of Europe, indicate the

---

1 Anthony D. W. The Horse, the Wheel, and Language: How Bronze-Age Riders from the Eurasian Steppe Shaped the Modern World. Princeton Univ. Press, 2007.
2 Khan R. R1a1a conquers the world in a few pulses. Discover, October 31, 2012.

Chapter 2: What Genes Tell Us

areas where this haplogroup occurs most frequently at present. Indeed, the frequency in these places even exceeds that in the northern Black Sea area where it originated. The map demonstrates only one dimension of the intensity of the Steppe-Folk's influence upon the local population, this being how they massively transmitted their Y chromosome to the local population. However, it cannot reflect their influence on the appearance, character, skin colour, eyes and other particularities of the local population which are formed by other (autosomal) sections of the genome.

By presenting peoples with the same haplogroup it is often speculated upon this basis that they are the same people. The absurdity of this approach is apparent. Among the modern Pashtuns of Afghanistan and the Polish in Europe, for example, haplogroup R1a1a occurs with above 50% frequency, but this does not mean they are the one and the same people. It only signifies that the Steppe-Folk did a good job in these areas. Yet another speculative prank, a transgression not infrequently committed by Russian publications, is the substitution of haplogroup R1a1a by the older haplogroup R1a in scientific articles. In consequence, a far broader circle of peoples and their territory are examined groundlessly by comparison with haplogroup R1a1a, thereby losing information and the character for an individual people and nullifying their particularity. This trick is akin to "looking through binoculars backwards" by means of which you seem to see more but see less distinctly; in this case the distinctions between peoples. Russians deploy this trick, for example,

WHO ARE WE UKRAINIANS?   Georgii Chornyi

Figure 2.9: A map of the distribution of haplogroup R1a1a

when trying to genetically prove the existence of the so-called cradle of the three "Fraternal" peoples.

The reason for the extraordinary prevalence of haplogroup R1a1a lies in the character of its bearers which were formed within the conditions of a strict, nomadic existence. There is a long standing, ingrained misconception in historical science that nomadism is something that is regressive and flawed. By contrast, odes have been written in praise of a settled, agricultural existence. However, the truth lies somewhere in the middle because the Steppe-Folk, when resolving life's problems, had to demonstrate no less ingenuity than the settled farmers. Here is a typical example which illustrates the remarkable skill possessed by the Steppe-Folk for adapting to the difficult conditions of nomadic life and solving the nutritional problem of their long campaigns.

Chapter 2: What Genes Tell Us

In late autumn, when the first frosts arrived, the Steppe-Folk cut the meat from slaughtered animals (horses and oxen) into thin lengths and hung it up to dry in the frosty air like linen. The stomachs of the animals were cleaned, washed and also dried. The dried strips of meat were then cut into smaller pieces and pulverised in a mortar. Spices were also dried and crushed and then added to meat. The resulting meat and spice powder was then poured into the dry stomach which was tightly tied shut. Almost all the meat of the slaughtered animal was processed like this. The powder-packed stomach was fastened to a horse-rider's saddle and always accompanied him on the road. All that was needed then was to boil some water and throw in a few spoons of powder to create a read-to-eat, nutritious, tasty broth.[1] They manage this without a fridge, kitchen or any logistics! Bravo, Steppe-Folk!

Subsequently, a well-educated Roman military officer, Ammianus Marcellinus, who lived in the fourth century AD showed his incompetence when describing the Huns as one of the groups descended from the Steppe-Folk in his book beneath the tentative title *Acts*. He could not imagine how the Huns managed in their long campaigns and wrote some twisted nonsense as if the Huns ate raw meat, preserving it between the horse's back and the rider's thighs. He had a bit of a clue but not much!

---

1 Боргардт А. А. *Бич Божий (Аттила – 5-й каган гуннов и его время)*. Донецк: Изд-во Донецк. физ.-техн. ин-та им. А. П. Галкина НАН Украины, 1998. p. 11.

2.18 The End of Trypillian Civilisation

We calculated that the date when the Steppe-Folk commenced their migration was approximately 5,200 years ago in the thirty-second century BC, which is only five centuries before the date that the Trypillian civilisation ended in the twenty-seventh century BC.[1] It is extremely likely that these five centuries were sufficient for the Steppe-Folk to conquer Trypillia and bring its civilisations to an end, and this assumption is confirmed by archaeological findings. The early Trypillian protocities of the fourth millennia BC located by the modern villages of Talyanka, Maidanetske and Legedzyne in Cherkasy oblast had no external fortifications to ward off enemies. However, a later Trypillian settlement by Kyiv in the third millennium BC had the appearance of a fortified settlement.[2] It is apparent that the Kyivan Trypillians already knew of the substantial threat that was approaching from the south-east and were preparing to defend themselves. However, they did not withstand the assault, the Steppe-Folk conquered them and went further into Europe (figure 2.10).[3]

---

1 Відейко М. Ю. *Трипільська цивілізація*. Київ: Академперіодика, 2002. p 31.

2 Климовский С. И. *Замковая гора в Киеве: пять тысяч лет истории* / предисл. М. В. Поповича. Киев : Стилос, 2005. p. 11.

3 Reich D. Ancient DNA Suggests Steppe Migrations Spread Indo-European Languages, Proceedings of the American Philosophical Society, no. 1, March 2018, vol. 162. Figure 15.

Chapter 2: What Genes Tell Us

Figure 2.10: The Steppe-Folk subdued the Trypillians and headed for Central Europe

So the blood brothers, the Trypillians and the Steppe-Folk, the descendants of common ancestors who once emerged together from the Ukrainian Climate Refuge encountered each other as foes a few thousand years later on the land of their ancestors and the Steppe-Folk triumphed in this duel. Their way of life turned out to be more resilient than that of the Trypillians, who were compelled to submit and accept the victors' terms. However, the substantial experience of the Trypillians in house building, pottery, metal work and their combination of agriculture and animal husbandry enriched and changed the life of the Steppe-Folk which raised the overall level of their culture and economy. The first state we know of, from written sources, Cimmeria arose on the territory of Ukraine was formed on the basis of the achievements of the Trypillians and Steppe-Folk. The Greeks called its population the Cimmerians (Κίμμέριοι), in Assyrian cuneiform they were known as the Hymirams and in the Old Testament the Gomer.[1] Our Kyivan chronicler Nestor referred to their descendants at the time of Rus' as the Sivery (Сѣвера).[2]

2.19 The Reverse Migrations of the Steppe-Folk

The written history of Ukrainians therefore begins with the state of Cimmeria and the scientists of the ancient world left fragments of this story in their works, including Hesiod, Herodotus, Strabo, Ptolemy, and others. In contrast to the artificial general name of Steppe-Folk, a mass of actual designations for peoples and tribes appear in the written sources. It is difficult, therefore, to determine to what race, to what haplogroup, they refer. In the works of these ancient authors, for example, the name of a people called the Scythians frequently occurs. Who were this people genetically? Whose ancestors were they? Let us examine in more detail how the process of Steppe migration, which was far from single vectored, occurred in order to address these issues.

When searching for territories suitable for a nomadic lifestyle, and over a period of time measured by more than a single century, the Steppe-Folk, or more precisely a portion of them, formed a separate people with a name

---

1 Книга Буття. X: 2, 3.
2 Повість врем'яних літ: літопис (за Іпатським списком) / пер. з давньоруської, післяслово, комент. В. В. Яременка. Київ: Рад. письменник, 1990. p. 12.

Chapter 2: What Genes Tell Us

either self ascribed or applied by their neighbours and migrated in the opposite direction towards their ancestral homeland. The descendants of the Steppe-Folk, who had not gone to new lands but remained, then encountered them as enemies that invaded their land. There were savage battles again to assert a people's supremacy and possess territory. There were several such reverse migrations by the Steppe-Folk and some of these were recorded by ancient historians in their works. However, there is unfortunately no written information about earlier events nor about when and how and in what waves the Steppe-Folk moved toward developing the Asian territories. In brief, the ancient historians only received information about the "arrival" of the Steppe-Folk. They could not glean details of their "departure" because in those early days writing simply did not exist. Therefore, we encounter a contradiction in Herodotus: on the one hand he says that the Scythians came from the east, from the Caspian Steppes, and on the other hand, according to his information, Scythian ploughers and farmers lived in the Dnipro region. They could not, having come from the east to the Dnipro area, suddenly be transformed from nomads to farmers. It is more likely that the Scythian ploughers and farmers were indigenous people, descendants of Trypillians who had never left their land. Furthermore, those who lived further to the east, as far as Southern Siberia, were considered Scythians and were named in the Turkic language as the Saka, Shakas, etc. The question of which Scythian tribes lived on the territories of modern Ukraine might be illuminated by genetic studies of their remains which have been found in the Dnipro region. Unfortunately, no such research has been undertaken. This issue will therefore be considered in the following section with the assistance of another historical witness - languages.

2.20 The Ancient Homeland of the Slavs

The question of the origin of those later inhabitants of Eastern Europe known as the Slavs is extremely complex and confused. The polemical discussions of scholars regarding where the Slavs originated and the whereabouts of their ancestral homeland have continued unabated for two hundred years. There is practically no hypothesis which has not been advanced by historians, archaeologists, anthropologists, linguists and ethnographers. However, the issue has remained unresolved since the time of Nestor the Chronicler who located the ancestral Slavic homeland on the upper and lower Danube. According to written sources, the world became aware of the Slavs in the sixth century AD when their expansion captured almost half of Europe. A paradoxical situation occurred because until that time no one knew anything about the Slavs, there were no records of them in the historical chronicles until suddenly there were countless numbers of them upon European territory. Where did they come from? Historians often have a stereotypical view of such issues and assume that a particular people came from somewhere. Then they begin "bringing" a people, according to various hypotheses, from

Chapter 2: What Genes Tell Us

everywhere: Asia, the Baltics, the Pripyat, the Vistula, the Oder, the Danube and other locations.[1] Two main hypotheses regarding the origin of the Slavs have recently become established among linguists. The first locates the Slavic homeland between the Vistula and the Oder, on the territory of modern Poland, the second situates it on the Central Dnipro Basin in Ukraine. The first hypothesis is based mainly on the analysis of the names of rivers in the area, the second hypothesis is more complex and uses the findings of comparative linguistics, botany, ethnology, and other sciences.[2]

A group of geneticists whose findings are presented in Rebala K. et al. (2007) sought to resolve this issue and researched the mutual genetic relationship of each pair of Slavic peoples.[3] Their research methods were based on special computer programmes which assisted with the calculation of the generic distance between each pair of Slavic nations. According to the results, the peoples who are genetically closest to Ukrainians are the Slovakians. The research showed that the southern Slavs (Bulgarians, Macedonians, Serbs, Bosnians, a section of the Croats), who are genetically distant from the rest of the Slavs,

---

1 Кобычев А. М. В поисках прародины славян. Москва : Наука, 1973. p. 168.
2 Schenker A. M. The dawn of Slavic: an introduction to Slavic Philology. New Haven – London: Yale University Press, 1995. p. 1–8.
3 Rebala K. et al. Y-STR variation among Slavs: evidence for the Slavic homeland in the middle Dnieper basin, Journal of Human Genetics 52, 2007, vol. 52, p. 406–414.

and at a much greater genetic distance internally than the western and eastern Slavs. It transpired also that the Polish, who are genetically closest to Ukrainians, are more distant from other Slavic nations. The article shows that the Y chromosome of Ukrainians has the largest number of close genetic distances with other Slavic peoples (up to 10) while the Polish have no more than three: one with Ukrainians and two, less close, with Slovaks and Lusatians (Sorbs). It is obvious that the migration routes of the Slavs began from the location where the largest number of genetically close pairings were created. Insofar as the largest number of such pairings, as shown by the results of the research, belong to Ukrainians, the location they live now is where the Slavs arose. The results of the Y-chromosomal studies of modern Slavic peoples therefore confirm that the second hypothesis is correct and that the Central Dnipro Basin is their cradle. Their rapid expansion which subsequently covered half of Europe began there.

The linguistic witnesses of the past in the form of the oldest known Slavonic names of rivers in the forest Steppe zone between the Dniester and the Dnipro help to establish the time of the Slavs' origin. The steady heredity of archaeological cultures of this area also assist and signify that the same related tribes lived in this area from the end of the Bronze Age up to the period of the Zarubynets tribes. It is, therefore, most likely that at the end of the first millennia BC when the Zarubynets culture already existed, the Slavs began settling from the Central Dnipro Basin to the north, south, west and south-west, although the first surviving reports of them, as we have noted, date from a more recent time in the sixth century.[1]

2.21 Ukrainians Through the Eyes of Archaeogenetics

Having analysed the studies in this section we can draw the following conclusions:

1. The main factors that significantly affected the development and formation of current European nations, including Ukrainians, were two natural disasters: the Last Glacial Maximum, which lasted for approximately 7,000 years (between 20,000 and 13,000 years ago), and the Great Flood which caused the formation of the Black and Azov seas (approximately 7,500 years ago). These two planetary-scale events became the impetus for the search and introduction of new technologies for human survival in extreme conditions before the emergence of two advanced civilisations, created by Trypillians and the Steppe-Folks respectively. The most resilient of these proved to be the Steppe-Folks' civilisation, which spread across the vast spaces of Eurasia and ended the Trypillian civilisation.

2. Ukrainians, like most European peoples, are the descendants of three main groups of ancestors who in various times came to the territory of modern Ukraine

---

1 История Украинской ССР. Киев: «Наукова думка», 1981. Т. 1. p. 139.

and gradually displaced their predecessors. The first group were the hunter-gatherers of 40,000 to 35,000 years ago, the second were the Anatolian farmers from modern Turkey who came about 8,500 years ago and the third were the Trypillians and Steppe-Folk who came about 7,000 years ago, although the Trypillians were the first to arrive. The first and second ancestral groups left modern Ukrainians with about 28% of their genetic make-up, the third left a more significant contribution of about 44%.[1]

3. The fact that the dominant haplogroup R1a1a originated from nowhere else but Ukraine suggests that it was not introduced externally and that some of its bearers did not migrate but remained on Ukrainian territory. This ensured the continuous transmission of this haplogroup from generation to generation until its bearers came to be called Ukrainians. This fact signifies the continuous, unbroken residence of Ukrainian ancestors on this land, which commenced about 10,000 years ago when the primeval father of Eastern Europeans who initiated the dominant haplogroup of modern Ukrainians, R1a1a, was born.

4. The fact that the Tarim Mummies share not only the haplogroup R1a1a with modern Ukrainians but also skin colour, hair and appearance, as can be seen in particular

---

[1] Haak W. et al. Massive Migration from the Steppe Was a Source for Indo-European Languages in Europe, Nature, 2015, vol. 522, no. 7555. Figure 3.

Chapter 2: What Genes Tell Us

from the reconstructed portrait of the Loulan Beauty, indicates that they shared common ancestors. Their forebears were the Steppe-Folk who began migrating approximately 5,200 years ago from the northern Black Sea and Azov Sea regions and gradually reached North-Western China. Archaeogenetics therefore proves the origin of Ukrainians from both the Trypillians and the later, but genetically related, Steppe-Folk. The ancestors of both these groups were the people who emerged from the Ukrainian Climate Refuge. Ukrainians adopted the peaceful nature of farmers and creators from the Trypillians and, from the Steppe-Folk, the character of indomitable warriors and defenders of their land. These qualities were clearly manifested in their descendants, the Scythians, Ruses, Cossacks and modern Ukrainians.

5. The degree of genetic influence of the migrant bearers of haplogroup R1a1a (the Trypillians and Steppe-Folk) on neighbouring peoples and those subdued by them depended on the geographical distance of these peoples from the Dnipro and the northern Black Sea regions, the duration of ethnic ties and other factors. The modern Asian peoples, for example, the Tadzhiks, Pashtuns, Indians, etc., whose ancestors were conquered by the Steppe-Folk, have a high percentage of this haplogroup. However, in terms of skin colour, hair and external appearance there are fundamental differences both among them and with their European conquerors. It therefore follows that the autosomal genes of the local

population predominated during the brief inter-ethnic relationship between these peoples and conquerors. The same observation could be made regarding the Mordovians, the Mari and many other peoples who live in Russia. They posses a high percentage of haplogroup R1a1a but differ in appearance from Europeans from whom they only took this haplogroup and the name "Russkye" while preserving their ethnicity. However, it is a different picture within Central and Eastern Europe. The Polish, Hungarians and Slovaks also have a high percentage of this haplogroup, however, in appearance they differ little from Ukrainians as a result of geographical proximity and prolonged inter-ethnic ties during which they repeatedly exchanged autosomal genes. The similarity of haplogroups between two peoples, therefore, does not mean that they are the same people. In order to reach such a conclusion the whole complex of indicators which characterise these peoples would need to be compared.

6. Insofar as our analysis has established that the ancestors of modern Ukrainians with the dominant R1a1a haplogroup continuously inhabited modern Ukrainian territory under different names for 10,000 years, a question naturally arises. From what point in time and under what name should they be considered Ukrainians? Should we begin with the Trypillian period or the Steppe-Folk, Scythians or the Ruses or from the first mention of Ukraine in the *The Tale of the Bygone*

Years? This is a complex and debatable question insofar as no convincing scientifically sound criteria have been established for its resolution. It is obvious that this issue cannot be resolved by genetic research alone because the genomic chain of Ukrainians, as already noted, extends far beyond 10,000 years back to the hunter-gatherers. In what link of this chain did this "forever local" people become Ukrainians needs to be determined by valid criteria. According to Ukrainian archaeologists, the main criteria of Ukrainian ethnicity is the "national self awareness" of an individual who, by their inner convictions, regards themselves as a Ukrainian. They simultaneously and questionably add that "ethnicity is primarily in the mind and not a matter of blood". This is a very dubious unscientific criteria bordering on the maniacal conviction of some psychiatric patient that he was Bonaparte. In my view, the criterion for the appearance of the first Ukrainians is that time and name in which the indicators of the genetic, linguistic, anthropological and archaeological historical witnesses to the past of Ukrainian ancestors converge. It is these indicators that can be realistically assessed rather than relying on the inner convictions which cannot be evaluated. We will therefore continue to listen to what we are told by the next witness to mankind's past, its languages.

Chapter 3: What Languages Tell Us

The people of our planet communicate by means of thousands of different languages and it is difficult to establish the exact quantity of them. Indeed, the number of languages range, according to various estimates, from 5,000 to 7,000. Languages are divided into different families which originated long ago in extinct maternal languages and each family is divided into separate language groups. The number of language families on the planet is over 15 but the exact number has not been determined due to insufficient research. The most widespread of these at present is the Indo-European language family which includes the Slavic group of languages to which Ukrainian belongs. We will consider how languages developed through history.

3.1 The Genealogical Tree of Indo-European Languages

Languages, similar to haplogroups, have the ability to branch out over time and sprout from one another. The branching occurred in human history when part of a tribe separated from their fellows and settled on new land. Their language was influenced by the new circumstances of their life, the languages of the local population in their new land, and became a dialect of their maternal language. Then, over

Chapter 3: What Languages Tell Us

a period of time, it developed into a separate, independent language known as a daughter language. The maternal language of those who did not migrate but remained on their land also changed over time, however, this was not as intensively as the daughter language because their living conditions did not change as substantially. After the branching occurred, both languages, the maternal language and the new (daughter) language, existed and developed in parallel for a period until a new branching occurred in one of them due to a subsequent separation of part of the tribe. There were then three languages and after a third branching, four etc. As we see, the process of language formation resembles the process of haplogroup formation. However, the difference is that the principle cause of branching is not a mutation but the separation of a part of the tribe. The resulting creation of new languages over the millennia are reflected by the genealogical language tree, which is similar to the haplogroup tree. Figure 3.1 depicts a fragment of the Indo-European genealogical language tree taken from the article by Gray R. et. al. (2011).[1]

It shows how two new languages of the primary order grew from the root maternal language approximately 9,000 years ago. One of these, the Hittite language, perished with no continuation, while the second branched again almost one thousand years later into two

---

[1] Gray R. et al. Language evolution and human history: what a difference a date makes, Phil. Trans. R. Soc., 2011, vol. 366. Figure 1.

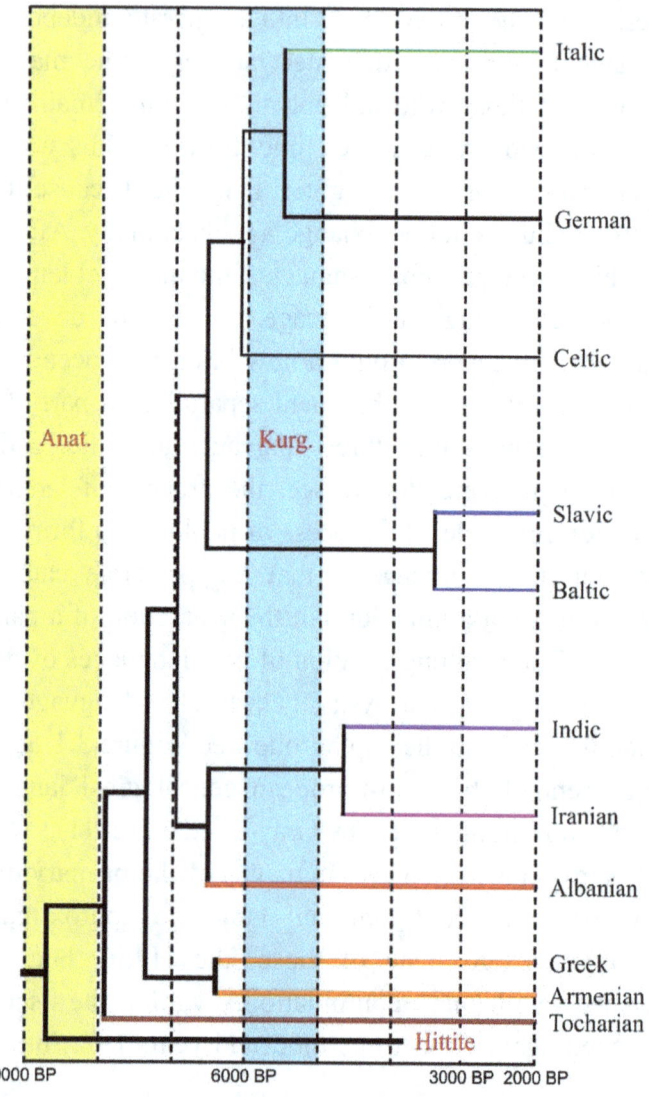

Figure 3.1: A fragment of the Indo-European genealogical language tree

Chapter 3: What Languages Tell Us

new secondary order languages. After this secondary branching one branch became the source for the extinct Tocharian languages while the other continued and flourished through new branches which formed a number of modern languages, including Armenian, Greek, Albanian and many others.

In order to construct a genealogical tree it is necessary to establish the actual branching, or non-branching, for both the living and extinct languages in relation to other languages in the family. This is undertaken by computer programme analysis using the so called Swadesh list, but what is this?

Morris Swadesh is a renowned American polyglot who identified a list of 200 basic concepts (or in some variations 110 or 100) which in his opinion exist in every language, ancient and modern, including those which are extinct. These include the concept of the individual and their sex (the individual, the man, and the woman), the anatomy (the head, the mouth, the leg, etc.), the closest animals to humans (the dog, lice, etc.) and natural human actions (eating, drinking and walking etc.). Swadesh's intuition told him that the words on his list were those that had been preserved over the longest period in each language during its contact with other languages. This stability allows scientific linguists to climb the words for these concepts, as if they were ladders, back down to those ancient words which predated branching. The technological approach consists of comparing the Swadesh list as written in dozens of languages of the same language family. Scientific linguists can then calculate, on the basis of the statistical computer analysis used to compare the list, the probability of a branching into different languages having occurred. They acquire this as a result of a graphic image of the language tree which is then calibrated to determine the time individual branches appeared using archaeological, historical and other data.

3.2 The Primeval Homeland of Indo-European Languages

Linguists have disputed where and when the maternal language of the Indo-European language family was born for over 100 years and there are currently two main hypotheses.

The first was established in 1956 by the archaeologist Marija Gimbutas, who claimed that speakers of that primeval maternal language lived between 5,000 and 6,000 years ago between the Dnipro and the Urals, from whence it spread to Asia and Europe. This hypothesis is favoured by archaeological research of the finds in burial mounds, or Kurgan, and is therefore termed the Kurgan Hypothesis, and a number of characteristic words in Indo-European languages, such as horse, wheel, axle, etc., which relate to Kurgan (burial mound) culture and the time the wheel was invented and the horse tamed. The hypothesis, as we see, coincides with the history of the expansion of the Steppe-Folk discussed in the previous section.

Chapter 3: What Languages Tell Us

The second hypothesis, known as the Anatolian, was established in 1987 by the British historian Colin Renfrew as a result of the radio-carbon analysis of the excavated remains of the ancient settlement of Chatal Guyuk in Turkey. He demonstrated that Indo-European languages originated earlier, 8,000 to 9,000 years ago, and came from Anatolia (modern Turkey). Renfrew does not believe that the spread of the maternal language was due to conquests, which became possible after the invention of the wheel and the domestication of the horse, he argues that it was supported by the spread of agricultural techniques for growing crops i.e. due to the transition from hunter-gathering to harvesting food.

In the previously cited article Gray R. et al., a linguistic investigation of both these hypotheses is conducted via a computer analysis of the Swadesh list as written in 87 Indo-European languages.[1] In the diagram of the fragment of the Indo-European Genealogical Language Tree (figure 3.1) acquired through this research, time intervals are divided by two bands which correspond to the Anatolian Hypothesis (9,000 to 8,000 years ago) and the Kurgan Hypothesis (6,000 to 5,000 years ago). The authors estimate that the first linguistic branch occurred approximately 8,700 years ago, which confirms the Anatolian hypothesis. However, one of the language branches of that primary branching did not

---

1 Gray R. et al. Language evolution and human history: what a difference a date makes, Phil. Trans. R. Soc., 2011, vol. 366. p. 1090–1100.

develop further and the language perished. The second of the branches initiated the beginning of new languages which were created subsequently beyond Anatolia and in the time period between the bands on the graphic, on the territory of modern Ukraine and Southern Russia. Given that the vast majority of Indo-European languages were not formed in Anatolia and that the process of language creation has no beginning nor end, it would be more legitimate to consider Ukraine and Southern Russia, rather than Anatolia, as the primeval homeland of Indo-European languages. An ever increasing number of researchers are taking this view. So the linguistic witnesses of the past confirm the truth of Marija Gimbutas's Kurgan Hypothesis.

3.3 Languages as the Mirror of the Steppe-Folk's Migrations

The process of the formation of Indo-European languages with a geographical connection to territories where their carriers reside or migrate to is demonstrated by a book written by American authors which was published in New York in 1986 and entitled *The Story of English*.[1] The schema of linguistic flows provided in the book (figure 3.2) practically reproduces the directions of the Steppe-Folk's movements during the time of their migration from the primeval homeland of Indo-European languages.[2]

---

1 Mc Crum Robert, Cran William, Mc Neil Robert. The Story of English. N.Y., USA: Viking, 1986. p. 384.
2 Ibid.

Chapter 3: What Languages Tell Us

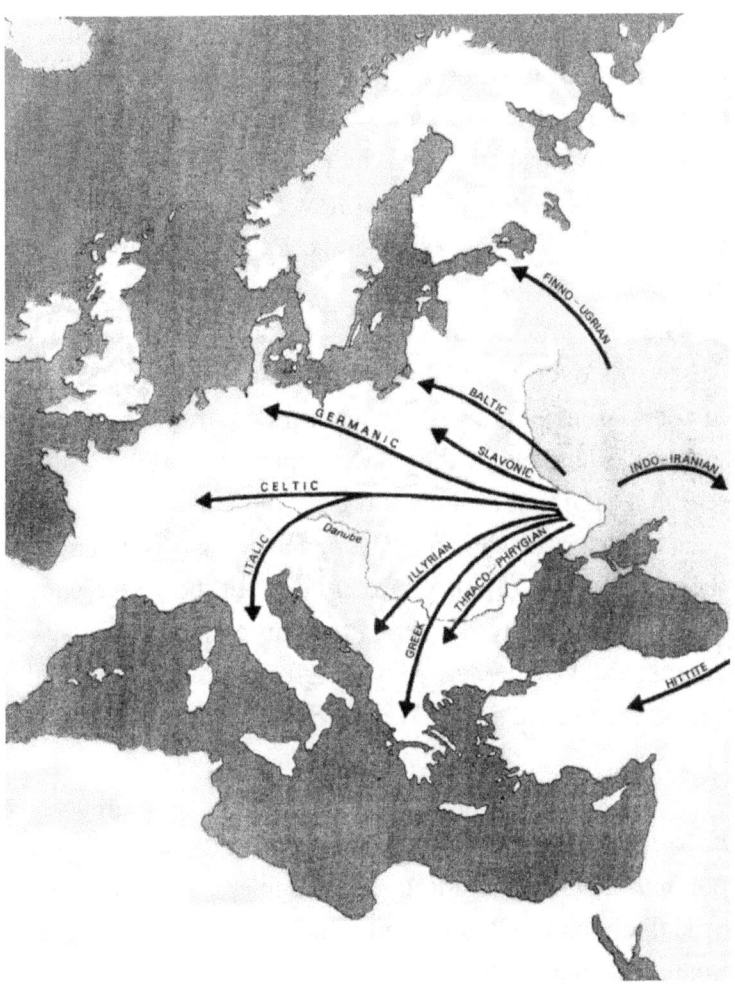

Figure 3.2: Schematic of the formation of the linguistic flows of Indo-European languages

The diagram reflects the period when the Steppe-Folk had already conquered Trypillia and established themselves not only in the Black Sea region but in the entire Dnipro area on both banks of the river. The migrations resulted in the formation of different Indo-European language groups as depicted in figure 3.1 and figure 3.2. These include the Italic, Germanic, Celtic, Slavic, Baltic and other languages. Let us examine in more detail how this occurred and what linguistic traces the Steppe-Folk left to Ukrainians and other peoples.

The descendants of those Steppe-Folk who headed westwards over a period of many centuries communicated in the Celtic languages, which formed from the ancient maternal language of those who emerged from the Dnipro region. In the first millennium BC, Celtic languages spread over almost all of Europe, from the British isles and the Iberian Peninsula to the Carpathians, but they were subsequently forced from the European continent by other languages. The modern day languages derived from the Celtic languages, Irish, Welsh, Scottish and others, have only survived in the British Isles.

However, over a period of several millennia, there are historic place names of Celtic origin that did not fade from popular memory, including, for example, the historic region of Halychyna in Ukraine and Poland, Gaul, which approximates to modern France, Galati in Romania, Galicia in Spain etc.[1]

---

[1] Мови Європи. Календар на 2001 рік (За матеріалами Лінгвістичного навчального музею Київського національного університету імені Тараса Шевченка) / уклад. К. Тищенко. Київ: Кальварія, 2001. p 20.

Chapter 3: What Languages Tell Us

The descendants of those Steppe-Folk who headed in a north-western direction spoke the newly formed Germanic languages from which modern German, Swedish, English and other languages originate. The Steppe-Folk initiated vast linguistic transformations as they headed first to the west and subsequently returned to the south towards the Apennine Peninsula. The Italic languages arose there, including Latin which subsequently became dominant in the Roman Empire and displaced the other Italic languages of that time. However, Latin was driven to extinction and is now a dead language not used for communication but only present in medical and scientific terminology. It is, however, the source of that large group of modern languages known as the Romance languages, including French, Spanish, Italian and others. Interestingly, almost one quarter of the vocabulary of modern Ukrainian originated from Latin and the Romance languages, overcoming, therefore, the path of the Steppe-Folk but in a different way.[1] It travelled without aggression by the path of linguistic borrowing during the course of prolonged inter-ethnic relations.

The descendants of those who advanced in the south-western direction, across the Balkan Peninsula, created the Illyrian, Ancient Greek and Thraco-Phrygian languages. Illyrian gave rise to modern Albanian, whereas Thracian-Phrygian became extinct and disseminated its traces in the language of its neighbours. It gave Ukrainian in

---

1 Ibid.

particular the fitting word *tiamyty*, to understand or become conscious of, and left traces in many other languages.[1] The last of the three languages, Ancient Greek, became widespread throughout the ancient world and gave modern languages numerous scientific and technical terms. *The New Testament* is written in Ancient Greek, along with the works of ancient poets, philosophers and scientists which have fortunately survived to the present day. The Greeks invented the modern form of the alphabet in which each graphic symbol/letter corresponds to a consonant or vowel sound.

The Steppe-Folk headed towards the shores of the Baltic where their descendants developed the Slavonic and Baltic languages. The scale of the expansion of the Slavonic languages in this direction is testified by the numerous Slavonic toponyms on German territory, including the name of its capital city Berlin, which developed on the site of two Slavonic settlements.[2] There are currently over one dozen Slavonic languages, including Ukrainian. However, only two modern languages remain from those derived from the original Baltic language group, Lithuanian and Latvian, the rest perished.

The Indo-Iranian languages formed in a south-east direction, thousands of kilometres from the Dnipro. One

---

1 Ibid.
2 Мови Європи. Календар на 2001 рік (За матеріалами Лінгвістичного навчального музею Київського національного університету імені Тараса Шевченка) / уклад. К. Тищенко. Київ: Кальварія, 2001. p 20.

Chapter 3: What Languages Tell Us

of them, Sanskrit, in which the oldest work of Indian literature, *The Vedas*, is written, is of particular interest to Ukrainians. The peculiarity of Sanskrit is that it has preserved a large number of words in their primal acoustic form, in the way they would have been spoken by our distant ancestors a few thousand years ago. Sanskrit has become as transparent as amber, preserving the ancient words of the tribes in the Dnipro area. How did this happen? The answer is suggested by another name for *The Vedas*, *The Shruti*, which translates as "that which is heard".[1] The fact is that *The Vedas* were transmitted orally over a long period by many generations of Brahmin priests and treated as sacred prehistoric revelations sent by God that could not be desecrated, i.e., changed, corrected or adapted to the local dialect. They were created in approximately the second to third millennia BC and written in Sanskrit at a much later date. *The Vedas,* therefore, due to the prohibition upon changing them, have eternally preserved the language of the Dnipro tribes. However, the language of those Dnipro area dwellers who remained on their territory throughout history changed far less compared to that of the re-settlers and conquerors. Thus these two languages, Sanskrit and the language of those who remained in the Dnipro region, due to different principles but with a similar result, have moved least

---

1 Наливайко Степан. Давньоіндійські імена. Назви. Терміни: проекція на Україну: довідник. Київ, 2009. p. 113.

from the original maternal language from among the Indo-European languages. This is probably why there are so many words in Sanskrit which are surprisingly similar to modern Ukrainian words spoken by the descendants of those who remained by the Dnipro. Here are a few examples, with the Ukrainian word preceding the Sanskrit word and the English definition (see next page):[1]

However, it is not only words that Ukrainians and Indians came to have common, they also shared ancient symbols of human existence which are known in Ukrainian as the svarga and the Trisuttâ/Tryzub or trident. The svarga, or swastika as it is more widely known, is the symbol of the god Svarog in whom the Dnipro tribes believed; the symbol of the solar circle and a sacred symbol of the Aryans or the Aryan sign. The Aryans or Arya in Sanskrit, was the name used by the tribes who invaded India 4,000 years ago, bringing the Sanskrit language, the oral *Vedas,* they had created and this Aryan sign with them.[2] This symbol is extremely popular in India, Indians decorate their homes with it and regard it as a talisman and a symbol of joy and happiness. The word "joy" in Sanskrit sounds like *svastia* and when modified became the word swastika.[3]

---

1 Ibid. pp. 3-4.
2 Силенко Лев. *Святе вчення. Силенкова віра в Дажбога.* Київ: АТ «Обереги», 1995 р. 47.
3 Ibid p. 126.

Chapter 3: What Languages Tell Us

Ukrainian	Sanskrit	English
Tato	Tata	Father
Mati	Matar	Mother
Nenâ	Nana	Mother
Narečena	Nara	Bride
Stan	Stana	State
Krasnij	Krìšna	Beautiful
Miša	Muša	Mouse
Oko	Ankha	Eye
Zerno, zbìžžâ	Bìdža	Grain
Ûška	Ûšìka	Soup
Kìš	Koša	Kish (Supreme Assembly of the Zaporozhian Cossacks)
Košovij	Kšatrìj	Koshoviy (The head of the Cossacks)
Bandura	Pandara	Bandura (a stringed instrument)
Perevertannâ	Parìvertana	Overturning
Kazati	Kagati	To say
Nišiti	Naštatì	To destroy
Čiluvati, Č'omati,	Čumatì	To kiss
Piti	Pìtì	To drink
Znati	Džnâtì	To know
Vìdati	Vedatì	To know
Sâati	Kšaâtì	To shine

There are extant images of the svarga/swastika in Kyiv. When you enter the Saint Sophia Cathedral, the first thing that captures your eye is a large, five metre image of Our Lady the Oranta composed of thousands of multi-coloured stones. She is dressed in a blue chiton and seems to float on a fairy-tale carpet from the solar gold oval of the main apse of the cathedral. Beneath the image of the Madonna, and in a decoration that extends over the image of the holy fathers of the church, Christian signs alternate with swastikas inlaid with yellow and red stones on a blue mosaic backdrop. Right-handed and left-handed swastikas are clearly visible, with the hooked ends pointing in a clockwise or anti-clockwise direction as well as swastikas without one link (triactre). This is a symbol of the earthly living flame, whose patron was Svarožič, the son of the god Svarog.[1] This suggests that the builders of Saint Sophia, who constructed the cathedral at the beginning of the eleventh century, still remembered and revered their Aryan ancestors who had lived there for several thousand years before them. They apparently insisted that the memory of the Aryans remained in this Christian temple despite the fact that Christianity did not tolerate any pagan manifestations and especially the pagan symbol of the deity of heavenly fire which Svarog was considered to be. The sacred

---

[1] Ілля Валерій. Сварга: поезії. Харків : Фірма «Майдан», 1996. pp. 170, 171.

memory of their forebears on this occasion overcame the canons of Christianity and left us a visible confirmation of the beginning of the Aryans' path from the Dnipro to India. The image of the svarga/swastika was consistently passed down from generation to generation, from the time of Trypillia to the present day (figure 3.3).

Figure 3.3: Svarga/swastika symbols on Ukrainian territory from Trypillia to the present: Symbols on Trypillian crockery in the fourth millennium BC. A symbol on the altar of Saint Sophia in Kyiv in the eleventh century AD. Symbols on a Ukrainian embroidered shirt in the nineteenth century AD.

In the nineteen-thirties and forties, the German Nazis, relying on brute force, tried to usurp the right to be the direct descendants of the Aryans and the owners of the Aryan symbol, the swastika. Their bloody crimes against humanity defiled this sacred sign and abruptly embedded an antipathy towards it in the souls of many Ukrainians. However, this should not be so. A decade and a half of fascist usurpation of this legacy cannot erase the millennial history of such high and noble conceptions as the Aryan and the swastika. A younger generation of Ukrainians armed with the truth about the past of their people will expunge this fascist filth from the ancient symbol of our ancestors.

Another Aryan sign is the *trisuttâ*, which is designated by the word *trisuta* in *The Vedas*. This symbol is based on three essences, or three conceptions, which the Aryans singled out as particularly significant. These consist of the spiritual essence of the individual, their material essence and the principles of spiritual and material existence. This sign is akin to a testament for their descendants: to improve your spiritual and physical strength by adhering to intelligent rules for living and just laws, enabling you to withstand life's challenges and do good.[1] After the Aryans, the sign came to be known by other names: the *triglav*, *trìjcâ* or more simply the Tryzub or trident. The Russian historian M. M. Karamzin, who possessed insufficient historical information, named this sign by the unfortunate mundane name of the *trezubec* or trident which does not, as we see, accord with the profound meaning of this symbol. However, there is nothing to be done about this error, the name he gave the sign has been too long established globally. The *trisuttâ* symbol was consistently inherited by the descendants of the Aryans who, remaining on the lands by the Dnipro, maintained their traditions: the Scythians, the Sarmatians, the Ruses, and finally the Ukrainians for whom it became the basis of their state emblem, the word

---

1 Силенко Лев. *Святе вчення. Силенкова віра в Дажбога.* Київ: АТ «Обереги», 1995 pp. 71, 72.

for emblem being "herb" in Ukrainian. This is quite natural because the word "herb" translates from the Polish as "heritage" (figure 3.4).

Figure 3.4: The inheritance of the trisuttâ symbol by the inhabitants of the Dnipro region: Symbol on the stones overlaying the Kamyana Mohyla in the fifth to eighth millennium BC. Symbol on a Sarmatian coin in the second century BC. The emblem of the Kyiv princes in the tenth century AD; The state emblem of Ukraine[1]

3.4 Mykhailo Krasuskyi on the Ukrainian Language

Every modern language has passed through certain formative stages before taking the form we see today. During the initial stages it separates from the maternal language, accumulates a certain amount of "daughterly" differences and becomes a proto-language for a modern language. Subsequently, as it acquires the features of an independent language, it becomes the ancient language relative to the

---

1 Велика ілюстрована енциклопедія України. Київ: Махаон-Україна, 2008. pp. 67, 72.

modern language. Finally, at the end of its formation, it becomes an independent language while retaining bridges to all three of its forerunners, the ancient language, proto-language and the original maternal language. The duration of the process of language formation and where the chronological boundaries lay between the stages of its formation is a very complex issue. The diagram (figure 3.1) illustrates that the Baltic-Slavic line of languages extend from the middle of the fifth millennium BC, i.e. from the period when the Trypillian civilisation existed. Therefore, at that point, the Trypillian language or several interrelated Trypillian languages existed. However, was there in the interconnections of these languages any element of the future Ukrainian language? This diagram alone cannot provide an answer. We will search for one in the work of polyglots who have a broad panoramic view of the history of the development of the languages of different peoples. The works of non-Ukrainian polyglots, who see Ukrainian from outside, and compare it to the other Indo-European languages and their own native language are exceptionally valuable in this context.

One such is Mykhailo Krasuskyi, he is Polish and a brilliant expert on the subject of many European and Oriental languages, both modern and ancient, including extinct languages. In 1880, he published a small edition of a brochure entitled *Drevnost' malorossijskogo âzyka*, or *The Antiquity of the Little-Russian Language* because Ukrainian was referred to as "Little-Russian" under

Chapter 3: What Languages Tell Us

Tsarism. In the Tsarist and Soviet eras the brochure was diligently suppressed and it was only when Ukraine became independent that it was successfully unearthed and republished.[1] Krasuskyi, from the height of his linguistic erudition, examined the inter-relations of words and expressions in different languages, including those long extinct, not only in his own Polish language but also in Ukrainian. He concluded that Ukrainian "was not only older than all the Slavonic languages, not excluding so-called Old Slavonic, but also Sanskrit, Greek, Latin and other Aryan languages". (It is apparent that he used the term Aryan for Indo-European.) Krasuskyi's linguistic research is reminiscent of archaeological excavations in linguistics where, instead of excavated remains, there are ancient words in different languages. His work confirms that the cradle of the Aryan tribes was not Central Asia, which was the view in his era, but the Sarmatian or Slavonic Valley. He noted that Little-Russians (Ukrainians), the inheritors of those Aryan tribes, still lived there. He scrupulously collated logical evidence, widely represented in his work, that the names in the numbers of the decimal system derive from proto-Ukrainian. It is worth noting that the brochure was published four years after the Russian Tsar had issued the Ems Ukaz, a decree which banned Ukrainian. The brochure seems like the reaction of a man who knew more

---

1 Красуский Михаил. Древность малороссийского языка. Індо-Європа, ч. 1. Київ, 1991. pp. 8–39.

than anyone else about the nature of the Ukrainian language. Utterly outraged by the decree, he was determined, albeit in this form, to open people's eyes to the quality of the language they were destroying. Krasuskyi, defending Ukrainians oppressed by Tsarist language policies, wrote that it was "in vain our ancestors were presented as divine slaves, in a word sheep. If that were so they would not have been able to organise such a strong and brave language by comparison with which Sanskrit, like Greek, appears weak and pale". His research proved that the ancient Ukrainian language created words for the other Slavonic languages.

Let us now compare the diagram in 3.1 with Krasuskyi's conclusion that Ukrainian is older than Greek or Latin. According to the diagram, the Greek language group separated from the Armenian one in the middle of the fifth millennium BC. At approximately the same time the Albanian language group separated from the Indo-Iranian languages and Balto-Slavic from the Celto-Germano-Italic languages. Such a large scale change, the simultaneous creation of six language groups, is not a coincidence. It was caused by a corresponding large-scale natural event, the Great Flood, which occurred in Europe in approximately 5,600 BC. This resulted in an avalanche of similar formations of a cascade of language groups in the Indo-European family. The ancestors of the bearers of these languages, driven out by the flood, were compelled to abandon the territory they inhabited and move to new lands, thereby displacing and mingling with the local population. This resulted in the creation of new language groups over a period of a millennia. This was a truly large-scale migration of peoples caused by a natural disaster that occurred long before the other major population relocations caused by the migrations of the Steppe-Folk. According to figure 3.1, the nearest maternal language older than Greek or the other languages was the language that branched out almost immediately after the Great Flood in about 5,400 BC (third branch in the diagram). Two language groups arose from one of these branches, as depicted lower in the diagram, Greek and Armenian, while from the second, at the top of the diagram, came from the rest of the Indo-European languages. As can be seen in the diagram, this higher branch was not only older than Greek and Latin, it was also older than Trypillian, for it had already diverged at the beginning of Trypillian civilisation in 5,400 BC. This was probably the language spoken by those who emerged from the Ukrainian Climate Refuge. Krasuskyi, therefore, when analysing the antiquity of the Ukrainian language, was in fact analysing some ancient mother language, that was no younger than Trypillian or was in fact Trypillian. Let us explore this question using the latest scientific advances from various fields.

3.5 When and Where Did the Ukrainian Language Originate?

Krasuskyi relied solely on his profound knowledge of various languages in his research. He would not, of course, have known of the achievements of genetics, modern linguistics, archaeology and other sciences. He possessed, instead, a brilliant linguistic erudition from the vantage point of which he could scan all the movements of languages in their development and interaction. In the quiet of his study he could reveal "at the nib of his pen" that which would later be excavated by archaeologists and determine the directions of the Steppe-Folk migration, whom he called the Aryan tribes. We will try to examine his conclusions based on the latest advances in archaeogenetics and linguistics.

In his fundamental work, *Lexicostatistic Dating of Prehistoric Ethnic Contacts,* Morris Swadesh demonstrates that the 200 basic words he selected (subsequently known as the Swadesh list) are replaced by new words at a relatively constant rate.[1] This varies for different languages at a rate between 15% and 24% per millennium. There is an analogy here with the rate of genetic mutations which occur at a relatively constant rate. Swadesh proposed evaluating the rapidity of linguistic substitution by means of the coefficient of lexical preservation *r*, which is measured as a percentage of the words (or a relevant part thereof) from his list that are preserved over a millennium. The constancy of the rate of lexical substitution is explained by the fact

---

[1] Swadesh M. Lexicostatistic Dating of Prehistoric Ethnic Contacts. Proc. Am. Philos. Soc., 1951, vol. 96, pp. 452–463.

Chapter 3: What Languages Tell Us

that while language is constantly developing and being enriched with new concepts and associated words, a certain portion of the old vocabulary is preserved to allow communication and comprehension between the regular generations of people. Within a language that has been separated from the maternal language there will, over the course of a millennia, remain a part of that maternal language's vocabulary which is equal to the coefficient of preservation r_1. Over the course of two millennia is preserved equals to the product of the previous balance on the same coefficient r_1. This gives us the equation $r_1 \times r_1 = r_1^2$ while over three millennia the corresponding equation for the preserved part of the maternal vocabulary results in r_1^3. This means that the process of decline in the preserved vocabulary occurs non-linearly according to the law of exponential function. Within the maternal language, after the branching of the daughter language, the process of replacement continues in a similar fashion. After the first millennia that part of the vocabulary which is preserved equals the coefficient r_2, after two millennia it will be equal to r_2^2, after three millennia it equals to r_2^3, etc. Although the substitution processes in both languages run in parallel, they differ so that in one of them a word that was common to both may be replaced, whereas in the other it might be preserved. Therefore, in the first millennium after the branching, the relative portion of preserved words common to both languages, denoted by c, will be equal to the product of their coefficients as per the result equation $r_1 \times r_2$. After two millennia it will be equal to $r_1^2 \times r_2^2$ and after three millennia $r_1^3 \times r_2^3$ etc., and in a general case:

$$c = r_1^t \times r_2^t \quad (3.1)$$

where t is the current time that has elapsed since the branching where the unit of time is one millennium.

After the logarithmic of expression above (3.1) we find that:

$$t = log c / (log r_1 + log r_2), \quad (3.2)$$

That is the time elapsed since the branching equals to the logarithm of the related part of the common words preserved in both languages divided by the sum of the logarithms of their coefficients of preservation. When the coefficients of preservation are equal ($r_1 = r_2 = r$) the expression (3.2) is simplified and has the following form:

$$t = log c / 2 log r \quad (3.3)$$

Subsequently, in a new work which refined his earlier studies, Swadesh reduced his list from 200 to 100 words and demonstrated the advantages of a shorter list which provides for greater accuracy in determining the time parameters. The practical application of the 100 word list showed that the coefficient of preservation, r, varies between 71% and 94% in different languages.

Using the formula (3.2) or (3.3) it is possible to calculate the time when the branching into two languages occurred, one of which became the daughter, subsidiary language, and continued its development as a partner of the first within the same language family. Before undertaking a calculation regarding the time the Ukrainian language was born it should be noted that, according to the genetic studies described in sub section 2.20, Slavonic people began their existence in the Dnipro river basin. Slavonic languages, therefore, began with the language of the indigenous population of the Dnipro region who, according to genetic studies, have lived there uninterruptedly for 10,000 years and now have their own language, Ukrainian. It follows logically that the language of the first Slavs, the natives of the Dnipro region, was proto-Ukrainian. The other Slavonic languages sprouted from that language during the period its bearers bearers left the Dnipro Basin and headed north, south, west and south-west.[1] However, according to figure 3.1, there was a branching of a maternal language, which is as yet unknown to us, much earlier, in the fifth millennium BC which marked the beginning of both the Slavonic and Baltic languages. Lithuanian is considered to be the oldest of the Baltic language group.[2] This means that the branching into the Baltic and Slavonic languages began with the divergence of the modern Ukrainian and

---

1   История Украинской ССР. Киев: «Наукова думка», 1981. Т. 1. p. 139.

2   Литовська мова URL: uk.wikipedia.org/wiki/Литовська_мова

Lithuanian languages, which are the oldest in their language groups. We will calculate the time of their divergence using the 100 word list provided by Swadesh written in Lithuanian and Ukrainian.[1],[2] In order to determine the coefficient of preservation *r* in Ukrainian we will use the vocabulary of the Old Ukrainian language in which the oldest of our chronicles, according to Ivan Franko, is written, *The Tale of the Bygone Years*.[3] The results of the evaluation of the coefficient of the preservation of vocabulary are shown in table 3.1. That portion of the common words that have survived in both Lithuanian and Ukrainian was at the level of 0.32 e.g. approximately one third of the words on the Swadesh list, 32, remained unchanged. They are marked with a plus sign in the sixth column. The remaining 68 words changed in either one or the other of the languages. When assessing the affinity of a pair of words using the Swadesh method, the inevitable orthoepic alterations in words which disguised their affinity, but not sufficiently so that it cannot be recognised, was not taken into account. This can be observed, for example, when we examine these pairs: malij – mažas, rìg – ragas, oko – akis, nìs – nosis, nìgot' – nagas, ruka – ranka, davati – duoti, voda – vanduo, dim – dūmai, vogon' – ugnis and others. The words in these

---

1 Appendix: Baltic Swadesh lists. http://en.m.wiktionary.org.
2 Appendix: Ukrainian Swadesh list. http://en.m.wiktionary.org.
3 Повість врем'яних літ: літопис (за Іпатським списком) / пер. з давньоруської, післяслово, комент. В. В. Яременка. Київ: Рад. Письменник, 1990. 558 с.

Chapter 3: What Languages Tell Us

Table 3.1: The hundred word Swadesh list in the Ukrainian, Old Ukrainian and Lithuanian Languages

English Meaning	Ukrainian	Old Ukrainian	Preservation	Lithuanian	Coincidence in Lithuanian and Ukrainian
I	Я	якоже и *азъ* (60/14↓)	-	aš	-
You (singular)	Ти	*ты* поставленъ от Бога (198/4↓)	+	tu	+
We	Ми	*мы ли, они ли?*(66/7↑)	+	mes	+
This	Цей, сей	*сий* же Ярослав (240/11↑)	+	šis, šitas	+
That	Той, те	и от *тѣх* Варягъ (28/2↑)	+	tas	+
Who	Хто	аще *кто* умреть (54/9,12↓)	+	kas	-
What	Що	кто убо *что* речеть (60/11↓)	+	kas, ka	-
Not	Не	*не* дадяше въпрячи (20/4↓)	+	ne	+
All	Все, всі	и помроша *вси* (20/7↓)	+	viskas, visa	+
Many	Багато, много	*мнози* бѣша христьяни (78/11↑)	+	daug	-
One	Один	законъ имамъ *одинъ* (24/14↓)	+	vienas	-
Two	Два	по *двѣ* жены (22/2↓)	+	du, dvi	+

Table 3.1: continued

English Meaning	Ukrainian	Old Ukrainian	Preservation	Lithuanian	Coincidence in Lithuanian and Ukrainian
Big/Great	Великий	обри тѣлом *велицѣ* (20/6↓)	+	didelis	-
Long	Довгий	в *долготу* лакоть (146/2↑)	+	ilgas	-
Small	Малий	ссудъ *мал* (22/5↓)	+	mažas	+
Woman (adult female)	Жінка	*женам* Дулѣбськымъ (20/3↓)	+	moteris	-
Man (adult male)	Чоловік, мужчина	въ 6 день створи же Богъ *человѣка* (144/13↓)	+	vyras	-
Person/Individual	Людина, чоловік	и удавиша кони и *человѣци* ци (122/12↓)	+	žmogus	-
Fish	Риба	*рыбы*, и овощемъ (44/5↑)	+	žuvis	-
Bird	Птах, птиця	*птица*, могущи вредити (60/4↓)	+	paukštis	-
Dog	Пес, собака	повелѣ *псомъ* глаголати (282/5↑)	+	šuo, šunis	-
Louse	Воша			utėlė	-
Tree	Дерево	добро *древо* (144/3↑)	+	medis	-
Seed	Сім'я, насіння	сътвори сѣ *мена* (144/3↓)	+	sėkla	-

Chapter 3: What Languages Tell Us

Table 3.1: continued

English Meaning	Ukrainian	Old Ukrainian	Preservation	Lithuanian	Coincidence in Lithuanian and Ukrainian
Leaf	Листок	листвием смоковнымъ (144/1↑)	+	lapas	-
Root	Корінь	отъ грѣховнаго корене (130/12↑)	+	šaknis	-
Bark	Кора			žieve	-
Skin	Шкіра	выня *кожю* с мясом (192/10↓), сдираху *хъзы* с конемь (242/4↑)	-	oda	-
Meat	М'ясо	*мясъ* не ядуще (22/16↓)	+	mėsa	+
Blood	Кров	се есть *кровь* моя (142/16↓)	+	kraujas	+
Bone	Кістка	ляжмы *костью* ту (112/3↑)	+	kaulas	-
Fat	Жир			taukai	-
Egg	Яйце			kiaušinis	-
Horn	Ріг	метала на *розях* (372/15↓)	+	ragas	+
Tail	Хвіст	Волчий *Хвост* (138/12↓)	+	uodega	-
Feather	Перо	птицы *пернатыя* (144/12↓)	+	plunksna	-

Table 3.1: continued

English Meaning	Ukrainian	Old Ukrainian	Preservation	Lithuanian	Coincidence in Lithuanian and Ukrainian
Hair	Волосся	и *власи* главнии (322/4↑)	+	plaukai	-
Head	Голова	посредѣ *головъ* (64/10↓)	+	galva	+
Ear	Вухо	ни *вхо* не слыша (318/18↑)	+	ausis	-
Eye	Око	ни *око* не види (318/18↑)	+	akis	+
Nose	Hic			nosis	+
Mouth	Рот	въ *рот* вливають (142/7↓)	+	burna	-
Tooth	Зуб	не дасть *зубомъ* (188/5↓)	+	dantis	-
Tongue	Язик	молвить *языкомъ* (134/6↑)	+	liežuvis	-
Nail	Ніготь	подъ *ногътемь* (264/4↑)	+	nagas	+
Leg/foot	Стопа, нога	попирающе подъ *нозѣ* (138/8↓)	+	péda	-
Knee	Коліно	си *колѣни* (380/16↑)	+	kelis	-
Hand	Рука	*руць* связавше (64/9↓)	+	ranka	+

Chapter 3: What Languages Tell Us

Table 3.1: continued

English Meaning	Ukrainian	Old Ukrainian	Preservation	Lithuanian	Coincidence in Lithuanian and Ukrainian
Belly	Живіт	въ *чресла* рыбьий хвостъ приросль (264/12↓)-	-	Pilvas, viduriai	-
Neck	Шия	ови до *шеѣ* (184/3↓)	+	kaklas	-
Breast	Груди	друзии до *персий* (184/4↓)-	-	krūtis	-
Heart	Серце	*сердце* свое (96/7↑)	+	širdis	+
Liver	Печінка			kepenys	-
To drink	Пити	ни *пьють* (136/17↑)	+	gerti	-
To eat	Їсти	и что *ясти* (256/7↑)	+	ėsti	+
To bite	Кусати	ми *укусилъ* (372/17↓)	+	kąsti	+
To look/ to see	Дивитися, бачити	*видяше* Бога (144/18↓)-	-	matyti	-
To hear/ to listen	Чути, слухати	се *слышав* царь (38/13↓)	+	girdėti	-
To know	Знати	а ты самъ *вѣси*(94/12↑)	-	žinoti	+
To sleep	Спати	и *успе* Адамъ (144/16↑)	+	miegoti	-
To die	Умирати	и *помроша* вси (20/7↓)	+	mirti	+
To kill	Вбивати	и *убиваху* (20/6↑)	+	žudyti	-
To swim	Плавати	начнеть *плавати* (138/11↑)	+	plaukti	+

Table 3.1: continued

English Meaning	Ukrainian	Old Ukrainian	Preservation	Lithuanian	Coincidence in Lithuanian and Ukrainian
To fly	Літати	и полетѣша (90/11↑)	+	skristi	-
To walk	Ходити	не хожаше (20/9↑)	+	eiti	-
To come	Приходити	приде в устье Днѣпръское (14/9↓)	+	ateiti, atvykti	-
To lie (down)	Лежати	и възлежи (210/13↓)	+	gulėti	-
To sit	Сидіти	всѣдоша въ лодья (104/3↑)	+	sėdėti	+
To stand	Стояти	она же стояше (94/5↓)	+	stovėti	+
To give	Давати	кому дань даете? (36/3↓)	+	duoti	+
To speak	Говорити	тѣм глаголаху (18/3↓)-		sakyti	-
The sun	Сонце	предъ солнцем (108/11↑)	+	saule	-
The moon	Місяць	створи мѣсяць (140/14↓)	+	mėnulis	-
Star	Зоря	зъвѣзды (136/14↑)	-	žvaigždė	-
Water	Вода	вода текущи (80/1↑)	+	vanduo	+
Rain	Дощ	молънья и дождь (234/7↓)	+	lietus	-

Chapter 3: What Languages Tell Us

Table 3.1: continued

English Meaning	Ukrainian	Old Ukrainian	Preservation	Lithuanian	Coincidence in Lithuanian and Ukrainian
Stone	Камінь	бѣ терем *каменъ* (82/8↓)	+	akmuo	-
Sand	Пісок	на рѣцѣ *Пищанѣ* (138/13↓)	+	smėlis	-
Earth/soil	Земля	*землю* розора (240/12↑)	+	žemé	+
Cloud	Хмара, оболок	на облацѣх сѣверьскых (144/6↓)	+	debesis	-
Smoke	Дим	яко *дымъ* (214/15↑)	+	dūmai	+
Fire	Вогонь	одѣржимъ огнем (58/1↑)	+	ugnis	+
Ash	Попіл			pelenai	-
To burn	Горіти	яко *изгаряше* (328/11↓)	+	degti	-
Road/Way	Дорога, путь	по грудну *пути* (400/6↓)	+	kelias	-
Mountain	Гора	сѣдяше на *горѣ* (16/9↑)	+	kalnas	-
Red	Червоний	*Чермному* морю (154/13↓)	+	raudonas	-
Green	Зелений			žalias	+
Yellow	Жовтий	будемъ *золотѣ* (118/4↑)-	-	geltonas	-
White	Білий	яко снѣг *обѣлю* я (356/2↑)	+	baltas	+
Black	Чорний	вранъ *черный* (304/1↓)	+	juodas	-

Table 3.1: continued

English Meaning	Ukrainian	Old Ukrainian	Preservation	Lithuanian	Coincidence in Lithuanian and Ukrainian
Night	Ніч	луна въ *нощи* (108/10↑)	+	naktis	-
Warm	Теплий	в *теплѢ* истьбѢ (344/8↓)	+	šiltas	-
Cold	Холодний	и *студень* (304/12↓)-	-	šaltas	-
Full	Повний			pilnas	-
New	Новий	и се быша *нова* (186/6↑)	+	naujas	+
Good	Добрий	*добрѢ* гости (82/10↓)	+	geras	-
Round	Круглий	яко *кругъ* бысть (328/9↓)	+	apvalus	-
Dry	Сухий	по *суху* (154/15↑)	+	sausas	-
Name (first)	Ім'я	*имя* ей Олена (94/9↓)	+	vardas	-
In total	Coefficient of vocabulary preservation in the Ukrainian language over the course of nine centuries: $r_{0.9}=(91-10)/91= 0.89$			The portion of vocabulary which coincides in the Ukrainian and Lithuanian languages: $c=32/100=0.32$	

pairs are recognised as those that have not been replaced since the divergence of the Ukrainian and Lithuanian languages and originate from the maternal language.

In the column "Old Ukrainian" the page numbers and lines (the up and down arrows indicate whether the count is from the top or bottom of the page) where the words that correspond to the Swadesh list occur within the chronicle are used. While surveying them it appears at first glance as if the Old Ukrainian language resembles Russian rather than Ukrainian. This is because Russian, by contrast with Ukrainian, borrowed many words from Church Slavonic, which was created to disseminate Christian teachings. These loan words have been adapted for the Moscow dialect when imported into Russian. The letter *ât'* (ѣ), which frequently occurs in the text of the chronicle, is usually pronounced *i*, less frequently as *ï* or *e*, but never as *ê*.[1] The following phrases provide examples: tìlom velicì, poletìša v gnìzda, do šeï, na rìcì Pìsanì and others could be cited. However, in Russian this letter, *ât'* (ѣ), is read as *ê* in the fashion of the Muscovite dialect. The phrases cited above would therefore read: têlom vêlicê, polêtêša v gnêzda, do šêê, na rêcê Pìsanê, etc. The letter *u* in Old Ukrainian is pronounced like *i* and the letter *ы* like the Ukrainian *u*, and the letter *e* is usually not softened (as in the following phrases: nì oko ne vìdì, nì vho ne sliša). In addition, the characteristics of the Ukrainian language are manifested in the soft verb endings in the chronicle text (umret', vlìvaût', nì p'ût', nì molvât') and the vocative case (Hriste Ìsuse, Bože naš, čelovѣkolûbče, otče, etc.). These two characteristics, which are present in the chronicle, are absent from the Russian language. If you take into account all these particular features when

---

1 Біленька-Свистович Л., Рибак Н. *Церковнослов'янська мова: підруч. зі словником для духов. навч. закл.* Київ: Криниця, 2000. p. 63

reading an ancient Ukrainian text it will be perceptibly Ukrainian and not Russian, as was emphasised not only by our Ukrainian researchers but also some Russian experts, including O. O. Shakhmatov, I. F. Buslayev and others. However, Russia's rulers and their faithful servants encroach on the history of the Kyiv state which existed in the ninth to the eleventh centuries when Muscovy was not yet in embryo. They do not refrain from "correcting" the chronicle texts with the Russian language, which in reality is falsifying them.

Therefore, the chronicle language has been distorted on the monuments to Princess Olha and the apostle Andrii, which were erected in Kyiv during Tsarism then subsequently destroyed by the Bolsheviks and has recently been restored. You can see how in the chronicle the word *hvalâ t'*, which has a soft sign, has been exchanged for a hard sign and the word *vъsiâêt'* has been replaced by *vozsiâêtъ* and also ends with a hard sign. The phrase attributed to St. Andrii "vidite gory siâ?" has been Russianised to "vidite – li gory sià?". Andrii's name is Russianised to render it Andrej, the Ukrainian word *svâtij* is abbreviated to *sv*. These changes are intended to hide that it is Ukrainian. The authors apparently worked hard to eradicate any trace of Ukrainian in the inscriptions. It is as if they were saying, "look, Ukrainians, at what is written here - we Russians were here in the princely era, our language was spoken here and today we will defend all who speak it on your territory". This "political landmine" was laid imperceptibly

Chapter 3: What Languages Tell Us

with the monuments right in the centre of our capital. This mine is a consequence of the colonisation of Ukraine by our northern neighbour because our forebears in their time could not hold out in the ferocious battle with their foes. However, the situation might have been different. The nineteenth century historian Vasily Klyuchevsky once fancifully said, "Imagine if Kyiv had not been captured and destroyed by the Tatars. It would be the capital of the first great Russian state... the official language would not be a mixture of Old Slavonic and Finnish but Slavic-Ukrainian. The Ukrainian author Hohol would not have had to write in Russian and Pushkin would have written in Ukrainian."[1] However, this is how it is. When a people cannot sustain their own statehood the occupier gradually eradicates all their national qualities. Let us now return to the analysis of table 3.1.

The chronicle does not include nine of the words in the Swadesh list so the vocabulary preservation of Ukrainian has been evaluated with 91 words, 10 of which were replacements. These words with their Ukrainian equivalents and English translations in brackets are azъ (ja/i), chъzy (škira/skin), čresla (živit/belly), persii (grudi/breast), vidjaše (bačiti/to see), věsi (znati/to know), glagolachu (govoriti/to speak), zъvězdy (zori/stars), zolotě (žovti/yellow), studenь (cholod/cold).

---

1 Бурячок Андрій. Мовоситуація в Київській Русі. Мова державто–мова офіційна: матеріали наукової конференції. Київ: Всеукраїнське товариство «Просвіта», 1995. P. 99

Nine centuries have passed since the chronicle was written, which corresponds to the calculated coefficient of preservation, $r_{0.9} = 0.89$ (see table 3.1). The numerical value of the coefficient r, which corresponds with one thousand years, is found with the equation:

$$0.89 = r^{0.9}$$

The solution to the equation is $r = 0.88$, which differs little from the average level of language preservation in Europe which is, according to Swadesh, 0.86. This entitles us to choose the same numerical value of coefficient r for the Lithuanian and Ukrainian languages the same and calculate, with the formula (3.3) the time (t_p) which has passed since their branching:

$$t_p = \frac{\log c}{2\log r} = \frac{\log 0.32}{2\log 0.88} \approx \textbf{45 centuries}$$

The result we derive demonstrates that Ukrainian and Lithuanian separated two centuries after the Trypillian civilisation ceased to exist in the twenty-seventh century BC.[1] It seems as if the Steppe-Folk, having conquered the Trypillians, squeezed a part of the Trypillian population to the north. These northerners, living in isolation from the

---

1 Відейко М.Ю. *Трипільська цивілізація*. Київ: Академперіодика, 2002. p.31

Chapter 3: What Languages Tell Us

other Trypillians, then developed a new daughter language, Lithuanian, which led to the formation of the other Baltic languages. It follows logically that the unknown language which launched the Baltic and Slavonic languages was Trypillian and this was the language in which the late Trypillians and Steppe-Folk communicated. Lithuanian branched off from this language and the maternal language of the Trypillians continued into proto-Ukrainian, which led to the formation of the other Slavonic languages. It follows logically that modern Ukrainian began with the Trypillian language. It originated in the depths of Trypillia and has ceaselessly developed until the present day.

Let us now consider again the conclusions reached by Mykhailo Krasuskyi. He lived at a time when nothing was yet known about the Trypillian civilisation. However, in spite of that, he accurately predicted the existence in Ukraine of an ancient language which, in his opinion, was older than Sanskrit or Latin. He named this language Little-Russian, i.e. Ukrainian. Working in conditions of an information deficit he naturally made an insignificant error because this language was not Ukrainian but its predecessor, the Trypillian language. This is confirmed by the mathematical calculations concerning the time of its branching into Ukrainian and Lithuanian above. However, he was certainly correct in his assertion that Ukrainian was older than all the other Slavonic languages. The results of the calculation also refine the schema in 3.1, indicating that the branching of the Trypillian language into the Baltic and

Slavonic languages did not occur in the second but the third millennium BC. This fact is indirectly confirmed by the genetic witnesses to the past who allow us to identify the mass influx of the Steppe-Folk into Europe in the middle of the third millennium BC (see subsections 2.16, 2.18 and figure 2.10).

Further evidence for the millennial antiquity of Ukrainian has also been acquired by other means. Our contemporary, the renowned Ukrainian philologist Kostiantyn Tyshchenko, who knows more than 25 Eurasian languages, has researched Ukrainian's toponyms and its lexical borrowings from neighbouring languages. He reached the conclusion that Ukrainian had an "eternal, at least four thousand year, existence here on the territory of modern Ukraine as the modern Ukrainian and the proto and ancient Ukrainian variants of the language of the local Slavs". After his subsequent analysis of the vocabulary of borrowed words and their links with toponyms, Professor Tyshchenko affirms that "this vocabulary could be combined with these toponyms over several centuries only by a single people. Although the name of that people has changed more than once, they are the same inhabitants of the Dnipro and Dniester whose ancestors were Slavonic Indo-Europeans but throughout this period they were the local people of this area".[1]

---

1 Тищенко К. *Мовні контакти: свідки формування українців.* Київ: Аквілон-Плюс, 2006. pp. 17, 18

3.6 The Trypillians and Their Language

Humanity has, since a certain period and during its intellectual development, begun recording information about its life. It invented symbols to allow its language to be reproduced in physical formats and applied these to a variety of media. These included natural stone, fired clay tablets and vessels, the bark and leaves of plants, parchment fashioned from animal skins, knotted ropes and many other similar devices. This is how the first written mementoes appeared, some of which have survived to the present. These inscriptions are written in ancient, extinct languages which are extremely hard to decrypt. A profound study of these relics allows the reader, albeit partially, to learn about those historical events that occurred in the distant past. We are of course primarily interested in written sources regarding the peoples who inhabited the territory of Ukraine in those ancient times. Scientists who have studied these sources have established that different peoples successively inhabited Ukraine, replacing each other, and had, among others, the following names: Trypillians, Aryans, Cimmerians, Scythians, Sarmatians, Antes, Huns, Ruses and others. We will subsequently look at what is said about these peoples in the surviving, written sources.

The prevailing opinion among scientists at present is that the enigmatic inscriptions on found Trypillian artefacts are pictographic writing which is not read but interpreted like, for example, a road sign provides information for road users. You may comprehend the meaning and purpose of the Trypillian signs but there is no possibility of determining in which language and with what words they are written. However, some information can be obtained about the Trypillian language by analysing the languages which originate from it. The 32 words in the Swadesh list, for example, which are preserved in both Ukrainian and Lithuanian are the words of the Trypillian language: in Ukrainian they are ti, mi, cej, toj, ne, vsì, dva, malij, m'âso, krov, rìg, golova, oko, nìs, nìgot', ruka, serce, ïsti, znati, kusati, umirati, plavati, sidìti, stoâti, davati, voda, zemlâ, dim, vogon', zelenij, bìlij, novij.[1]

The calculated result of forty-five centuries obtained by the formula under 3.3 allows us to display graphically the chronology of the substitution process for Trypillian words from the Swadesh list with Proto-Ukrainian, Ancient, and modern Ukrainian words from the moment that Lithuanian branched away. Figure 3.5 presents a graph of the exponential function c where $c_1 = r_1^T$ which reflects this process mathematically.

---

[1] Translator's note: these words mean respectively; you, we, this, that, not, all, two, small, meat, blood, horn, head, eye, nose, nail, hand, heart, to eat, to know, to bite, to die, to swim, to sit, to stand, to give, water, earth, smoke, fire, green, white, new.

Chapter 3: What Languages Tell Us

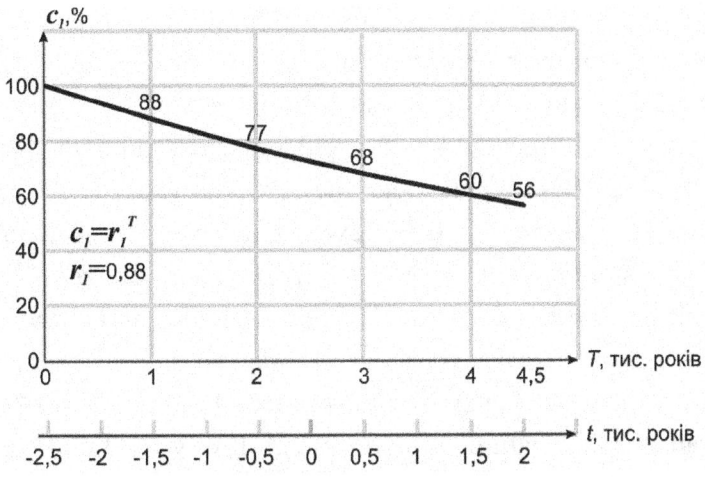

Figure 3.5: A graph illustrating the preservation of Trypillian words from the Swadesh list

The graph uses two time axes: T - the absolute time from the branching apart of Ukrainian and Lithuanian, while t is the calendar time according to modern chronology (both BC and AD) with the units of both being a period of one millennium. The percentage of preserved words from the Swadesh list is plotted on the ordinate axis. The graph demonstrates that, in middle of the first millennium BC, when the Persian Emperor Darius tried unsuccessfully to subdue the Scythians, the percentage of preserved Trypillian words in the Scythian language was 77%. The equivalent figure for modern Ukrainian is 56% i.e. 56 words from the 100 on the Swadesh list have been retained. These include the 32 words referred to above which survive in both Lithuanian and Ukrainian. There are in addition 24 words from among those marked with a plus sign in the preservation column on table 3.1. It is logical to conclude that these 24 words should be added to the list of the most utilised Trypillian words. Although they were replaced in Lithuanian they have survived in all the Slavonic languages without exception. These words are as follows: *odin, riba, voša, listok, korìn', kora, kìstka, âjce, pero, zub, âzik, piti, spati, lìtati, ležati, sonce, doŝ, kamìn', pìsok, popìl, čornij, nìč, teplij, povnij, kruglij, suhij, ìm'â.*[1] Professor Tyshchenko, whom we cited earlier, speaks of the Pan-Slavonic nature of these words.[2] However, it transpires that the number of preserved Pan-Slavonic words on the list, 27, slightly exceeds 24. This slight discrepancy should be attributed to errors in discretely assessing the match/mismatch of words in different languages that actually do not change discretely but continuously and the insufficient information for the calculation (we used 91 words rather than 100 and a time period of nine rather than ten centuries).

It is worth remembering that the Swadesh list consists of the words that are preserved the longest and, beyond it, words are replaced at a much higher rate. Therefore, the high percentage of preserved Trypillian words from the list

---

[1] Translator's note: the English meanings of these words are; one, fish, lice, leaf, root, bark, bone, egg, feather, tooth, tongue, to drink, to sleep, to fly, to lie (as in lie down), sun, rain, stone, sand, ash, black, night, warm, full, round, dry, (first) name.

[2] Тищенко Костянтин. *Всеслов'янськість мови українців*. Український тиждень, № 39 (256), 28.09–04.10.2012. p. 53.

we have calculated (56% as defined theoretically by the formula $c_1 = r_1{}^t$ and 59% (32+27) as determined in reality taking into account the number of Pan-Slavonic languages) does not mean that over half of the Ukrainian language is composed of Trypillian words. The percentage of Trypillian words for the entirety of the Ukrainian language is far lower due to the intense process of word substitution outside of the Swadesh list. Swadesh's method and his list are just tools which, like a polygraph, reveals hidden events on the historical path of a people and their language by analysing certain linguistic characteristics. In the present case, the lists and Swadesh's method have helped clarify when the Baltic and Slavonic language groups branched apart and established the Ukrainian language's Trypillian origins, which, it transpired, stretched back for 4,500 years and even to voice more than 50 preserved Trypillian words.

3.7 The Aryans

The word Aryans derives from the self designation of one of the Steppe tribes which is written in Sanskrit as *Arja* in the ancient collection of Indian religious songs, the *Rigveda,* and occurs throughout that text on several dozen occasions. The Aryans bore their name and several other words to India when they invaded its northern areas via the mountains of the Hindu Kush in the middle of the second millennium BC. They subdued the local population and brought with them a patriarchal and tribal system, faith in the heavenly gods and heroic oral epics which were the basis for the creations of one of the oldest books on earth, *The Vedas*. They also brought with them their language which became a prototype of Sanskrit.

However, Aryan words also occur far away from India in the form of borrowings in the Finno-Ugric languages. The Finns and the Estonians, for example, refer to a cow as *vasa* which derives from the Aryan word *vatsa*. Similarly, the Mordvins have a word *azor* which means "lord" and derives from the Aryan word *asura*, which means god or lord. There are also known and reverse borrowings from the Finno-Ugric languages: the Indian texts describe natural events which are not typical of Indian latitudes, The Northern Lights, white nights, leaf fall in winter, birds migrating, etc. This indicates that the Aryans lived for a prolonged period near the Finno-Ugric peoples who inhabited a forested strip between the River Vistula and the Eastern Urals. It follows that the Aryans lived south of this area, in the forested Steppe zone suitable for a semi-nomadic way of life. This is confirmed by the word *ar'âla*, which derives from the word Aryan, but means southern in the Sámi language spoken by a Finno-Ugric people of Northern Europe.[1]

The word "horse", which is closely related to the lifestyle of the Aryans, has not escaped the attention of philologists. When analysing this word in various ancient

---

1 Клейн Л. От Днепра до Инда. Знание – сила. Москва, 1984. № 7. p. 18.

Chapter 3: What Languages Tell Us

languages (Old Irish, Old English, Gothic, Tocharian, Sanskrit, Old Persian, etc.) and how it has changed since antiquity, they established that the forebears of the Aryans lived for a long period in the area where the horse was first domesticated and became part of their daily lives. The most ancient place where the remains of a domesticated horse were found is near Deriyivka village, Kirovograd oblast on the right bank of the Dnipro. The American archaeologist Marija Gimbutas concluded, on the basis of the findings from an excavation of a cemetery near the village, that the wild horse was first tamed in this area 6,000 years ago.[1] All of this indicates that the Aryans originally dwelled on their primeval homeland in South Ukraine, from where they embarked on their long journey to India and elsewhere.

Traces of the Aryans' historic habitation have been found far from both Ukraine and India on the territory of the modern states of Syria and Iraq. There is also a fourteenth century tract entitled *Training Book* which has survived to the present day and was authored by one Kikkuli, a representative of the local people of Mitanni in Syria. The work is a treatise on horse training and includes words borrowed from the Aryan language but slightly modified to the local, Mitanni language. These words include *ajka-vartana, tera-vartana, panca-vartana*, which

---

1 Parpola A. The Problem of the Aryans and the Soma: textual-linguistic and archaeological evidence. The Indo-Aryans of Ancient South Asia: Language Material Culture and Ethnicity, Berlin – New York: Walter de Gruyter, 1995. pp. 354, 355.

mean one circle, three circles, five circles respectively. The word *vartana* originates from the verbs "to turn", "to return" (in Ukrainian these are *vertìti, povertati*) and means to pass a horse through a full circle. These words are preceded by Sanskrit numerals *eka* (one), *tri* (three) *pancha* (five) and slightly modified under the influence of the local Mitanni language. The information found in the interstate treaty of one of Mitanni's rulers is of crucial significance. He sealed the treaty with an oath to four gods whose names are almost identical to those of Indian gods, *Indara* (similar to the Indian god *Indra*) and *Mitira*, *Nasatia* and *Uruvna* (*Varuna*). Furthermore, in documents dating from this period which have been found in Syria and Palestine, the names *Purusha* and *Indarota* (*Indrota*) are also identical to Indian names. The Aryans appeared on the territory of Syria no later than their incursion into India and in all probability simultaneously in the middle of the second millennium BC. These names, therefore, were probably borne to Syria and India from the same area, the homeland of the Aryans, the territory of Ukraine.[1] This conclusion is supported by the external appearance of a Mitanian Aryan whose image is preserved on a relief depicting captured soldiers from the Saqqara Tomb of the Egyptian Pharaoh Horemheb who lived in the fourteenth century BC (figure 3.6).[2]

---

1 Клейн Л. *От Днепра до Инда*. Знание – сила. Москва, 1984. № 7. p. 17.
2 See https://ru.m.wikipedia.org.

Chapter 3: What Languages Tell Us

Figure 3.6: The depiction of an Aryan on the tomb of Pharaoh Horemheb

The image depicts a large Cossack-style forelock dangling from his head, the sign of a warrior defending his land. The portrait stands out from those of the other warriors by virtue of its European appearance: the straight nose, the high, flat forehead and the round head. The descendants of the Aryans continued the tradition of wearing a forelock. The Byzantine historian Leo Diaconus described the appearance of the Kyivan Prince Svyatoslav Khorobryj, who lived 2,500 years after the Aryans, as follows: "his head was completely bald but a forelock hung down one side, the sign of nobility." This tradition was continued at an even later date by the Zaporozhian Cossacks and you can meet people now on the streets of Kyiv, Dnipro or Zaporizhzhia with the same hairstyles. This tradition, which is characteristic of Ukrainians and their ancestors, has therefore existed for no less than 3,500 years.

The traces of ancient Aryan habitation are preserved by linguistic relics in another area far removed from the locality of their ancestral homeland, on the territory of

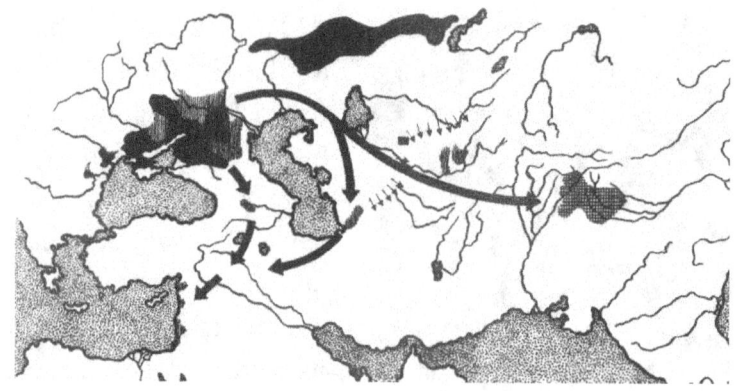

Figure 3.7: The three streams of Aryan migration

Persia, which now bears a name derived from the word Aryan, Iran. A collection of religious songs similar to the *Rigveda* was created here but at a later date than its Indian counterpart. This book known as *The Avesta* presents the Aryans as the ancestors of the Iranians. The linguistic sources we have referred to show that the Aryans migrated in three streams. The first stream passed over the Caucasus and Anatolia to Syrian and Palestinian territory where the state of Mitania was created. The second stream ran through Central Asia and the mountains of the Hindu Kush to North India where the Indo-Aryan state Aryavarta was created. Finally, the third stream, which departed a little later than the first two, passed by the Caspian Sea to the territory of Persia which later became known as Iran (figure 3.7).[1]

---

[1] Клейн Л. *От Днепра до Инда.* Знание – сила. Москва, 1984. № 7. № 7. p. 19.

Chapter 3: What Languages Tell Us

What compelled the Aryans to resettle so rapidly in different areas? The most probable cause was climate change and in particular a drought which lasted until the seventh century BC.[1]

The resettlement of the Steppe-Folk, including the Aryans, is vividly and richly portrayed in the book *The Wonder That Was India* by the renowned Indologist Professor A. L. Basham. An excerpt from this book is given here:[2]

About 2000 BC, the great steppeland which stretches from Poland to Central Asia was inhabited by semi-nomadic barbarians, who were tall, comparatively fair and mostly long headed. They had tamed the horse which they harnessed to light chariots with spoked wheels of a much faster and better type than the lumbering ass-drawn carts with four solid wheels, which were the best means of transport known to contemporary Sumer. They were mainly pastoral, but practised a little agriculture. There is no evidence that they were in direct contact with the Sumerians, but they had adopted some Mesopotamian innovations, notably the shaft-hole axe. In the early part of the second millennium, whether from

---

1 Брайчевский М.Ю. *Когда и как возник Киев*. Киев: «Наукова думка», 1964. pp. 21, 22.
2 Basham A. L. The Wonder That Was India. 3rd revised edition. New Delhi: Sidgwick & Jackson, 2000. p. 29.

the pressure of population, desiccation of pasture lands, or from both causes, these people were on the move. They migrated in bands westwards, southwards and eastwards, conquering local populations and inter-marrying with them to form a ruling class. They brought with them their patrilineal family system, their worship of sky gods and their horses and chariots. In most of the lands in which they settled their original language gradually adapted itself to the tongues of the conquered peoples. Some invaded Europe, to become the ancestors of the Greeks, Latins, Celts and Teutons; others appeared in Anatolia, and from the mixture of these with the original inhabitants there arose the great empire of the Hittites. Yet others remained in their old home, the ancestors of the later Baltic and Slavonic people. And yet others moved southwards to the Caucasus and the Iranian tableland, whence they made many attacks on the Middle Eastern civilisations. The Kassites, who conquered Babylon, were led by men of this stock. In the fourteenth century BC there appeared in North-East Syria, a people called Mitanni, whose kings had Indo-Iranian names, and a few of whose gods are familiar to every student of Indian religion: Indara: Uruvna (the Vedic god Varuna), Mitira and Nasatiya. As well as those of the Mitanni, other chiefs in Syria and Palestine had names of Indo-Iranian type.

Chapter 3: What Languages Tell Us

The marauding tribesmen gradually merged with the older populations of the Middle East, and the ancient civilisations, invigorated by fresh blood and ideas, they rose to new heights of material culture.

The Aryans sent separate parts of their tribe to develop new territories while simultaneously adapting to the arid climate of the drought referred to above. They never left their homeland, as evidenced by haplogroup R1a1a which was preserved by them and their descendants on our land to the present day. Ukrainians are grateful to their Aryan ancestors for *The Vedas* created by them, for the signs of Svarog, which adorn Saint Sophia, and for the symbol of the Trisuttâ, which became Ukraine's state emblem. They are especially grateful for the language which the Aryans received from the Trypillians and became the property of Ukraine, its state language.

3.8 The Cimmerians

The earliest reference to the Cimmerians is found in *The Odyssey*, the epic poem by the legendary Ancient Greek poet Homer who lived in the eighth century BC. The poem describes the adventures of the Greek wanderers led by Odysseus whose boat was driven to the shores of Cimmeria:

At last we reached the deep current of the River Oceanus

There lies the city and the land of the Cimmerians
Arriving, we moored our boat and drove
Sheep along the currents of Oceanus, the river moved...[1]

Homer's words convey a great deal. Firstly, they contradict the official view that the Cimmerians were a nomadic people who never built cities and only ruined those of others during military campaigns. Homer is, after all, describing a Cimmerian city and their settled mode of life. Secondly, these words helped orientate the search for the location of their city. The River Oceanus could be an estuary that extends the river's current into the sea. So, marvellously, twenty-eight centuries after Homer, archaeologists have found evidence confirming his words. The remnants of an ancient Cimmerian city were discovered in 1927 where the convergence of the Southern Bug and Ingul rivers forms the Bug estuary, almost in the centre of the modern oblast town of Mykolayiv.[2] This event is of similar significance to the discovery of Troy by Heinrich Schliemann, which also occurred not least due to the description of the city's location in Homer's *Iliad*. Archaeologists found further confirmation of Homer's words on the slopes of the Opuk mountain in Crimea, near the city of Kerch, when they discovered the remains of a Cimmerian

---

1 Original text taken from: Гомер. Одіссея / пер. Б. Тена. Харків: Фоліо, 2001. ХÌ, 13, 14, 20, 21.

2 See uk.wikipedia.org/wiki/Місто_людей_кімерійських

Chapter 3: What Languages Tell Us

city which predated the Greek settlements in Crimea.[1] The Cimmerians, therefore, had cities and, like their forebears the Aryans, led a partially nomadic life.

The name Cimmerians is derive from the Greeks and in their language it sounds like Kimmerioi (Κιμμέριοι). However, in the cuneiform texts of Assyria, from the seventh to eighth centuries, there is also a reference to this people but their name is pronounced slightly differently as Gimirri.[2] The extremely similar names for one and the same people acquired from two sources, Greek and Assyrian, which are very remote from each other, indicate that the Cimmerians/Gimirri is the name this people called themselves and it is given differently in foreign languages. But what was their actual name?

If the linguistic bridges that connect the modern world with the remote past, between which their lie millennia, were not preserved it would be almost impossible to determine this name and through it the descendants of this people. However, we have a fortunate chance circumstance here in the surviving ancient Indian manuscripts written in Sanskrit. The renowned Ukrainian Indologist Stepan Nalyvaiko, who researched the ancient Indian epic *The Mahabharata*, drew attention to the strange similarity between the name of the Suvira people it refers to and the name of the Sivera (or Severa) people Nestor described in

---

1 УРЕ. Київ 1980. Т. 5. p. 186.
2 Гаврилюк Н. Гіміррі. Енциклопедія історії України. Т. 2. http://history.org.ua/?termin=Gimirri.

The Tale of the Bygone Years: "a druzii že sědoša na Desně i po Semi i po Sulě i narkošasja Sěvera."[1] ("The others settled along the Desna, Sema and Sul and were called the Severa.)The similarity of these names provided an impetus to further linguistic and historical research which resulted in the Indologist developing a convincing hypothesis regarding the "self naming" of the "Cimmerian People".[2] We will now consider its fundamental elements.

The vowel sound *u* in Ukrainian is often transferred into other vowel sounds in Sanskrit such as i-a-o, etc. The following pairings, with the Sanskrit word preceding the Ukrainian and the English definition, illustrate this vowel change: *sunu-syn* (son), *chatura-chotyry* (four), *bgru-brova* (eyebrows), *bahuta-bahato* (many). If we take this into account it becomes clear that the words Suvira and Sivera are the same name in which the vowels have been changed. However, it is a mystery how this name came to be shared by two peoples who were not only geographically distant but who have a chronological gap of one and a half to two millennia between them (from Homer to Nestor). *The Mahabharata* helps us conjecture how this might have occurred. The fact is that in this epic the Suvira people are definitely mentioned together with the Sindhi people and

---

1 Повість врем'яних літ: літопис (за Іпатським списком) / пер. з давньоруської, післяслово, комент. В. В. Яременка. Київ: Рад. письменник, 1990. p. 8

2 Наливайко Степан. Таємниці розкриває санскрит. Київ: Вид. центр «Просвіта», 2000.pp. 10–17.

Chapter 3: What Languages Tell Us

they shared a territory and rulers with each other. When it describes the life of these peoples, *The Mahabharata* practically equates them. However, the Sindhis are known outside India and, according to Ancient Greek historians, also lived in the area of the present day Taman Peninsula i.e. where the Cimmerians lived. Furthermore, several centuries later, at the beginning of the first millennium AD, when the world had seemingly forgotten the Cimmerians, Greek historians noted that they, and the Sindhis, lived on the Taman Peninsula. Dionysius Periegetes, who lived in the first and second centuries AD, for example, wrote in his historical chronicle that "the Sauromates neighbour with the Sindhis, the Cimmerians and those who live near the Euxine". (Author's note: Euxine refers to the Black Sea.)[1].It appears that the tandem of the Suvira and the Sindhi, which developed in India, was the equivalent of the tandem of the Cimmerians and the Sindhi who lived on the Taman Peninsula. It is logical to conclude, therefore, that the word Cimmerians is the self designation of the Sivera people transmitted through the medium of Ancient Greek. Similarly, it is the word which 1,500 to 2,000 years later than the Assyrians and the Greeks was rendered by Nestor as "Sĕvera".

Why did the Greeks change the name of the Sivera so profoundly? The fact is that, as time passed, the

---

1 Латышев В. В. Известия древних писателей греческих и латинских о Скифии и Кавказе. Санкт-Петербург: Тип. Императорской Академии Наук. 1890. Т. I. Греческие писатели. p. 184

pronunciation of words in the maternal language varies in different zones that it extends to. The linguistic boundary which separates these zones is termed the isogloss. The characteristic isogloss for Indo-European languages is termed the *centum-satem* which derives from the pronunciation of the word for 100 in the Latin (centum) and Avestan (satem) languages. Ukrainian, Sanskrit and other languages belong to the *satem* group; Greek, Italian and some other languages belong to the *centum* group. The geographic isogloss seemingly divides Indo-Europeans into eastern and western groups. The consonantal sound *s* in Eastern Indo-European words is often replaced by *k* in Western Indo-European words, including Greek. This is apparent in the following Ukrainian words when contrasted with their Greek equivalents, both given here in the Latin alphabet: *serce – kardìo, desâtnik – dekan*.[1] The *v* sound is often replaced by *m*, so, for example, we can assume that the word "Nemogardas" in Greek (Νεμογαρδάς) is the equivalent of Novgorod in Ukrainian but pronounced in a Greek fashion. This explains how the Sivera became the Cimmerians for the Greeks.

When analysing the names of different peoples, as well as the events described in *The Mahabharata*, Stepan Nalivaiko concludes that some of the occurrences described took place on the northern Black Sea coast with

---

[1] The word pairings mean "heart" and "Dean" respectively.

Chapter 3: What Languages Tell Us

the participation of the forebears of modern Ukrainians.[1] Stories describing these events were borne orally to the territory of India and described in the epic *The Mahabharata* and the Cimmerians/Sivera were one of the local Trypillian tribes who had eternally dwelled on the northern Black Sea coast. They, like their forebears the Aryans, sent units of their tribesmen to distant India where their name was corrected to fit the local language norms: the Sivera became the Suvira.

Herodotus, writing in the fifth century BC, outlined the boundaries inhabited by the Cimmerians from the Dniester to the Taman. Subsequently, Nestor, writing in the eleventh century AD recorded their northern expansion to what is now Chernihiv region. The territory they inhabited is testified to by modern place names: Sivershchina, Novhorod-Siverskyi, Siversky Donets. Similarly, some ancient place names allude to them: the Cimmerian (Siversky) Bosporus (now the Kerch Strait), as well as the name of the ancient city on the Kerch Peninsula which may have been called Siverik but which the Greeks transmitted in their fashion as Cimmeric. This list can also include the name of the city of Severodonetsk which was unfortunately distorted by its transference through a foreign language, in this case Russian. It would be correct, therefore, to name the city Siverodonetsk,

---

1 Наливайко Степан. *Давньоіндійські імена. Назви. Терміни: проекція на Україну*: довідник. Київ, 2009. p. 233.

from the name for the associated river, Siversky Donets. It is possible that the name of the Crimean Peninsula (Krym in Ukrainian) originates from the name of the first state on its territory because the word Crimea in modern Chinese sounds like "Kemiliya" which is very similar to "Cimmeria".

Stepan Nalivaiko's hypothesis, which equates the Taman Cimmerians and the Chernihiv Siverians, reveals a new view of the history of our ancestors. It becomes clear why the Tmutarakan principality, which is remote from Chernihiv on the Taman Peninsula, was ruled mainly by Chernihiv princes. This probably occurred because both the Sivera and the Tmutarakan people were descendants of those same Cimmerians. The cherished dream of Prince Ihor "to seek the city of Tmutarakan, or else to drink with their helmets from the Don" becomes comprehensible. *The Tale of the Host of Ihor* uses these playful metaphors to reveal Prince Ihor's yearning to break across the Polovtsian Steppe and regain his sovereignty over the Tmutarakan principality, which had been lost 100 years earlier. However, the Polovtsians, who had their own interests in Tmutarakan, which did not coincide with that of the Siverans, obstructed him and, as we know, his plans were not realised. He was not helped by the family ties between many Siverans and the Polovtsians, because of a widespread tradition among them for taking a Polovtsian wife. Ihor had inherited much from the Polovtsians because both his grandfather and father were married to the daughters of Polovtsian Khans,

Chapter 3: What Languages Tell Us

so he had, in part, Polovtsian blood in his veins. All of this illustrates the ethnic proximity of the Siverans and Polovtsians, indicating that both were descendants of those ancient Cimmerians and Sindis who were written about by the Greeks and Assyrians. It is evidence that they were not nomads who came to this land but indigenous peoples who had long lived on Ukrainian territory and were the direct descendants of the Cimmerians. The Polovtsians, like the Siverans, made a noteworthy contribution to the formation of the Ukrainian nation.

Another important aspect of the Cimmerians should be noted, this being the special, important position of women in their families and society. Cimmerian women did not only manage family affairs, they often led military campaigns and participated in battle alongside the menfolk. This circumstance has engendered countless legends about the warlike Amazons who allegedly killed the boys they gave birth to and let only the girls live. They supposedly burned one of their breasts with a copper instrument at a young age so that it did not develop and hamper their mastery of weapons. There were also many other fables about their practices.

The independent status of a Cimmerian woman, her equality with men, which distinguished her from the women of other peoples, has existed for millennia, since Cimmerian times, and persists to the present. Even now the echoes of ancient legends in the antique songs of Polissya which praise the "vojs′ko dìvoc′koê" (maiden army) can be heard. In some places in Ukraine, and in particular in Volhynia, an ancient tradition has been preserved which gives a girl the right to pay suit to a boy by taking him to live in her or her family's house. She sends suitors to his parents and she herself goes to them and shows her ability to manage the household then requests the groom and his parents to agree to the marriage. The parents, respecting the custom of their ancestors, do not have the right to reject her without knowing her abilities as a mistress of the household or the kind of person she is.[1]

The equality of men and women within marriage is eloquently testified to by the Ukrainian word for marriage, *šlûb,* which derives from *zlûb, zlûbitisâ*, the words for being and falling in love and contrasts with the Russian word *brak* which derives from to take. The word *šlûb* very accurately reflects the tradition Ukrainians have of getting married or choosing someone out of love and not to please someone else's will. The tradition of not marrying upon someone as the Russians say but being married to someone underlines the equal rights of the partners within Ukrainian wedlock. This Ukrainian tradition begins in the Cimmerian period and these differences illustrate that Ukrainians and Russians had different ancestors whose family structures were significantly different.

---

[1] Романюк Ніна. *Слідами волинських амазонок.* Україна молода. 08.09.1999. 08.09.1999.

3.9 The Scythians

The name of the Scythians (which is Skitoi, Σκύθοι, in Ancient Greek) and the name they gave themselves, Skoloti (which is Σκολότοι in Ancient Greek), was recorded by the "Father of History" Herodotus in book four of his histories, *Melpomene*.[1] Most philologists believe that both terms derived from the word *skuda* (to shoot) whose root has survived to the present in some Indo-European languages. It may be logically assumed that this word was present in the ancient Scythian language which is one of the representatives of the Indo-European language family. Unfortunately, there is no extant and deciphered Scythian text at the present time. Philologists are therefore compelled to study a very limited array of personal and geographic names which have been preserved in texts concerning the Scythians in Ancient Greek, Syriac-Babylonian and other ancient languages. The research demonstrates that in Scythian, by comparison with the languages above, the consonantal sound *d* becomes *I*. The Scythians probably, therefore, pronounced the word *skuda* as *skula* and their self name Skoloty derives from that pronunciation. Furthermore, in Ancient Greek the pronunciation of the consonantal sound *d* changed a little over time, with its ringing crisp sound

---

[1] Walter Blanco, *Herodotus: The Histories: The Complete Translation, Backgrounds, Commentaries*. Edited by Jennifer Tolbert Roberts. New York: W. W. Norton, 2013. (Book 4, VI)

changed to the muted theta ϑ (theta) and the pronunciation of the word *skuda* changing to *skutha* (σκύϑα). The most common weapon at that time was the bow, so the self name of the Scythians, Skoloti, most probably meant archers. Therefore, it is probable that Herodotus gave the name of these archers in two languages, with the Greek pronunciation Skify and then as it was pronounced by the Scythians themselves, Skoloty. (Because the pronunciation of the Greek word [*theta*] is closer to the pronunciation of the Cyrillic letter *m*(t) rather than *ф*(f), authors of Ukrainian texts in recent times write Skyty rather that Skify, Ateny (Athens) rather than Afiny, and Eter rather than Efer (Ether) etc.).

The self naming of the Scythians as Archers is not incidental. In the legend of the origin of the Scythians, as narrated by Herodotus, it is said that the mighty Heracles, whom the Scythians considered their ancestor, carried two bows. He left one of them with his sons and gave them the following task: whichever of them could draw the bow when he became an adult would become the ruler of the land. Only one of the sons, the third and youngest who was called Skif, could fulfil this task. He began the dynasty of those who became the Scythian emperors. It is no wonder that the gold and silver vase from the Kul-Oba burial mound, this outstanding masterpiece of ancient jewellery, depicts, among other daily scenes, how the bow, one of the main instruments of the Scythians, is prepared (figure 3.8).

Chapter 3: What Languages Tell Us

Figure 3.8: The depiction of a Scythian on the Kul-Oba vase

The bow became the main symbol of the Scythians and led to their self designation as archers.

It follows from this analysis that Scythians (the archers/shooters) is not the name of a separate ethnic group or people, it is a collective name belonging to the tribes and peoples who were part of a large state union which acquired the name Scythia (or, in Nestor's chronicle. Velikaâ Skufъ). This is confirmed by the fact that Herodotus, who was aware of the specific character of each Scythian people he described, gave them double names: Scythian-Ploughers, Scythian-Farmers, Scythian-Nomads, Scythian-Royals, and other designations. Who were these peoples, were they indigenous or did they come from elsewhere?

According to the historical records, the Scythians, as described by Herodotus, ruled the territory of modern Ukraine from the seventh to the third centuries BC.[1] Therefore, they were on this land when, according to genetic and toponymic research, Slavs were already present (see section 2.20). It is probably these Slavs, that Herodotus named Scythian-Ploughers and Scythian-Farmers thereby emphasising their main characteristic their agricultural occupations, which originated with their Trypillian ancestors. The Slavs clearly constituted the majority of the Scythian population, judging by the fact that at the end of the first millennium BC they began settling from the Middle Dnipro Basin to the south, west and south-west due to overpopulation.[2] It follows that the main element of the Scythian population was the Slavs, the indigenous residents of the Dnipro region, the descendants of the Trypillians and the settled Steppe-Folk. The ruling positions in Scythian society, according to Herodotus, belonged to the royal Scythians. He noted that they organised their greatest holiday annually in honour of the Scythian war god Ares, on the territory of what is now the Kirovohrad region in the locality of Ekzampai, which translates as "Sacred Paths". Here, on the soil of the Kirovohrad region, there

---

[1] *Словник-довідник з археології* / під ред. Н. О. Гаврилюк. Київ: Наукова думка, 1996 р. 252.

[2] *История Украинской ССР*. Киев : «Наукова думка», 1981. Т. 1. р. 139.

Chapter 3: What Languages Tell Us

was a central Scythian sanctuary, the sacred centre of Scythia.[1]

It is very regrettable that the residents of the former Kirovohrad, probably due to a lack of historical awareness, did not support the writer and publicist Serhiy Plachinda's excellent proposal to rename their city Skifopol, thereby engraving topographically the presence of these Ukrainian forebears on their land. The name Skifopol would be a worthy memorial to our Scythian ancestors who are known throughout the world. It is lamentable because when Ukrainians are indifferent to their historical values and do not protect them the apologists of the "Russian World" persistently promote their vision of Great Scythia. They allege that it stretched from Transnistria to Southern Siberia and that "its borders correspond approximately with the borders of the Russian Empire".[2] There was no such state in reality, just as there were no Scythians as envisaged by the Russian poet Aleksandr Blok:

> Yes, the Scythians are us
> Yes the Asiatics are us
> With slanted
> And gluttonous eyes!

---

1 Петрук Володимир. *Екзампай. Сакральний центр Великої Скіфії*. Київ: Київськ. націон. університет імені Тараса Шевченка, 2006. p. 241.

2 Васильева Н. И. *«Великая Скифия». Новый взгляд на историю Древнего Мира*. Москва: Метагалактика, 1999–2000. 304

Let us consider the portrait of a Scythian reconstructed from a skull discovered by archaeologists (figure 3.9).[1]

There are no "slanted eyes" and indeed it is a typical European visage. There are indeed countless numbers of people with similar faces among us Ukrainians.

There even arose a dispute between the Scythians and the Egyptians as to which people was the more ancient according to the Roman historian Gnaeus Pompeius Trogus, who lived five centuries later than Herodotus. In his work *Philippic Histories and the Origin of the Whole World and the Places of the Earth,* Pompeius, who is also known as "the second Herodotus" wrote about a protracted quarrel between the Scythians and the Egyptians regarding which was the elder, which race was more ancient.[2] The ancient world regarded the arguments advanced by the Egyptians as mistaken and therefore Pompeius wrote in

Figure 3.9: The facial reconstruction of a Scythian

---

1 Сегеда Сергій. *У пошуках предків. Антропологія та етнічна історія України.* Київ : Наш час, 2012. p. 207.

2 The original Latin title is *Historiae Philippicae et Totius Mundi Origines et Terrae Situs.*

Chapter 3: What Languages Tell Us

his history that "the Scythians were always regarded as the more ancient people".[1]

Let us examine his account in more detail. The most ancient Egyptian kingdom only began its existence in the twenty-second century BC, at exactly the point when the Trypillian civilisation ceased to exist. It transpires that the Scythian advantage over the Egyptians in terms of longevity signifies that they remembered their ancestors from the time when the Trypillian civilisation still existed. They clearly traced their lineage from the Steppe-Folk who destroyed Trypillia (see section 2.18). The Steppe-Folk, as was shown in section two, are the indigenous people of the Black Sea and Azov Steppes. It follows therefore that the Scythians regarded themselves as indigenous to this area.

The fact of this dispute between the Egyptians and Scythians, as recorded in these histories, illustrates how aware the ancient world was of the people known as the Scythians. The world then knew of their strength and invincibility and the wisdom of Scythian philosophers such as Anacharsis, and which peoples inhabited Scythia and their customs etc. Ukraine, therefore, has such an ancient and detailed description of its history, of a kind which is not possessed even by the developed countries of Europe such as France, Germany, England, etc.,

---

1 *Justini in historias Trogi Pompeii epitomarum.* Lubecae; Lipsiae: Widemeyerus 1702. Lib. 1–2.

because the first records of the people of these countries were only produced at the end of the first millennium BC. Herodotus may rightly be considered not only the "father" of world history but also the father of the ancient history of Ukraine.

However, in addition to his work, there are chroniclers who later than him recorded the military prowess of the Scythians and, in particular, Paulus Orosius who lived in the fourth century AD. In his book *The History of the War against the Pagans,* Orosius described the Scythians victory over the army of Zopirion, one of the deputies of the renowned Alexander of Macedonia, in 331 BC.[1] The Scythian triumph over the Macedonian army had an extraordinary resonance in the world of that time: their army, which did not succumb either to the Persian Emperor Darius the First's or Alexander the Great's army, was considered invincible. In the first century AD, when the Roman Emperor Trajan managed to defeat them at a point when Scythian power was already in decline, he was gloried as the "One who Triumphed over Scythia".[2] Trajan honoured his victory by building a monument that was unprecedented in scope at that time and consisted of a massive stone cube, 40 metres long, wide and tall, with a 15 metre relief sculpture of himself thereon.[3]

---

1 The original Latin title is *Historiarum Adversum Paganos.*
2 Eusebius Pamphilus. *Chronicon.* p. 193.
3 Боргардт Олександр. *Дві культури.* 5-те вид. Київ : Видавничий дім «Простір», 2016.p. 18.

3.10 The Sarmatians

Herodotus, the father of history, narrated a beautiful legend concerning how the marriages between young Scythians and martial Amazons gave rise to a new, tenacious tribe whom he named the Sauromatians but which his successors termed the Sarmatians. He asserted that the Sauromatians spoke the Scythian language because the male Scythians could not learn "Amazonian". However, it transpired that the women were smarter and mastered Scythian.[1] The legend in fact reflected the reality that the Sarmatians were one of the related Scythian tribes which belonged to the Scythian state union and there was in fact no significant difference between these two peoples. They not only had a common language but there was little difference between their lifestyles, burial rites and even their clothing. The sole difference was in the period of their dominance over other tribes. The leading role in the state union, which covered the territory of modern Ukraine, was passed from the Scythians to the Sarmatians at the end of the fourth century BC. They ruled the state union from the third century BC into the third century AD and this resulted in even the name of the state changing. Western historians no longer termed it Scythia but instead used the name European Sarmatia.

The name Sarmatians, like the name Scythians, is a general designation for certain peoples known from the

---

1 Herodoti. *Historiarum*. Libri IX. Lipsiae, 1890. Lib. 4. p. 114, 117.

works of ancient historians who divided them into different peoples such as the Iazyges (or Ias), Roxolani (White Alans), Siraces, Aorsi, Alans and other tribes. In particular, the ancient Roman historian Strabo wrote about the first state union of the Sarmatians in the territories of modern Ukraine, which was formed at the beginning of the second century BC between the Iazyges and the Roxolani. They subdued the Scythians and expanded their domain on what is now the territory of modern Romania, Bulgaria and Hungary, approaching the border of the Roman Empire with which they were almost constantly at war. The periods of conflict were sporadically interrupted by periods of peace during which armed Sarmatian detachments, mainly cavalry, entered the service of the Roman army and civilian Sarmatians settled throughout Europe on the lands of the Roman Empire. At the beginning of the AD period, the Aorsi drove the Roxolani from the territory of Southern Ukraine and in the second century AD all the Scythian-Sarmatians were conquered by the Alans, which resulted in a new state union being formed.

From where does the generalised term Sarmatians originate? There are several versions concerning the source of this term. The most probable of them, in my view, seems to be that proposed by the scientific Russian linguist Oleg Trubachov who derives it from the Indo-Aryan word *sar* (woman) and the suffix "ma(n)t" which conjoined approximate to "feminine" in meaning. This version is supported by the fact that in excavated

Chapter 3: What Languages Tell Us

Scythian-Sarmatian graves 20% of the skeletons are those of women who were buried in the same clothing and with the same weaponry as the men.[1] In addition, the historical chronicles contain stories about Sarmatian women leading military campaigns and, in parity with the men, participating in battles. The ancient Greco-Roman historian Polyaenus, in a work entitled *Strategemata* (military ploys), tells the story of Amage, the wife of one of the Sarmatian kings in the second century BC. The tenacious Amage rode at the head of 100 riders, whom she gave three horses each, travelling 1,200 stade (190 kilometres) to defend the inhabitants of Tauric Chersonesus from the harsh arbitrary rule of the Scythians.[2] The unexpected onslaught of the Sarmatians broke through the Scythian guard, penetrated the palace and dealt with the people who were oppressing the Chersonese people.[3] This allows us to see how, by contrast with other peoples, the position of women is a characteristic feature inherent in the societies of the Cimmerians, Scythians and Sarmatians. This trait was probably developed across several millennia in the harsh conditions of the nomadic life of the Steppe-Folk. The obligations and the skills of both the female and male

---

1 Anthony David. *The Horse, the Wheel, and Language. How Bronze-Age Riders from Eurasian Steppe Shaped the Modern World.* Princeton University Press.

2 Translator's note - A Roman unit of measurement also known as a furlong – some sources say 100 stades (roughly 184.81 kilometres).

3 Симоненко О. В. Амага. *Енциклопедія історії України.* Т. 1: А–В. Київ: Наукова думка, 2003.

sexes were compelled to equivalence by nature itself. This characteristic also speaks to the common origin of these Steppe tribes who returned from the Asian Steppes to their homeland. The ancient historians regarded them as natives of Central Asia, but this was in fact a return to their native habitats, albeit a savage one with war and victims.

The first written reference to Kyiv, a city which in all times played a central unifying role in the lives of Ukrainians, occurs during that period when the Sarmatians already ruled Scythia. The reference occurs in Claudius Ptolemy's work *Geography*, in the middle of the second century. Although Ptolemy was a contemporary of the Sarmatians, he lived far away from them in Alexandria, therefore, the information about Kyiv reached him through intermediaries and appears slightly distorted, as a result he records Kyiv under the name of Metropolis. We will address how this occurred later, but now let us try to investigate the origin of the name Kyiv.

3.11 From where does your name come, Kyiv?

This section will show how the linguistic witnesses of the peoples of the world, in accord with their genetic witnesses and with the knowledge derived from certain natural sciences, jointly reveal the origin of the name Kyiv. They simultaneously contradict the legend of the founder of the city, the mythical prince Kyi. Their disclosure begins with the oldest linguistic witness, toponyms.

Chapter 3: What Languages Tell Us

Toponyms that are similar to the word Kyiv occur in the vast areas stretching from Poland and Czechia to Siberia and Finland. There are, for example, the mountains of Kieve and Kijov in Poland, Kiy Island in the White Sea, the Kevė river and Kivijärvi lake in Finland, the Keyva Mountains in Russia's Murmansk oblast, the Kiya and *Kievskii Egan* rivers in Western Siberia, the historic Kijski Mountains (which are now termed Kuznetsk-Alatau) and many others.[1] These names are thousands of years old and originate from a very ancient word which is close to the modern word *kivi* in Finnish, *kev* in Mordovian, *kiv* in the Mansi language and related words in other languages. All of these words mean "stone". Names similar to the word Kyiv have been inherited by the current generation of proto-Finnic tribes which inhabited these vast areas before the Indo-Europeans emerged on them. Proto-Finns or primeval Finns are the ancient forebears of the Finno-Ugric peoples: the Hungarians, Finns, Estonians, Mordovians, Udmurts, Mari, Khanty, Mansi and others. The extremely ancient habitation of the Eurasian territories by the proto-Finns is evidenced not only by the toponyms listed above but also by the linguistic witnesses in the form of numerous borrowings from Finnish vocabulary, phonetics and grammar in Indo-European languages.[2] It

---

1 Тищенко К. Мовні контакти: свідки формування українців.Київ Аквілон-Плюс, 2006. 416 с. pp. 65, 66.

2 Ibid pp 57,58.

is also supported by the genetic witnesses which show the far greater antiquity of the proto-Finns compared to Indo-Europeans.[1] As we have already remarked, the descendants of the proto-Finns were the neighbours of the ancient Aryans in the second and third millennia BC. However, subsequently, Claudius Ptolemy recorded their presence in the Dnipro region in the second century AD and termed them the Finni (Φίννοι).[2] He also refers to their neighbours the Bulans (Βούλανες), perhaps these were the Polianians or Volhynians.[3] Later still, the Slavs spread to the north-east and displaced the descendants of the proto-Finns from the Dnipro region. The primary occupations of the proto-Finns were fishing, hunting and fruit picking. The names they gave to the surrounding geographical features, therefore, were primarily intended to ease the navigation of the terrain and simplify the mutual agreement of the plans and details of joint ventures in these areas. There were convenient and notable landmarks for them, such as a large stone or group of stones, a stone outcrop, boulder or rocks. These acquired a general name articulated in one short word which would be close to the modern Finnish word *kivi.* It is probable that this word also referred to a place

---

[1] Cavalli-Sforza L. L. et al. The History and Geography of Human Genes: Princeton University Press, Princeton, 1994. pp. 268–270.

[2] Claudii Ptolemaei. Geographia. Edidit Carolus Fridericus Augustus Nobbe. Lipsiae, 1843, vol. III pp. 5, 20.

[3] Translator's note: these were two ancient Slavonic tribes.

Chapter 3: What Languages Tell Us

where Kyiv is now located. But where was that stone which gave Kyiv its name?

It is known that the central area of Ukraine lies on the Ukrainian Shield or Ukrainian Crystalline Massif, which formed billions of years ago as the result of the rising of the hard granite rocks. The shield stretched in a broad strip towards the south-east from Prykarpattia to Donbas. It directly affects the direction of the flow and the character of the Dnipro. The river crosses Belarus in an almost meridional direction before encountering the shield in Kyiv's vicinity and is compelled to adjust its flow in a south-easterly direction, bypassing the northern edge of the shield. It is only when it reaches the area of the cities of Dnipro and Zaporizhzhia, quite distant from Kyiv, that the river finally crosses the granite massif of the shield. It then leaves in its course numerous rapids and so called fences, separate outcrops of crystalline rock now flooded by the waters of the Dnipro reservoir. Separate protrusions of this shield, exposed by the washing away of light rocks, were probably notable near Kyiv in the past in the area where the Dnipro river's rapid flow collides with the solid granite. This assumption is, importantly, confirmed by the chronicles.

Let us recollect the words of Prince Volodymyr who, on the eve of the mass christening of the Kyivans, ordered that the wooden image of the god Perun be cast into the Dnipro. He also ordered that, "If the image lands somewhere thrust it from the shore until it passes the **rapids** (author's emphasis) then leave him."[1] People ran along the shore and, turning to Perun, begged him not to depart, Emerge, God, "emerge!" The village of Vydubychi later arose at the site of his departure. What rapids did Prince Volodymyr have in mind?[2]

The Dnipro rapids are mentioned on many occasions in the chronicles, most frequently when they speak about the military campaigns of the Kyivan princes against the southern nomads. On these occasions there is no doubt that they are referring to the southern rapids located on the lower reaches of the Dnipro. However, in the incident with the wooden image of Perun, it is unlikely that Prince Volodymyr, when giving his order, could have meant the southern rapids. Why not? Firstly, the Pechenegs held sway over the southern rapids. Prince Svyatoslav, Volodymyr's father, had died at their hands and in order to send the image of Perun to that area it would have been necessary not just to thrust it away from the shore but also to send a military force capable of battling its way to the rapids surrounded by their foes. The inexpediency of conducting such an operation is, I think, obvious. Secondly, it says in the chronicle that the image of Perun was cast by the wind

---

[1] *Повість врем'яних літ: літопис (за Іпатським списком)* / пер. з давньоруської, післяслово, комент. В. В. Яременка. Київ: Рад. письменник, 1990. 558 с., p. 183.

[2] Translator's note: The village's name alludes to the imperative verb *Vidibaj* which the Kyivans cried at Perun and which I have rendered as "emerge".

Chapter 3: What Languages Tell Us

into Perun's ditch which, judging by the name, could not be situated in the land of the Pechenegs because they had another faith. The chronicle thus refers to the rapids and ditches (sandbank) which were near Kyiv and not on the lower reaches of the Dnipro. It is certain that in the ancient period when the proto-Finns dwelled here the rapids would also have existed as stone ledges in the centre of the river that served as a landmark for those primitive fishers. Furthermore, near the rapids where the current of water narrowed, fishing nets were arranged which meant a secure living for a large group of people. So it is probable that the first fishing settlement of the proto-Finns arose on the banks of the Dnipro, near the future village of Vydubychi, and was named after stone in the form of the Dnipro rapids. It seems, therefore, that the first Kyivans were proto-Finnic fishers.

The Finnish language, like all other languages, has changed over the millennia. Therefore, the modern Finnish word *kivi*, the Mordovian word *kev* etc meaning stone, was probably pronounced differently, just like in the bible, at the time the proto-Finns lived. When Jesus, in *The Gospel according to John*, addresses Simon he says, "You will be called Cephas, which means stone".[1] The Gospel was characteristically written in Greek but the author did not use typical Greek words for stone such as *litas* (λιθάς) or *petros* (πέτρος), but instead used the foreign word *Κήφας*

---

1 The Gospel according to John, 1:42.

[ki:fa or kefa – without the letter *s* attached by Greeks], and explained what it meant. Ivan Franko proved convincingly that biblical stories are not original, back in his day they are borrowed from the Babylonians, Assyrians, Egyptians and other peoples.[1] The biblical word *Κήφας*, in the opinion of linguists, originates from the Aramaic language. The Aramaeans, the ancestors of the modern Syrians, lived several centuries later than the proto-Finns. The Finnish word *kivi* or the Mordovian word *kev* and other knowledge derived from the proto-Finns may have reached them via linguistic contacts with other peoples. This applies in particular to the Aryans who left the Dnipro region and crossed the Caucasus, reaching Syria and Palestine where they encountered the Aramaeans. This assumption concerning the southward spread of the words *kivi* and *kev* is supported by the Finnish epic the *Kalevala* which narrates the tale of how a young girl became pregnant by swallowing a berry which resembled a strawberry.[2] An important element of this legend is that the word "berry" in Finnish sounds like Maria (*marja*). This indicates that the Evangelists who wrote the gospels borrowed not only the word *Κήφας* from the Aramaeans but also this story about an immaculate conception, in addition to the Finnish word for berry which became the name of the Mother of

---

1 Франко І. Я. Сотворення світу в світлі науки. Нью-Йорк : Оріяна, 1969. 119 с, 1969.

2 *Калевала*: фін. нар. епос / пер. Є. Тимченка; передм. Д. Павличка; іл. О.-Й. Аланена. Київ: Основи, 1995. p. 331.

God. These facts are supported by the greater antiquity of the Finnish tale compared to the biblical story as well as the Aramaeans's borrowing of the word *kivi (kev)* which passed through them into the bible.

The name of the original fishing settlement on the banks of the Dnipro has also undergone some changes, over the millennia it was pronounced and subsequently written in various ways by those who heard of it or who lived there as guest or conqueror. The wise people, the Chinese, who have lived in their ancient land for millennia and observed the lives of other peoples by recording information about them in their unfathomably complicated and simultaneously flexible hieroglyphic writing, have perfectly conveyed the original name of our city as preserved in their language. The name Kyiv in modern Chinese is pronounced midway between *tifu* and *jifu*. This is extremely similar to the biblical word *Κήφας* [ki:fa]. and indirectly confirms that the name of our capital originates from the word for stone.

3.12 How Kyiv was hidden beneath the name Metropolis

In this section, which concerns Kyiv, we can trace a certain connection between Ptolemy's *Geography* and the *Gospel According to John*. Let us compare the two texts. The gospel was written at the end of the first century AD and Ptolemy wrote his work between 50 and 60 years later, both text are written in Ancient Greek. The word *cephas (Κηφάς)*, which John borrowed from another language, was probably familiar to Ptolemy, a scholar with wide erudition in various areas. However, for John it simply meant a stone while for Ptolemy it was the name of a city. So why did he substitute it with another word for the name of the capital, Metropolis? In order to answer this question let us consider what significance the Ancient Greeks embedded in the concept of a capital city.

The word *Asti* was used in Ancient Greek in order to denote the most prominent capitals in the world. Ancient Greek dictionaries indicate that an ancient Greek only had to hear the word *Asti* to understand that the renowned Greek capital Athens was being referred to. They also glorified another outstanding capital, Rome, with this word. However, other, less prominent, capitals were referred to by the word Metropolis. But the array of words which meant capital extended beyond these two terms. There was still one more interesting word which the Greeks borrowed from Latin, *Caesarea*, which literally translated means the city of Caesar.[1] The word Caesar began its life as the proper name of one of the patricians of ancient Rome. However, it soon became a universal term which mean the ruler of a country in various languages: in Old Slavonic Цѣсарь, in Greek Καίσαρας, in German *Kaiser* etc. The word's pronunciation varied according to the country and language. Insofar as the ruler typically lived in the capital

---

1 *Древнегреческо-русский словарь* / сост. И. Х. Дворецкий. Москва: Гос. изд-во иностр. и национ. Словарей, 1958 р. 858.

Chapter 3: What Languages Tell Us

city, the word *Caesarea* came to mean the capital city. The Greeks therefore had three words similar in meaning, *Asti*, *Metropolis*, and *Caesarea*.

The most common word of the trio was *Metropolis*, which occurs more than a dozen times in the work of Ptolemy; the word *Caesarea* is also occasionally used. However, the array of words, synonyms, for capital city was not limited to with these three terms. It transpires that the economical Greeks also used an abbreviated version of the word *Caesarea, Kiasa* ((Κιάσα).[1] We can see that this word differs from the word *Κήφας* [ki:fa] because there is an additional *a* in the centre and different consonants with *σ* replacing *φ*. This kind of difference in a word is occasionally due to the unclear handwritten text of an original document. The Byzantine Emperor Constantine VII Flavius Porphyrogenitus (905-959), for example, once referred to Kyiv as Kioba in his work *On the Administration of Empire* (*De Administrando Imperio*). On a second occasion in this text he referred to Kyiv as *Kioaba* (Κιοάβα) with the same additional letter *a* in the middle of the word and substituted by the sound *b*.[2] (The sound *v* is absent in Greek, so while in Ukrainian we say *Vîzantîâ*, the Greeks say *Byzantium*). It is probable that the name of our city also reached Ptolemy with an *a* in the centre of the

---

1 Claudii Ptolemaei. *Geographia*. Edidit Carolus Fridericus Augustus Nobbe. Lipsiae, 1843. Lib. III. p. 63.

2 Constantine Porphyrogenetus. *De administrando imperio*. http://books.goog le.com.ua.

word and sounded like *Kiafa*. He therefore decided that it was not the city's name but an abbreviated version (*Kiasa*) of the Latin word *Caesarea*. Therefore, it was worthwhile replacing this word with the Greek equivalent *Metropolis* which was understandable to the general Greek public. This is how the real name of our city in Ptolemy's time, which we can conjecture was *Kiafa* or a similar word, did not enter into Ptolemy's book. It was substituted by the word *Metropolis* for almost one thousand years until its first mention in Nestor's chronicle.

3.13 The Distorted translation of the Chronicle's Phrase Concerning Kyiv

The question arises, did Nestor know that in the location where he created his chronicle a large city had existed for one thousand years before him and which Ptolemy called *Metropolis?* It appears that he knew as can be seen from Nestor's phrase in the pages of his work, when he solemnly said via the mouth of Prince Oleg: "Se budi mati gorodom Ruskym" or "the Ruses' mother city".[1] Let us note that the words *gorodom* and *Ruskym* are written in the singular in Nestor by contrast with the classic Russian translation, followed subsequently by all other renderings where these words are represented in the plural as "mat' gorodov russkih" or "mother of Russian

---

1 *Повість врем'яних літ : літопис (за Іпатським списком)* / пер. з давньоруської, післяслово, комент. В. В. Яременка. Київ : Рад. письменник, 1990. p. 34.

cities".[1] Thus, at first glance, a slight difference (singular – plural) significantly changes the meaning of Nestor's phrase because the word *city*, written in the singular, joins with the neighbouring word to form the characteristic word combination *mother-city*. This is an exact copy, as if through tracing paper, of the Greek term *meter-polis*. When we translate it correctly, Nestor's phrase sounds completely different from the fallacious renderings and reads, "This will be the Ruses' metropolis". Oleh, in order to consolidate the primary position of Kyiv within the state of Rus', declared that it would be the the Ruses' metropolis, to the capital of the state of Rus' by contrast; it follows with its earlier status as an ordinary Polyane town.[2] The similarity to Ptolemy's phrase, "the metropolis of all Egypt," (Αἰγύπτου πασης μητροπολις) is obvious here.[3] The similarity of phrases and the carbon copy of the Greek suggest that Nestor or his predecessors in the chronicles, who certainly knew Ancient Greek and were familiar with the works of many ancient Greek authors, may have known about the ancient Sarmatian town on the Dnipro from them and possibly about Ptolemy's *Geography*. However, they were silent on that theme,

---

[1] This Russian "translation" exploited the resemblance between the name of the kingdom of Rus' and the name the Duchy of Muscovy artificially created for its state, "Russia".

[2] Translator's note: Polyane refers to the association of East Slavonic tribes in the Dnipro region from the eighth century AD onwards.

[3] Claudii Ptolemaei. *Geographia*. Edidit Carolus Fridericus Augustus Nobbe. Lipsiae, 1843. Lib. IV. pp. 5, 9.

referring only to the ninth century Byzantine historian Georgios Hamartolos who laid out human history from a Christian view point. Why did they keep silent? Because they could not express themselves freely in their works, the censor was hanging over them instilling the idea that humanity, prior to the adoption of Christianity, could not have any valid history or culture. This denial of the achievements of past generations, which their successors often permit themselves, almost resulted in the loss of Nestor's own name because it disappeared from one of the editions of the chronicle. The abbot, Sylvestr, attributed the sole authorship of the text to himself. Fortunately, other editions survived and Nestor was not lost to the world.[1]

With regard to the fallacious phrase "Mother of Russian Cities", it remained throughout every era as a solemn and glorifying epithet for our city, although Nestor imbued the phrase uttered by Oleh, as you can see, with quite another meaning. If Nestor had wanted to express the sentiment in the way they have translated him he would have made Kyiv a father rather than a mother. Similarly, the name Almaty means "The Father of Apples" for the Kazakhs and the word Mississippi means "The Father of the Waters" in the language of the Alconquin Native Americans and there are other instances of such patriarchal nomenclature among

---

1 Літопис руський / пер. з давньорус. Л. Є. Махновця ; відп. ред. О. В. Мишанич. Київ: Дніпро, 1989. p. VII.

Chapter 3: What Languages Tell Us

various peoples.[1] The Greek word *polis* is not masculine but feminine, therefore the Greeks placed the word mother next to it to create the compound word from *meter-polis*. Nestor, borrowing this uplifting Greek expression, rendered it in the Old Ukrainian language in the form of a complex noun, mother-city, *mati-gorod* or more precisely, *mati-gorodom* in the instrumental case used in the text: "This will be the Mother-City of the Ruses". However, the lack of grammatical correspondence between the word for city in both languages, which is feminine in Ancient Greek and masculine in Old Ukrainian, was not taken into account. Nestor was probably relying on the reader accurately understanding this well-known expression which meant metropolis, the main city, the capital. However, their successors tried too hard by translating the whole line into Russian, splitting the compound noun referred to into separate concepts, replacing singular words with plural and changing the case of some words. In consequence, the city of Kyiv, which bore a masculine noun, became a "mother". As we see, Nestor did not name the city thus, this change emerged in the translations, it seems, intentionally.

The unfortunate aspect of this is not that Kyiv was referred to as a "mother" but that the

translation substituted the essence of what Prince Oleh had said with another meaning. Instead of the

---

1 *Новый энциклопедический словарь* / под ред. К. К. Арсеньева. Петроград: АО «Издательское дело бывшее Брокгауз-Ефрон», 1915. Т. 26. p. 692.

prince's main idea, his intention to change the status of the conquered city, which was, it could be said, a Polyane town and would be the capital of the state of Rus', the translation voices a completely different, tendentious, thought - here will be a city that will become the mother of Russian cities. This distorted Russian translation conceals a devious political meaning. First the word "will" means that the ancient history of Kyiv, known since Ptolemy's time, is ignored. It is as if there were no Sarmatian Kyiv-Metropolis or a city which was recorded by eastern geographers referring to it as *Kujaba* or German historians who termed it *Kuene, Kianugard, Kunagard* and other names. Secondly, this, for Russians, is of the most fundamental significance. The title of the Mother of Russian Cities endows them with the right to consider Kyiv the ancestor of Russian cities and the Kyivan lands their ancient homeland. This in turn permits them to encroach on the Kyivan history of the ninth to twelve centuries under the name of Rus'. This distorted translation is intended on the one hand to abbreviate the history of Kyiv so that in terms of duration it is less distinct from the history of Moscow and, on the other, to seize Kyiv as the starting point for the history of Russia.

3.14 The Huns, the Kuns, the Kyians, the Kuyavs, the Antes

It seems that the most confusing, vague and falsified segment in the history of Ukrainians is the first half of the

Chapter 3: What Languages Tell Us

first millennium AD. This is in particularly with regard to the Huns, concerning whose origin the encyclopaedias say is not "ultimately clarified". Let us try to establish if this is really the case.

The first report of the people whom historians have accepted were the Huns occurs in the second century in the work of the ancient Greek scientist Claudius Ptolemy. It is contained in a short phrase in his *Geography* when he says that "between the Bastarnae and the Roxolani – the Khunoi" (*Χούνοι*).[1] The last word is translated into Russian and Ukrainian languages as "Huns" and into equivalent terms in other European languages. On the map of Sarmatia, which was renewed with textual information from Ptolemy, the Bastarnae are shown as dwelling in the Carpathian area while the Roxolani are situated north of the Sea of Azov, in what is now the modern Donbas. The map shows a people who dwelled between those two tribes naming them as the *Chuni* (see figure 3.10). The inscriptions on the map are in Italian, however, the word *Chuni* is absent in the Italian-Ukrainian dictionary. There is instead the word *Unni* which translates into Ukrainian as Huns. The Ptolemaic word *Χούνοι* is also absent from the Ancient Greek to Russian dictionary, there is instead the word *unnoj* (*Οὖννοι*) without the consonant at the beginning of the word and with a double Greek *n* (νν). This word rather than the word *Χούνοι* is translated as Huns. It therefore

---

1 Ptolemy's Geography. Book 3, chapter 5, § 25.

Figure 3.10: The map of Sarmatia, reconstructed Italian author Gastaldi in 1548 according Ptolemy's Geography

follows that Ptolemy was not referring to the Huns in the phrase we have quoted but another people with a similar name. Who were they?

It must be noted that Ptolemy's work, written in the second century, could not have survived to the era of book printing if it had not been written by hand repeatedly on several occasions to replace worn-out copies. It was inevitable that errors would occur while it was rewritten, especially with regard to the consonants **k** and **x** which usually alternate with each other. Therefore, in Ptolemy's original text, the name of that people may have been written as *Κούνοι* with the letter **k** at the beginning of the

Chapter 3: What Languages Tell Us

word. In that case the word would have to read as *Koiunoj* dependent on the presence of a particular sign above the diphthong *oú* without which it would read like a long *u*. If the sign were present the diphthong would read as two sounds, *o* followed by *yu*. It is easy to guess that the words *Kunoj* or *Koiunoj* mean Kyivans pronounced in the Greek manner, that is the population of Kyiv and the Kyivan land. We encounter similar names for Kyivans, modified when adapted to foreign languages, not only in Ptolemy but also in other European texts.

In German and Scandinavian folk tales of the time, for example, including sagas and other folk genres, the Kyivans were called the Quene, Cunni, Koueve and the Choani. The Kyiv area was called Kueneland and Kunaland, and the city of Kyiv was named Kuenae, Kianugard, Hunagard and other similar names.[1] The German chronicler and Christian missionary Adam of Bremen who lived in the eleventh century called the capital of Rus' Chiven.[2] This was how foreigners learned to pronounce the name of Kyiv. It is obvious that all these names, in Ptolemy and in the sagas and other folk literatures, are lexically derived from the word Kyiv.

Therefore, the people referred to in Ptolemy's work who lived between the Bastarnae and the Roxolani, were most likely Kyivans whom he referred to as the Kunoj or

---

1 Вельтман Олександр. *Аттіла і Русь IV та V століть*. Основа. Київ, 1996. № 30 (8). pp. 97–106. p. 105.

2 Ibid p. 104.

Koiunoj. There are several cases in history where the name of a people is created from the name of a city or, conversely, a people have transferred their name to a city. The name for the city of Moscow, for example, is the origin of the name of a people - the Muscovites. Then, conversely, the name of a medieval tribe, the Parisians, is the origin of the name of the French city Paris.[1]

There is a similar instance of the transfer of names in the case of Kyiv. This can be indirectly confirmed from the reports of Persian and Arab geographers in the ninth and tenth centuries which referred to three separate groups of Ruses.[2] One of these groups was referred to as the Kuiavia and their capital, where their king's residence was sited, was called Kuiava (Kuiaba). The name of this city was the origin for the name given to the Kyivan lands, Kuiavia, and their inhabitants were probably collectively named the Kuiavy.[3]

However, why are none of these words, kyiani, kuny, khoani kuiavy kuene, kunni and other similar terms, encountered in any translations of Ptolemy's work into the relevant languages? In all the translations of Ptolemy only two words figure, *huny* or *khuny* (Huns in English). The

---

1 France. A Phaidon Cultural Guide. New Jersey : Prentice-Hall, 1985. p. 474.

2 Translator's note: Ruses here refers to the people rather than the state of Rus'.

3 Диба Юрій. *Географія початкової русі за східними джерела ми. Княжа доба: історія і культура.* Львів, 2016. Вип. 10: Святий Володимир Великий 1015–2015. pp. 10, 11.

Chapter 3: What Languages Tell Us

reason for what we might term the "hunning" of Kyivans was probably the first and, unfortunately, inaccurate, translation of Ptolemy's work into Latin. We will examine how this happened.

Ptolemy's *Geography* was written in Ancient Greek in approximately AD 150 and the first translations into other languages appeared in the fifteenth and sixteenth centuries, almost one and a half millennium after it was written.[1] The dominant language in Europe during that period was Latin and the first translations of Ptolemy's work were written in that language. At that time the shock caused in Europe by the blows of the Hun chief's armies against the military of the slave-owning state of Rome in the fifth century had been forgotten. There remained only the memory of the people who had swept like a whirlwind across Europe and their name, which was pronounced fearfully and in various ways as Khuny, Kuny, the Huns etc., according to the language used. Europe, violated by the Huns and recovering from its fear of them, avidly absorbed the most fallacious myths about its violators. This was clearly a kind of moral compensation for the terror they had suffered. One of these myths regarded the Huns as alien, Asiatic in origin, semi-wild nomads who never dismounted their horses day or night and ate raw meat, which they kept under their saddles. This myth

---

1 Бронштэн В. А. *Клавдий Птолемей: II век н.э.* Москва: Наука, 1983. pp. 149–153.

sank deeply into the consciousness of Europe and became the norm of historiography concerning the Huns. The translators of Ptolemy were not embarrasseded by the difference between the word *Χούνοι* in Ptolemy's work and the word *Οὖννοι* in dictionaries of Ancient Greek, and did not delve into their origins. They simply deployed the common Latin word *Hunni* which was recognised by everyone and that, of course, had no lexical link to the name Kyiv by contrast with the terms noted above. That is how the Kyivans of Ptolemy's time, which, as noted, was the second century AD, became known to the world as the Huns after his work had been translated.

It might seem that there was nothing untoward in this misnomer, indeed, every people in the course of their history has more than once acquired new names dependent on the circumstances which have arisen. However, issues connected to the use of the name Huns eventually became apparent. An absurd theory concerning this people was proposed in the eighteenth century, three hundred years after the first translation of Ptolemy's work. Joseph de Gounier, a French scholar, speculated that the Huns were descendants of the Mongolian tribe the Khunn whom the Chinese comprehensively defeated and pursued relentlessly to the banks of the Volga in the second century AD. Subsequently, in the fourth century AD this people, already known as the Huns rather than the Khunn, supposedly invaded the northern Black Sea coast. This was a ridiculous and evidence-free version of their history, based only

Chapter 3: What Languages Tell Us

on the similarity between the words Huns and Khunn, but nevertheless was widely supported. We have a paradox here! We will subsequently examine why this occurred but, for now, we are interested in the views of those who lived closer in time to the Huns and were better acquainted with them.

The third century Byzantine historian Marcian of Heraclea left us the following account: "Next to the Alans, the so called Khoani (Χοανοι) live around the Dnipro."[1] If the Khoani, according to Marcian, already lived near the Dnipro in the third century, how could they penetrate the area where they already dwelled in the fourth century? This account by Marcian completely refutes De Gournier's absurd version. The Danish chronicler Saxo Grammaticus, who lived in the twelfth century, regarded the Huns and the Ruses as one people.[2] The Scandinavian folk literatures speak of Hun warriors with the names of Jarisleifr and Jariczar (which are equivalents for the Ukrainian names Yaroslav and Yarozhyr).[3] These names undoubtedly suggest that the Huns were Slavs. Furthermore, in one of the northern folk tales it says directly "our ancestors spoke of the Slavs under the name of the Huns".[4]

---

1 Вельтман Олександр. *Аттіла і Русь IV та V століть.* Основа. Київ, 1996. № 30 (8). p. 103.

2 Ibid p. 104.

3 Вельтман Олександр. *Аттіла і Русь IV та V століть.* Основа. Київ, 1996. № 30 (8). p. 105.

4 Ibid p. 104.

The Byzantine historians Jordanes, Procopios of Caesarea, Menander and others who lived in the sixth century reported the existence of a so-called Antes Union of Slavonic tribes in the fourth century. This union was the origin of a general name for the Eastern Slavs, the Antae or Antes in Latin. In addition to the Antes, the medieval historians recognised a western group of Slavs, called the Sklaueni in Latin, who spread to the west and south-west from their ancestral home in the Central Dnipro Basin and inhabited the Balkans and the area north of the Danube. Jordanes, in his work *Getica,* reported that Vinitar, the Goth king, led his numerous army onto the terrain of the Antes, the modern day Kyiv region, in AD 380. He was defeated in his first battle but then, as Jordanes wrote, acted more resolutely and, achieving victory, crucified the leader of the Antes, Bozh and his sons, and seventy elders of the Antes to terrorise the conquered population.[1] This brutal massacre did not pass by without a fitting response. The combined forces of the Antes and the Huns rose to avenge themselves for the death of Bozh and his associates. They were led by King Bolemyr and in the year 390 defeated Vinitar's army and killed him. Jordanes, who gives the obviously Slavonic two-word name of Bolemyr (which is similar to Bole-slav, Vladi-mir) in Latin as Balamber, describes the event thus: "Balamber, stealing

---

1 Иордан. *О происхождении и деяниях гетов. Getica* / вступ. статья ; пер.; коммент. Е. Ч. Скржинской. Москва: Восточная литература, 1960. {246}, {247}, 610, 611.

Chapter 3: What Languages Tell Us

Figure 3.11: Monument to the Antes near Rokytne village. Photo credit: Khort.

up to the River Eryk, fired an arrow and, wounding Vinitaria in the head, slew him."[1] The mutual revenge of the Antes and the Huns proves once more that they were a pairing of related tribes who had the common task of defending their land from foreigners. A monument to our ancestors, the Antes, has been erected on the site of Bozh's death near the village of Rokytne in Kyiv oblast (figure 3.11).[2]

The River Eryk referred to by Jordanes was probably the Ros', which calls into question the hypothesis that the name of Rus' derived from its name. Indeed, during the era of Jordanes in the sixth century, the name of the Scandinavian Roses was a well-known term in the Dnipro region. The Scandinavians, who, at the beginning of the millennium mastered the "amber pathways" on the Dnipro, Pripyat and other rivers were called Roses

---

1 Ibid {249}, 614.
2 Monument to the Antes near Rokytne village. Photo credit: Khort.

in Greek pronunciation. This route later became part of the route "from the Viking to the Greek" and the Ros' river probably had the older name Eryk in this period. Jordanes, incidentally, although he describes the Huns in unflattering terms as an appalling monstrosity, also provides valuable information about them. He describes two groups of Huns living in two separate locations. The first group, according to Jordanes, roamed the southern area of Ukraine near the Black Sea coast. He does not provide details of the location of the second group but gives their name as the Saviri.[1]

The Huns/Saviri presumably lived to the north of the southern Huns in exactly the same place where Claudius Ptolemy located a tribe with a very similar name, the Savari. It is easy, on the basis of the linguistic similarity, to recognise in these two names, Saviri and Savari, the Sivery, those descendants of the Cimmerians we discussed in subsection 3.8. Jordanes's report therefore links separate elements of the long, ancient pedigree of the Ukrainian people: the Cimmerians of Homer's time (the eighth century BC), the Savari (Σαύαροι)[2] of Ptolemy's era (second century AD), the Huns/Saviri of Jordanes's time (sixth century AD), Sivery of Nestor the Chronicler's period in the eleventh century and, finally, the indigenous Ukrainians

---

1 Иордан. *О происхождении и деяниях гетов. Getica* / вступ. статья; пер.; коммент. Е. Ч. Скржинской. Москва: Восточная литература, 1960. {37}, 120.

2 Ptolemy's Geography. Book 3, chapter 5, paragraph 22.

of the Sivershchyna of our days.[1] We have before us a unique instance in human history where the name of one branch of the Ukrainian people remains almost unchanged and uninterruptedly accompanies them on their historical path across three millennia. This journey from the Cimmerians to the Ukrainians illustrates the long antiquity of the Ukrainian nation. Jordanes's report also indicates that, because the Huns/Savari were one of the links in the long chain of descendants that stretches from the Cimmerians, they could not be the descendants of the Mongols who appeared one thousand years after the Cimmerians. They also could not be the ancestors of the Hungarians who, in Jordanes's era, lived between the Volga and the Urals and only after one and a half centuries, in 893, left their settlements and, searching for new territory, reached the Danube. Jordanes's report concerning the Huns/Savari thereby illustrates that the Huns were the indigenous inhabitants of the Dnipro region whom Ptolemy called Kyiani, according to the area they resided (see the map in figure 3.10 where they are termed in Italian as the Chuni).

Therefore, the names written in the heading of this subsection and referred to in the text, the Huns, the Kuns, the Kyians the Kuyavs, the Antes and others are names for one and the same people. These terms reached historians from different sources and with different pronunciations. They were the name of that people, proto-Ukrainians, who

---

[1] A North Ukrainian region in the middle and lower Desna basin.

were the ancestors of modern Ukrainians. Let us compare the instance of the Turks, the Osmans, Ottomans, Saracens, Mohammedans and others. Our ancestors, similarly, were called different names during their history.

3.15 The name Ukraine is older than the name Rus'!

In the work *Getica*, written in the sixth century by the Byzantine historian Jordanes, there is a phrase which reveals the origin of the name Ukraine: "Scythiae terras quae lingua eorum Oium vocabatur."[1] This translates from the Latin as "the land of the Scythians which is called Oium in their language". Let us consider two important aspects of this phrase.

Firstly, Oium is the name of the land not in the Gothic but in the Scythian language, as is evident from Jordanes's phrase. The word *land* (*zemlja* in Ukrainian, *terros* in Latin), is often used in Slavonic languages to signify a country, a land or a state. Let us reconsider the phrase uttered in the chronicle "otkudu estь pošla Ruskaja zemlja i chto v nej počalъ pěrvěe knjažiti" which translates as "where did the Rus' land come from and who first began to rule there?".[2] It is apparent that the words "Rus' land" in

---

1 Иордан. *О происхождении и деяниях гетов. Getica* / вступ. статья; пер.; коммент. Е. Ч. Скржинской. Москва {27}.

2 *Повість врем'яних літ: літопис (за Іпатським списком)* / пер. з давньоруської, післяслово, комент. В. В. Яременка. Київ: Рад. письменник, 1990.р. 6.

Chapter 3: What Languages Tell Us

the chronicle refer to the Rus' state, the Rus' country, the Rus' principality.

Secondly, a peculiarity in the Latin text of Jordanes is that proper nouns in his work often end in the syllable *um*. The name Dnipro, for example, or Danapr in Latin, is written as Danaprum in his text. The Dniester river, or Danastr becomes the Danastrum, the Caspian Sea is the Caspium and the Caucasus is the Caucasum.[1] It follows therefore that the Scythians called their country Oi in their own language, without the Latin suffix *um*.

As we have previously discussed, the Scythian language was probably proto-Ukrainian, one of the Slavonic languages which characteristically have the synonyms *kraj, zemlja, kraïna* which are interchangeable for country, land or state. The Scythians, therefore, clearly called their land Oi-kraïna or Kraïna-Oi. The name Oikraïna subsequently became the main term and eventually they began pronouncing it as Oukraïna.[2] That is how it is written in the Hypatian Chronicle for 1187 when the Prince of Pereyslav, Volodymyr Hlibovych died: "o nem že Oukraina mnogo postona" or "Oukraine moaned much for him."[3] Therefore, the date of the first appearance of the name Ukraine in

---

1 Иордан. *О происхождении и деяниях гетов. Getica* / вступ. статья; пер.; коммент. Е. Ч. Скржинской. Москва {30}.

2 Translator's note: *Ukraïna* is the scientific transliteration into Latin from Cyrillic of the word Ukraine in Ukrainian.

3 *Полное собрание русских летописей (ПСРЛ)* / под ред. А. А. Шахматова. 2-е изд. Санкт-Петербург: Типография М. А. Александрова, 1908. Т. 2. Ипатьевская летопись. Стб. 653.

written sources should not be regarded as this twelfth century reference in Nestor's chronicle, instead we should note that it was first recorded in the sixth century in 551 by Jordanes in his *Getica,* although it was not completely formulated as Oi-kraïna. It appears that the name Ukraine was handed to us as the legacy of our ancestors, the Scythians. In 2051, 1,500 years will have passed since the first reference to the name Ukraine in the work of Jordanes.

In order to understand the concept the Scythians embodied in the word *Oi,* let us recollect that the descendants of the ancient Dnipro inhabitants flowed from the territory of modern Ukraine in wave upon wave. They created new nations in Europe, Asia Minor, Central Asia, India and other remote regions of the globe. It was akin to the wondrous paradise Egg spoken of in one Ukrainian folk tale which engendered new peoples, new languages and new countries. The Scythians who lived on that land and the other peoples who emerged from there seemingly remembered their origin well and called their ancestral homeland by a name which was close to the word egg. Indeed the word for egg in ancient and modern European languages is short and sounds similar to the Scythian word *Oi*: *oion* (ὠόν) is egg in Ancient Greek, *óvu* in Italian, *ovum* in Latin, *ou* in Romanian, *ouef* in French, *ei* in German etc.[1] Any of the words for egg we have listed, when combined with

---

1 Glosbe – багатомовний онлайн-словник; Каганець Ігор. Свастика і таємниці імені «Україна». http//:observer.sd.org.ua, 2007.

Chapter 3: What Languages Tell Us

the word for country which is used in Slavonic languages, including proto-Ukrainian (Scythian), could eventually develop into the name of *Ou-kraïna* as it was later written in the chronicle. There are traces of that one syllable Scythian word for egg in modern Slavonic languages: *jajko* in Polish, *jaje* in Serbian, *âjce* in Ukrainian etc.

The name "egg-country" probably originated long before its appearance in the work of Jordanes. Its age is measured by more than a single millennia and it was transmitted orally, by word of mouth, from generation to generation. It was finally written by Jordanes in the sixth century as *Oi-kraïna* and in the twelfth century by Nestor as *Ou-kraïna*. The interpretation of the name of Ukraine as the *окраїна*, i.e. the frontier areas, periphery of Poland or Russia., is just a political fiction created to justify invasions which attempted and continue to attempt to seize Ukrainian territory. Indeed, Ukraine could not be the periphery of another state which was not even in embryo at a time when the name Ukraine already existed.

Further confirmation that the name Ukraine derives from the compound word egg-country is the Ukrainian *Pysanka* egg.[1] It represents conceptions of the universe and human existence and is perceived globally as the visiting card of our state and as a symbol of Ukraine.

---

1 Translator's note: a *Pysanka* is a painted egg painted with folk motifs and part of Ukraine's Easter traditions but long predates Christianity and is pagan in origin.

One more important conclusion follows from Jordanes's account is that the name of Ukraine is older than the name of Rus', which was first referred to in the *Annales Bertiniani* in 839, almost three centuries after Jordanes's account.[1] Therefore, the name of Ukraine, inherited from the Scythians, was replaced by a subsequent name Rus' for an extended period of one thousand years. However, it was preserved in folk memory and has returned from historical oblivion.

The question arises, how did the name Ukraine at first surrender its place to the younger name of Rus' and then regain its position again? The fact is that in the first millennium AD Scandinavian conquerors imposed the name Rus' on the local inhabitants of the entire Dnipro region. When the locals regained their statehood in the ninth century they retained the Scandinavian name Rus'. However, the old Scythian name of Oi-kraina did not disappear without a trace, it was transmitted orally, from generation to generation, from parents and grandparents to their children and grandchildren. In the words of Taras Shevchenko, "Thank you Grandfather that you hid/ The Cossack glory in your century old head/ And which I have now your grandchildren told."

When Muscovy completely occupied the land on both sides of the Dnipro in the eighteenth century, destroying

---

[1] *Annales Bertiniani. Monumenta Germaniae hist orica* / Ed. G. H. Pertz. Hannoverae: Bibliopolii Alvici Hahniani, 1826. Vol. 1. S. 434.

the Zaporizhzhian Sich and ascribing itself the name Rus', it simultaneously cast the fallacious name "Little Russia" on the inhabitants of this territory. The local population, indignant at this humiliation, recollected and renewed the name which originated from its Scythian ancestors, Ukraine. In consequence the name Rus', which had been dominant on our land for a temporary but quite prolonged period of approximately one thousand years, ceased being used and the more ancient name of Ukraine was revived instead. Events transpired in accord with the old saying, "If there were no good fortune then misfortune helped". If the Muscovites had not appropriated the name Rus', then we would have retained the name brought to us by the Scandinavians for a longer period and, like the French, it would have been unlikely that we could have returned the designation of our ancestors. So an unfortunate occurrence helped us regain our true name.

3.16 Where was the Capital of the Huns?

The extraordinary impression that the Huns made on Europe during the period of their victorious campaigns under King Attila has engendered a mass of speculation, myths and obviously false information. Who were the Huns, where did they originate, where was their capital? The controversy about these and other disputable issues connected to the Huns has never ceased. One of the eyewitnesses of the life of the Huns and the sole one who left written memoirs about this people was Priscus of Panium

(Πρίσκος Πανίτης in Ancient Greek), an assistant to the Byzantine Ambassador. He described the Byzantine Embassy's journey to the residence of King Attila, the reception of the guests invited into his palace and the daily life and customs of the Huns. However, the excerpts from his work *The History of Byzantium* (Ἱστορία Βυζαντιακή in Ancient Greek), which have survived to the present, unfortunately contain very little information that would allow us to trace the route taken by the Embassy to the capital of the Huns and its location.[1] Researchers looking into the history of the Huns believe that the Embassy journeyed to the Danube in Pannonia (in present day Hungary) where the ever-restless Attila had, for a second time, relocated his residence, moving on this occasion from a town on the Tisza river. However, an attentive reading of Priscus's work gives us grounds for disputing the researchers' view and also for re-evaluating certain controversial issues relating to the history of the Huns. These are extremely important questions because we are discussing "blank spots" in the history of ancient Ukraine. Let us try to find answers to them by using the map and those meagre scraps of information that remain from the works of Priscus, Ptolemy, Jordanes and other ancient historians.

Priscus describes certain events beginning in 433 when Attila's uncle, King Rugila (whose name translates as Rua

---

[1] *Сказания Приска Панийского* / пер. Г. С. Дестуниса. Санкт-Петербург, 1860.

Chapter 3: What Languages Tell Us

when translated into Russian from Ancient Greek and Roas, Rugila, Roua in other languages) stood at the head of the Hun state (the Antes union). Rugila was the fourth ruler of the Huns after Bolemir, who we have previously referred to as the founder of the Hun state who chose Kyiv for its capital.[1] Attila was born there and raised at the court of his uncle.[2] It is interesting that during this period Flavius Aetius, the young son of a Roman noble who would in the future command Roman legions, was being held as a hostage at the court.[3] So here, in Kyiv, teachers experienced in military affairs taught Aetius, Attila and their peers riding skills and the masterful use of a sword and a bow. The superlative skills acquired by Aetius in Kyiv impressed his allies in Europe on more than one occasion.[4] Aetius and Attila had friendly relations from childhood onwards until the renowned battle of the Catalaunian Fields when the former friends became foes and opposed each other as the heads of their armies.

Attila inherited sovereignty over the Huns after the death of Rugila in 434. He continued the course set by his

---

1 Боргардт Александр. *Бич Божий (Атилла – 5-й каган гуннов и его времня).*Донецк: Изд-во Донецк. физ.-техн. ин-та им. А. П. Галкина НАН Украины,1998. p. 234.

2 Ibid p. 255.

3 Григорий Турский. *История франков* / пер., примеч. В. Д. Савуковой. Москва: Наука, 1987. Кн. 2.

4 Боргардт Александр. *Бич Божий (Атилла – 5-й каган гуннов и его времня).*Донецк: Изд-во Донецк. физ.-техн. ин-та им. А. П. Галкина НАН Украины,1998. p. 266.

uncle and attacked the army of Eastern Rome (Byzantium), ravaged the Byzantine cities and demanded an annual tribute from Constantinople in accord with previous truces. Theodosius, the Byzantine Emperor, sent a High Embassy, which included Priscus, to King Attila in 448 in order to resolve this interstate dispute.

According to Priscus, the Embassy departed from Constantinople, modern day Istanbul, and travelled to Sardica, which is now Sofia, the Bulgarian capital. The Embassy travelled from Sofia to Nais, which is now Niš in present day Serbia and from there to the River Istra, which is now the Danube. The river was the border between the lands of Scythia and Byzantium. Priscus noted that the route from Constantinople to Sardica could be professionally marched along in 13 days and from Nais to the Danube in five days. According to the map, the distance from Constantinople to Sardica in a straight line is approximately 495 kilometres and then 110 kilometres from Nais to the Danube. Therefore, the march along the first route would have needed to reach a distance of 38 kilometres daily along a straight line and 22 kilometres daily along the second part of the route, reaching an average daily speed of 30 kilometres. It may be logically assumed that the Byzantine Embassy could not move at the speed of a march because, as Priscus writes, it included "baggage on pack animals". This would have reduced the average daily speed. In order to calculate an estimated distance we shall assume that the average speed of the progress of the Embassy was about 80% of that of

Chapter 3: What Languages Tell Us

a pedestrian march, i.e. 24 kilometres daily. However, the actual daily journey would have been longer because it included winding roads and ascents and descents which would have significantly lengthened it. Having crossed the River Istra, the Embassy was received by Attila at his field camp but not without some diplomatic difficulties. The ambassadors were then instructed to head to the northern territories of Scythia to the court of King Attila where, it was promised, they would be given a written response to the message of the Byzantine Emperor.

The Embassy travelled on, crossing many rivers on boats fashioned from single trees, and rafts, the three most significant of these rivers are named as the Drecon, Tigas, and Tiphesas. The names of these rivers are not encountered in Ptolemy's *Geography,* which was written three centuries earlier than Priscus's account. They were probably left-hand tributaries of the Danube. The description of the Embassy's route from that point onwards does not include any geographical names, by contrast with the detailed account of the journey's beginning. It is as if the subsequent geographic names were deliberately deleted in order to deprive it of a link to Scythian territory and to remove the history of the Huns from Ukraine's past. However, I anticipate that something will remain in Priscus's work which will not permit the truth to be lost.

In particular, as he writes, the Embassy, having crossed the rivers he names, travelled along a smooth road on "the area of a plain". They did not, therefore, traverse the spurs of the Carpathians into Hungary but headed north-east along the Danube plain into the territories of modern Romania and Moldova. Priscus subsequently narrates that after a prolonged journey a terrible nocturnal adventure occurred on the banks of a lake near a Scythian settlement ruled by the wife of the deceased Bleda, Attila's brother. The Scythians rescued the Byzantine Embassy from a powerful nocturnal thunderstorm and its accompanying deluge. Priscus, alas, does not report the duration of the journey from the Danube's shores to the Scythian settlement or how far they travelled during that period. Let us try to logically deduce the location of the settlement to which this refers.

Firstly, the settlement could not be in the extreme south of Scythia on the Black Sea Steppes where one of the Scythian tribes, the Akatziri, resided. At this point Attila had only just established his rule over that tribe and intended his oldest son to become their ruler. The wife of Bleda's dominions could not have been among the Akatziri, who were unconquered at that time, nor near to them; it had to be to the north of the Black Sea regions. Secondly, this settlement could not be along the northern edge of Scythia because, as Priscus writes, the Embassy travelled to those lands, after the nocturnal incident, for a further seven days. They were then compelled to halt and wait for Attila and his convoy to advance. After Attila advanced, the Embassy had to continue to follow in the wake of his people "crossing some rivers". The northern peripheries of Scythia were, therefore, still far

Chapter 3: What Languages Tell Us

away. Thirdly, the settlement must have been in an area where no vines were grown because in the villages where the Embassy passed through they were offered a drink which the Scythians called *med* rather than wine. This means that the settlement must have been distant from the territories of modern Romania and Moldovia where from ancient times grapes have been harvested and wine produced and via which, apparently, the Embassy had already had time to pass. If we compare the arguments above we can assume that the settlement ruled by Bleda's wife was near the central line that divided Scythia into its northern and southern halves. It would have been, more specifically, near the line which connects the modern cities of Haivoron, Ulyanivka and Holovanivsk in Kirovohrad oblast, which is where the sacred centre of Scythia, Ekzampaeus, was based during Herodotus's era.

The Embassy travelled further to the north, from the Scythian settlement referred to above, and in the seven day period mentioned; they successfully travelled 168 kilometres at an average speed, as we have calculated, of 24 kilometres per day. When we draw a line 168 kilometres long on the map from the central line of Scythia we have determined we find the probable location where the Embassy awaited Attila's progress. It transpires that the site was near the modern city of Bila Tserkva.

The Embassy then, by "crossing some rivers", which were probably the modern water courses of the Ros', the Stugna and their tributaries, finally reached a "huge settlement". The name of this town has been removed here but the text retains a very important distinction from other settlements with these words: "a huge settlement wherein lay Attila's palace". It was, they assured us, "the most magnificent of all the palaces compared to those Attila had in other places". This huge settlement was certainly Kyiv which, in the opinion of Kyivan archaeologist Illia Samoilovskyi, already existed in the second century BC. Evidence for Samoilovskyi's argument exists in the numerous traces of settlements from that time on the territory of Kyiv and two large cemeteries found in the area of the Korchuvatyi and Karavajev Dachas.[1] Additional evidence that the end point of the Byzantine Embassy's route was not Pannonia where modern Hungary is situated is provided by Priscus. He notes that Onigisius, the second most important person in the Hun state after Attila, transported the stones for the construction of his bath from "Paeonian land", that is from Pannonia because there was no material of that kind near the Hun capital. Thus, even the meagre information that was not removed from Priscus's work indicates that Kyiv was the Hun capital. It was in that city that our glorious forebear, King Attila, was born, grew up and ruled the Hun state.

---

1   Самойловський Ілля. Коли виник Київ (До 1100-річчя першої літописної згадки про Київ). Науково-інформаційний бюлетень Архівного управління УРСР. Київ, 1961. № 4. p. 19–23. (Translator's note - the terms refer to historical locations in Kyiv.

3.17 Why has the truth concerning the Huns been silenced?

Priscus's stories about the Huns, their way of life, culture and traditions, create the impression that they might have been written about the lives of Ukrainians in the princely and Cossack eras. The same custom of greeting important guests with a choral song and bread and salt, but also, in the case of the Huns, wine and dishes on a tray with which they greeted Attila is reminiscent of Bohdan Khmelnytsky who "under the ringing of the bells of Saint Sophia entered Kyiv on a white horse".[1] The foreigners afflicted by bad weather were treated by the Scythians according to Ukrainian customs, hospitably received, granted the warmth of a fire and a comfortable bed. They did not live in nomad style Yurts nor in simple village huts warmed by burning reeds. Scythian men cut their hair in a Ukrainian style in a circle around the crown. The warm reception of the guests in Attila's palace resembles a banquet in the tower of a Kyivan prince. While the Byzantine Embassy was on the way to the capital they were given traditional Ukrainian food of millet and *kvas* with barley and *med*, an intoxicating beverage still popularly called *medovuha* in Ukraine (mead in English). Everything occurs just how it would in a customary Ukrainian environment. Priscus alternately calls the people with whom the Embassy interacts

---

1 From a song with lyrics by Valerij Marchenko.

the Huns, the Scythians, the general term barbarians, seemingly not seeing any difference between these terms, regarding them as different designations for one and the same people. In addition to the familiar Ukrainian words *med* and *kvas,* which are referred to by Priscus, another interesting term characteristic of the Ukrainian language is passed to us by Jordanes. That word is *strava* or dish.[1] When describing Attila's funeral, Jordanes writes of the Huns: "after such lamenting and groaning they lay dishes (in his Latin writing *stravam*) on his grave, as they call them and conduct a huge banquet."[2]

Everything that is said of the Huns in these texts proves convincingly that they are not alien but indigenous to the Dnipro region. However, the world does not want to admit this. It is more convenient for everyone to agree with the baseless hypothesis of Joseph de Gournier and stubbornly ignore the objective, historical evidence of Ptolemy, Priscus, Jordanes and other ancient historians. Why has this occurred? The answer is very simple: it is advantageous for the world to believe this. The Germans, the present day descendants of the Goths, would rather perceive the terrible defeats of their ancestors not as a response to Gothic aggression but as a natural disaster, divine punishment sent for some unclear reason from

---

1 Translator's note: dish in the sense of a menu item e.g. a fish dish etc.

2 Иордан. О происхождении и де яниях гетов. Getica / вступ. с татья ; пер. ;коммент. Е. Ч. Скржинской. Москва: Изд-во вост. лит., 1960. 1960. {258}.

Chapter 3: What Languages Tell Us

Mongolia in the form of the half-wild people called the Huns. It is also advantageous for the Russians to amputate part of Ukraine's ancient history and hand it to fictional aliens from Asia, while misappropriating the rest and graciously permitting Ukrainians to clamber out of the triple cradle of the "brotherly peoples" in the fourteenth century. This manoeuvre was also advantageous for Orthodox Christianity which, under Prince Volodymyr the Baptiser, became the state religion of Rus' in 988. In the main chronicle of Ukraine, *Tale of the Bygone Years,* written by the preachers of this faith, there is no reference to the Huns. There are details of the Ugre, both the white and black, the An'glian (English), the Agarian (Arabs), the Polian, Drevlian, Kryvych and many others, yet there is not a single word about the Huns. This is despite the fact that all Europe spoke of the Huns and European historians wrote that the Huns were the Ruses, Slavs that bore the Slavonic names Yaroslav and Yarozhyr, and that their capital was Kyiv. Why did the church keep silent about all this? We find the answer in the chronicle which states that prior to the adoption of Christianity, the people were pagans and "forgot who created them and lived like farm beasts".[1] This says, therefore, that the people could not have had a decent history or culture and their true history only commenced with the adoption of

---

1 *Повість врем'яних літ: літопис (за Іпатським списком)* / пер. з давньорусь-кої, післяслово, комент. В. В. Яременка. Київ: Рад. письменник, 1990. р. 146.

Christianity. Censorship obviously prohibited the introduction of any information about the Huns into the chronicle. The circumstance of the Huns misappropriation is even beneficial to the Hungarians who, though unconnected to the origin of the Huns, are suddenly bestowed with a meteoric radiance of Hun glory. They did not reject this unwarranted association but, on the contrary, advertise it well and give their new born boys the name of Attila en-masse. They also began to search the least indications that might confirm their belonging to the descendants of the Huns. This obscuring of the truth is only disadvantageous to we Ukrainians, the descendants of the indigenous peoples who lived in those days on the territory of modern Ukraine, the descendants of the Huns-Kyians. It is therefore our sacred task to restore the truth by breaking through the thickets of historical falsifications. One of our tasks is to restore the truth about the legendary leader of the Hun state, Attila, details of whose origins have been falsified by both Ukrainian and foreign historians. He is as outstanding a compatriot for Kyivans as, for example, Julius Caesar is for Romans or Charlemagne for the inhabitants of the German city of Aachen. The sole difference is that the current inhabitants of Rome or Aachen know of and respect their great countrymen whereas the origins and birthplace of Attila are known only to a few Ukrainians. This is a consequence of the historical silence concerning, and the falsification of, the facts by Tsarist and Soviet ideologies.

Chapter 3: What Languages Tell Us

Attila did not succeed in defeating his chief opponent, the Western Roman Empire, he died suddenly at the height of his power in 453 and was probably poisoned. However, the final nail in the coffin of the empire's existence was hammered in by his successor Odoacer (431-493), which is sometimes also spelled Odovacer or Odovacar, the son of a state functionary in Attila's government.[1] Attila's plan was realised and the slave-owning state of Rome fell. Nevertheless, Attila, against the backdrop of that event, has been coarsely designated "the scourge of God". This name, with which Attila was thanked by Europe for his efforts, looks like an iniquitous curiosity. After all, Europe, which is proud of its democratic freedoms, should surely recollect that the first people who brought its peoples liberation from Roman slavery were our ancestors. They were known at different times as the Scythians, Sarmatians, Huns and subsequently Ruses. They were freedom loving, independent and had an ancient tradition of a national gathering whose leaders they chose for themselves. They hated slavery and fought stubbornly for centuries against slave-owning Rome. The power of the Romans gradually melted away and the counterweight to them grew in force. The blows struck by Attila shook the foundations of the Roman Empire and lead to its collapse. The first act committed by Odoacer after he had captured Rome was the liberation of the slaves. It was

---

[1] Боргардт О. *О. Дві культури.* Донецьк: Вид-во Донецьк. фіз.-техн. Ін-ту ім. О. П. Галкіна НАН України, 1999. p. 23.

obviously for this reason that the slave owners of Europe left their descendants a malevolent image of Attila and his associates.

However, those were the views of slave owners. Our Ukrainian chroniclers of the Cossack era were, on the contrary, proud of the deeds of our "Sarmatian-Cossack forbears", "those ancient Ruses" as they called them. Samijlo Velychko, in his famous *Chronicle*, while describing the war waged by Bohdan Khmelnytsky for the liberation of Ukraine from Polish enslavement, recollects the events of a millennia ago when a military unit of Ruses who lived on the Baltic or German Pomeranian land seized ancient Rome under the leadership of Prince Odonacer (Odoaker) and held it in their power for fourteen years. Velychko draws a parallel with Bohdan Khmelnytsky's war of liberation against Polish enslavement and writes, "thus we follow the example of our ancient ancestry those long ago Ruses, and who can forbid us from being warriors and demean our chivalry and courage!"[1] These were just words and so topical today when Ukraine, with weapons in its hands, defends its independence and territorial integrity, in this instance in the war with the Russian aggressor.

3.18 The Origin of the Name Rus'

One thousand years ago when the forebears of the Ukrainians were colonising the territory of the Finno-Ugric

---

1 Величко Самійло. *Літопис*. Київ: Дніпро, 1991. Т. 1. pp. 26, 82.

Chapter 3: What Languages Tell Us

peoples, they recklessly and indulgently agreed that the colonised people could call themselves "Ruskii" (after the name of state-coloniser, the Rus'). It was akin to indulging a child to stop them crying. However, the child grew up, grew stronger and began to lay claim to the heritage of Ukrainians, to their land, their history and the right to "defend" the Russian-speaking population of Ukraine and to establish the "Russian World" there. Ultimately, they escalated to the open seizure of Ukrainian territories. That is the significance of that one tiny word recklessly left to the misfortune of their inheritors. It is no wonder that the confrontation between Greece and Macedonia over that one word and name, Macedonia, lasted for so many years. This is because the name of a country often determines destiny, as we can observe in Russian-Ukrainian relations. The Greeks, perhaps knowing of the difficult relations between those two countries, displayed a prudent concern for the fate of their inheritors and steadfastly insisted that the neighbouring state changed its name, Macedonia, which was identical to the designation of a historical region of Greece. Ultimately, a compromise was found in 2019, the Macedonians submitted and began calling their state the Republic of Northern Macedonia.

Where did this fateful word "Rus'" originate? There are over one dozen different versions that can be reduced into two main groups. The theories in the first group assert that the name Rus' was borne to Ukraine by incomers from Scandinavia who had long been called Norsemen/

Normans which, in translation, means people from the north. The second group of theories asserts that the name is local in origin. The supporters of the first group came to be known as "Normanists" while the second group were designated "Anti-Normanists". The supporters of both groups have a substantial volume of arguments to support their theory. The Normanists rely mainly on information from the chronicles. There is, for example, a record in AD 862 which speaks of a summons to the Varangians (the Eastern Slavonic name for the Vikings) to become princes of and to rule the local population: "and they went by the sea to the Varangians, to Rus', because those Varangians were called the Rus' (…) and the land is named Rus' after those Varangians."[1] The Anti-Normanists substantiate their theories with the ancient names of rivers concentrated in the Dnipro region (the Ros', Rosava, Rosavka, Rostavytsya rivers), as well as the accounts of Byzantine and Arabic authors concerning ancient peoples who lived on the territory of modern Ukraine and had the root-syllable "ros" in their names (the *rosy*, *rosomany*, and *roxolani*). The dispute between the Normanists and the Anti-Normanists has endured for over two hundred years. It was initiated by the Russians to prove that Rus' is their ancient name and existed before the origin of a state called Rus' on Ukrainian territory. However, initially, the Russians could not dispute

---

1 *Повість врем'яних літ : літопис (за Іпатським списком)* / пер. з давньоруської, післяслово, комент. В. В. Яременка. Київ: Рад. письменник, 1990. p.28.

Chapter 3: What Languages Tell Us

this matter with Ukrainians because Ukraine at that time was mute and had no voice under the oppression of Russian occupation. They therefore pursued their argument with German scientists who were invited into Russia and who, on the basis of information in the chronicles, claimed that Rus', the Kyiv state, was created by the incomers, the Varangians. Perhaps they hinted thus at the inability of the Slavs to create their own state. The Russian scientist Mikhail Lomonosov reacted angrily to this German attack. In his work *Kratkoj rossijskoj letopisec* (*A Short Russian Chronicle*) he is outraged by this German version according to which "the Swedes gave us Princes... and the Chukhna, a name".[1] Lomonosov asserts that in 862 Rurik was invited to rule the Slavs not from Scandinavia but from the southeastern shore of the Baltic Sea where the Slavic tribe of the Rus' resided.[2][3] In this work he not only groundlessly points towards the Baltic tribe of the Rus' but also permits himself to be arrogant towards the Finns, using the insulting term the Chukhna. However, the position outlined in his work, which began the Anti-Normanist theory, was seized upon by Russian historians in the Tsarist era and continued during the Soviet period. They preached, on the basis of

---

[1] Translator's footnote: an outdated term which had pejorative overtones for the Baltic/Finnish peoples in the Novgorod region.

[2] A Varangian chieftain who founded the Rurik dynasty which ruled Rus'.

[3] Ломоносов Михаил. Краткой россійской лѣтописецъ съ родословіемъ. Сочинен ие Мих айла Ломо носова. Въ Санктпетербургѣ при Импер аторской Академіи Наукъ, 1760 года.

Lomonosov's version, that the name Rus' first appeared in 862 in Novgorod where Rurik was called to rule. The name then passed to Kyiv when Oleh, after insidiously killing Askold, took possession of the Kyiv throne in 882. This account gave the Russians the opportunity to speak of the secondary quality of the history of Kyiv and its entry into Russian history. On the basis of this version, in 1862 the Russians built a pompous monument weighing 10,000 tons and called "A Millennium of Russia" in Novgorod. However, recent archaeological research has shown that the name Rus' was present in written sources, when Novgorod did not exist, it only appeared in the eleventh century. So the version of Old Man Lomonosov fell apart and the Russians began feverishly searching for a substitute.

The attention of archaeologists and even the Russian president turned to Stara Ladoga where the remains of a Scandinavian settlement, a trading post dating to the eighth century were revealed. In order to use this discovery the Russians had a sudden "enlightenment", turned to the Normanist version and began saying that the word Rus' was brought by the Varangians but first to Stara Ladoga, then to Novgorod, which, incidentally, did not exist at that time, and thence to Kyiv. However, with a careful reading of *The Tale of the Bygone Years,* you can note that the episode concerning the call to the Varangians to rule over the lands of the tribes of the "Rus', Chud', Sloveny, Kryvychi and Ves'" is a fiction added, as it were, in retrospect for the artificial elevation of Novgorod in its rivalry

Chapter 3: What Languages Tell Us

with Kyiv. It is easy to observe this device when you read an earlier account in the chronicle dating from AD 852. It states that the chronicler learned of the name of the Rus' land from a Byzantine source: "in the year 852, in the fifteenth indict when Mykhailo began his reign, they began to nickname the realm the Rus' land.[1] We learned of this from a Greek chronicle in which it is said that the emperor of Rus' came to Tsaregrad."[2],[3] It is clear that the chronicler who added the episode concerning the summons to the Varangians did not note the report dating from 852 and, fortunately, did not redact it from the chronicle. The inauthenticity of this subsequently added episode is also debunked by historical events recorded from this period. There is an account, for example, of how the Rus', led by Prince Askold of Kyiv, ventured on a campaign against Constantinople (which Tsaregrad is synonymous with) in 860.[4] Therefore, the new Russian theory concerning the origin of the name Rus', which is associated with Stara Ladoga and built on the fiction of a Novgorod contributor to the chronicle, is an obvious fiction. However, this did

---

1 Translator's note: an indict is an Ancient Greek chronological unit equivalent to fifteen years.

2 *Повість врем'яних літ : літопис (за Іпатським списком)* / пер. з давньоруської, післяслово, комент. В. В. Яременка. Київ: Рад. письменник, 1990.p. 27.

3 Translator's note: Tsaregrad was the Slavonic name for Constantinople in this period.

4 Котляр М.Ф., Плахонін А.Г. *Походи русі на Візантію* // Енциклопедія історії України у 10 т., Т.8 : Па–Прик. Київ: Наукова думка, 2011.

not prevent Russians from celebrating the supposed 1,150 year anniversary of Russian statehood, which they had invented, in 2012. A child, as we see, who has supposedly grown up continues to play.

It is now believed that the oldest written source in which the name Rus' (or *Rhos* in Latin) first appeared is the *Bertin Annals* or *Bertin Chronicles* named after the location of their discovery at the Abbey of St. Bertin in Northern France. In 2018, France transferred some excerpts from the chronicles to Ukraine, recognising that they directly relate to Ukrainian history. In particular, it is recorded in the annals that in 839, representatives of the Byzantine Embassy arrived in France together with representatives of a state called Rhos whose king bore the title Khagan (*Chacanus* in Latin).[1] This title was characteristic not only for the Turks, the rulers of Kyiv were sometimes called *Khagan* (Great Khan). For example, in the full title of the work by Metropolitan Ilarion, *Slovo pro zakon i blagodat,* there are the following words: "praise be to our Khagan Volodymyr that we were baptised by him."[2] There is a strong possibility that those who called themselves the Rhos were from the Kyivan principality and that their Khagan was the predecessor of Askold whose name has been lost. These were probably ambassadors of Prince Bravlin who, at the end of the eighth – beginning of the

---

1 *Annales Bertiniani. Monumenta Germaniae historica.* historica / Ed. G. H. Pertz.Hannoverae: Bibliopolii Alvici Hahniani, 1826. Vol. 1. p. 434.

2 Translator's note: this translates as "The Word of the Law and Grace".

Chapter 3: What Languages Tell Us

ninth centuries, led his army in a Crimean campaign which devastated several Crimean cities. This episode is recorded in the *Žitïi Stefana Suroz'kogo*.[1] [2] However, Louis I, the Emperor of the Franks, investigated the mission of these guests and established that they came from the Swedes (*Sueones*). This can be explained by the fact that people who spoke foreign languages were recruited for the ambassadorial mission and some of these may have been of Swedish origin.

The Normanists have one very significant trump card to play in support of their theory. It is the work *De administrando imperio* (*On the management of the Empire*) by the Byzantine Emperor Constantine VII Flavius Porphyrogenitus which was written in the middle of the tenth century.[3] In this work he uses the term Ros to refer to the people who conquered the Slavonic tribes of Kyiv and other territories. This people, he notes, took tribute from them, fed at the expense of the subjugated people each autumn and winter, and in spring loaded boats fashioned from a single tree, took goods from them and transported these via the Dnipro for sale in southern lands, overcoming the river's rapids. Who were these people? The key to

---

[1] Котляр М.Ф. *Бравлін* // Енциклопедія історії України у 10 т., Т.1 : А–В. Київ: Наукова думка, 2003.

[2] Translator's note: the text referred to is, in translation, *The Life of Stefan of Surozh* which dates from the ninth century

[3] Constantine Porphyrogenetus. *De administrando imperio*. http://books.goog le.com.ua.

their identification was left by Emperor Constantine VII himself. When describing the rapids on the Dnipro he gives them two sets of names, Roski, which is adjectival associating them with the Ros people (*Ρωσιστί*), and Slavonic (*Σκλαβηνιστί*). However, in the nineteenth century, the outstanding Ukrainian linguist Omelyan Partytsky proved convincingly that the Roski names for the rapids originates from the Scandinavian languages. The fourth group of Dnipro rapids, for example, are referred to by the Emperor using the Ros term as the *Ejfor* (*Αειφόρ*) and by the Slavonic term as the *Neaset* (*Νεασήτ*). In Partytsky's opinion, the Roski name derives from the ancient Swedish term e*ifor*, which means "dangerous".[1] The Slavonic name will be clear to Ukrainian speakers without being translated, it means insatiable. These rapids of inglorious fame were flooded by the waters of the Dnipro reservoir in the last century.

What compelled the learned emperor to provide two-fold names for the rapids? The obvious reason is that, during his lifetime, there was a bilingual situation on Kyivan territory. The incomers from Scandinavia spoke the Ros language and the local population spoke Slavonic or, more precisely Old Ukrainian, which had already developed as we demonstrated earlier (see section 3.5). Its existence is also confirmed by the ancient Ukrainian word *Neaset*. Although the ancient Ukrainian language subsequently displaced the

---

1 Партицький Омелян. *Скандинавщина в давній Руси*. Львів, 1887.

Chapter 3: What Languages Tell Us

Ros language, the name Ros was nevertheless ascribed to the local population. The Ros subsequently returned to their natural name of Rus. They were called the Ros by the Greek-Byzantines perhaps because the letter *u* is absent from Greek; the Greek letter Ypsilon *y* was pronounced like the Ukrainian letter *ю (yu)*, therefore the pronunciation of Ros was closer to the name Rus than the pronunciation of *Ryus* would have been. It emerges that we have another instance here of how the name of the conquerors is transferred to those they conquered: the Dacians became the Romanians, the Gauls became the Franks, the Sivery who relocated to the Balkans became the Bulgarians, the colonised Finno-Ugric peoples of the Moscow area became the Russians, the Slavs who lived in the Pannonia became the Hungarians and in this last instance, as we have just considered, the Antes and Huns of the Kyiv region became known by the generalised name of Ruses, and the name of their state is recorded in the Kyiv chronicles with a softened ending as the Rus'. The word Rus' did, therefore, most likely come to us from Scandinavia, not via Ladoga and Novgorod but across Kyiv and its lands.

That Novgorod chronicler clearly knew of the temporary dominion of those Scandinavians over the Kyiv region and consciously twisted the text in favour of Novgorod, fabricating a legend about a call to the Varangians to rule there. However, even there he made some reckless errors. While searching for evidence of his fabrication in foreign sources he came across a phrase in the Gothic language which related to King Rurik and runs as follows: *"Konung Roegrik med sine hus ok troe vern"* which means "King Rurik with his home and his faithful military unit".[1] The words in the text were not separated properly with spaces at that time and the chronicler had the impression that the sentence referred to two other people in addition to Rurik; Sineus (sine hus) and Truvor (troe vern). He generously endowed these two virtual guests from overseas with local cities: one was given as a "gift" Biliozero and the other was presented with Izborsk. However, subsequently, regaining his senses and realising that none of the descendants of Sineus and Truvor had ever existed or interacted with anyone, by contrasts with Rurik's many descendants, he gives his fictional characters another two years to live, for a veneer of plausibility, and then ruthlessly, while they are still young, "kills" one after the other. Rurik's status at this point increases, he is "commanded" from Ladoga to rule over Novgorod, which only appeared 100 years after the king "sent" to rule there. It only remains for us to thank the chronicler for being too lazy to delete, or perhaps in such haste that he did not notice, the evidence which completely cancelled out everything he had added to the text.

There is another similar curiosity in the chronicle. It appeared either due to a lack of awareness on the part of the chroniclers or was introduced knowingly to hide

---

1 Боргардт Алекса ндр. Бич Божий (Ат ти ла – 5-ый каган гун нов и его время). Донецк: Изд-во Д оне цк. фи з.-техн. ин-та им. А. П. Галкина НАН Украины, 1998. p. 316.

trivial details of ancestral lives which would have been unpleasant for their descendants to read. The oddity we have in mind affected the name of King Askold al-Dur, an immigrant from the northern countries who succeeded in seizing the Kyivan throne for a period of time. The authors of the chronicle created two princes from one, Askold and Dir. They perceived the surname Dur as the first name of another person. They then read the word Dur with a Swedish *u* in the middle via the old Ukrainian *u* which is the modern Ukrainian *i*. Askold received the addition to his name of the characteristic Arabic article *al* when he served as chief of the guards in the Emirate of Córdoba in Spain. His name features in the chronicles of the Emirate as "Askold al-Dur".[1] The compilers of the chronicle realised that the contemporary residents of Kyiv knew of only one princely grave, that of Askold situated in a prominent place on a hill and no one had heard of Dir's grave. They were therefore compelled to "bury" Dir in what seemed to them an inconspicuous place "by sacred Orina".[2] The question naturally arises, why would they have been buried separately? They ruled together, fought together, were slain together and were buried apart? The awl really protruded out of the sack!

---

1 Боргардт Александр. *Бич Божий (Аттила – 5-ый каган гуннов и его время)*. Донецк: Изд-во Д онецк. физ.-техн. ин-та им. А. П. Галкина НАН Украины, 1998. p. 316.

2 *Літопис руський* / пер. з давньорус. Л. Є. Махновця ; відп. ред. О. В. Мишанич. Київ: Дніпро, 1989. p. 13.

3.19 The Kyiv Stronghold of Sambatas

Even though over one thousand years have passed since they resided in Ukraine, there are still traces left by the Scandinavians on our land. One of these is the same yellow and blue colours on the flags of Sweden and Ukraine. A second relic of their presence is that enigmatic account by the Byzantine emperor of how the single tree boats of the Ros gathered at the Kyiv fortress (καστρον) called Sambatas (Σαμβατας) every spring.[1] Where was this fortress, whence and from what language does its name originate and is that name a secondary designation for Kyiv? Historians have many questions here but no convincing answers. The Academician B. Rybakov generally regards the origin of the name Sambatas as unclear, despite the dozens of variant interpretations thereof, and locates the fortress in Kyiv's Podil area.[2]

The chronicles have not borne this name to our time but it is preserved in popular memory in the word Samburky, which they give to an area on the southern outskirts of Kyiv. There are several places in this area whose names are similar in structure to the name Samburky: Nyvky Hrushky, Teremky, Poznyaky, Osokorky etc. Each of them delineates a particular area of Kyiv based on its characteristic features. Teremky, for example, which means towers, is a locality where a princely tower was situated. Similarly, the location

---

1 Constantine Porphyrogenetus. *De administrando imperio*, cap. 9.
2 Рыбаков Б. А. Город Кия. *Вопросы истории.* Москва, 1980, № 5. p. 41.

Chapter 3: What Languages Tell Us

where Sambat was situated (which would not have had the characteristic Greek suffix "as" ascribes to it by the emperor) would probably have been called Sambatky, with the pronunciation subsequently changing to Samburky. After all, proper names are not permanent and immutable, they change as time flows over the generations. The Dolobske lake, for example, which appears in the chronicles is the modern Dovbychka lake near Kyiv. Similarly, the area called Zhelan in the chronicles became the modern Zhuliani and the chronicles' Shelvove village near Bork gave its name to the area of Kyiv called Shulyavka etc. It is not, therefore, surprising, that the name Sambatky was "corrected" by subsequent generations of our ancestors over the centuries and became Samburky. The modern term is a slightly distorted reflection of the name of that ancient fortress.

The name Sambat was most probably introduced by the Varangians-Scandinavians whose presence in Rus' at the end of the first millennium was extremely conspicuous. Let us recollect the Varangian Cave in Kyiv or the peace agreements made between the Kyivan princes Ihor and Oleh and Byzantium in AD 912 and 945.[1] It emerges from the texts of the agreements of "love between the Greeks and the Rus'" that the vast majority of those who participated in the interstate negotiations on behalf of Kyiv were of Scandinavian origin as their names testify: Vuiefast, Shygobern,

---

1 *Київ. Енциклопедичний довідник* / за ред. А. В. Кудрицького. Київ: Гол. редакція УРЕ, 1981. p. 87.

Sfandr, Adolb and others.[1] The name Sambat is clearly a term in the Ros language, the emperor does not provide the Slavonic alternative name and perhaps did not know what that was. Similarly, he provided only one name for the third set of Dnipro rapids, Gelandri (Γελανδρί), which linguists consider to be in the Ros language.[2] He probably did not know the Slavic name either but he interpreted it for his Greek readers as follows: "The Slavonic name means the noise of the rapids." These rapids were known in our time as the Dzvonetsky or simply the Zvonets.[3] Everything we have considered here suggests that we should search for a Scandinavian origin in the name Sambat.

In the modern Swedish and Norwegian languages the prefix "sam" is utilised to form words which signify compatibility and aggregation. Samla, for example, means to collect, samman means together, near to one another. Sambat, therefore, is a gathering of boats, their mooring, pier or, as our ancestors said in the ancient Ukrainian language, a *prityka*. So, the location of the *prityka* is suggested by the popular memory of the toponym Samburky. This conclusion is also confirmed by the modern names of places located adjacent to Samburky, the Galerna

---

1 *Літопис руський* / пер. з давньорус. Л. Є. Махновця; відп. ред. О. В. Мишанич. Київ: Дніпро, 1989. p. 26.

2 Скляренко Віктор. *Русь і варяги: Історико-етимологічне дослідження*. Київ: Довіра, 2006. p. 80.

3 Translator's note: the names relate to the Ukrainian words for bell and the verb to ring.

Bay and Galerny Island on the Dnipro. These preserve the memory of the military rowing boats called galleys which once docked there. According to historians, the river bed of the Dnipro retreated to the east in this area and the present day Samburky became further remote from the banks of the Dnipro and its inlets.[1] The fact that in earlier times the Dnipro's course lay significantly further to the west than at the present time is shown by a topographic map of Kyiv in the nineteenth century. Furthermore, there is an account of how in the twelfth century a retaining wall had to be built urgently under the Vydubetsky Monastery to prevent it from falling in the precipice created by the swift Dnipro current. It is difficult even to imagine now the massive threat that hung over the church then when the monastery is so far away from where the Dnipro flows in its present day course.

3.20 The Early States of the Ruses

After Attila's death, the vast Hun state (Hun Kingdom), which included the Antes Union, disintegrated into a number of smaller state unions. The Antes Union persisted for a while but was soon eliminated by a people who came from Asia, the Avars, who are termed the Obry in the chronicle. The Obry tormented the subjugated Antes and harnessed their women to carts instead of using horses or bulls. However, as the chronicle says, "God destroyed

---

1 Вакулишин Сергій. *Кінець світу*. Столиця. 09.08.2001.

them all and today there is not a single Obryn". There remains only a bad memory of them in the folk proverb "perish like the Obry".[1] Thus, the Antes alliance, founded by Prince Bozh in the fourth century, ceased to exist at the beginning of the seventh century and since that time the name Antes became another designation for our ancestors who, of course, never moved from their native Dnipro region but came to be called by a new name, the Ruses (or Rus in the singular), after they were conquered by the Scandinavians. The process of developing new state associations on the territory of modern Ukraine continued but under a different name ascribed to our ancestors, who became the Ruses.

In the seventh to the tenth centuries, the countries of the Arab Caliphate saw a further development of the historical and geographical sciences which are based on the work of the ancient scientists. Some of the works of the Arab and Persian writers have survived to the present albeit with meagre, often contradictory but nevertheless significant, information about our ancestors. Almost all the Arab and Persian authors who wrote about the topic made a distinction between the Slavs and the Ruses, often setting them in opposition to one another. The process whereby the Slavs branched into different groups continued in full swing at that time. The Slavs, while relocating from

---

1 *Літопис руський* / пер. з давньорус. Л. Є. Махновця; відп. ред. О. В. Мишанич. Київ: Дніпро, 1989. p. 20.

Chapter 3: What Languages Tell Us

the Dnipro region in all directions, were initially divided into the Antes and the Sklavenes. Subsequently, they separated into the western, eastern, northern and southern Slavs, simultaneously acquiring various names (the Poles, Lusatians, Serbs, Croats, Bulgarians, etc.).

The people who would later become the Ruses remained on their ancestral terrain of the Dnipro region, including the Kyiv region. Kyiv has a very favourable strategic position at the intersection of water and land routes in Eastern Europe and has always been a unifying centre throughout our history, including the Sarmatian era, when Claudius Ptolemy referred to the city with a synonym for capital city, Metropolis, and during the period of the Kyivan princes Bozh and Bolemyr, who rallied the Kyivan army against the foreign Goths, and during Attila's time. It was the city where he grew up and from whence he commenced his renown as the wise leader of the great Hun state. After that realm collapsed, and after the defeat of the Antes by the Avars, Kyiv gradually regained its power and unified a circle of disparate tribes. It is at this point that eastern geographers report the information concerning a new state formed by the Ruses in the eighth to ninth centuries, it was known as Kuyabia and had its capital in the city of Kuyaba. Thus the Arab geographer al-Istakhri, who lived in the first half of the tenth century but relied on the works of his earlier predecessors such as al-Balkhi, Ibn Khordadbeh and others, wrote in his work *Routes of the Realms*: "The Ruses. There are three groups. One group is closer to Bulgar and their king dwells in a city called Kuyaba, and it is larger than Bulgar. The most remote group is called as-Slavia and (the third) group is called al-Arsania and their king dwells in Arsa. They neighbour on the northern borders of Ruma.[1] There are so many of them and they are so powerful that they have imposed tribute on the border regions of Ruma."[2]

We see that there was a king at the head of each group of the Ruses and that, therefore, each of them had their own state. It is probable that these three groups formed the core of the future Kyivan state which arose in the ninth century and was named Rus'. The geographical location of Kuyabia is clearly the Kyiv area and researchers are almost unanimously agreed on this issue. With regard to the location of the other two states, there are numerous theories most of which are obviously wrong because they propose locations situated geographically distant from Kuyaba and the border regions of Ruma (Byzantium). These groups are, after all, related to each other and the territories they inhabited must have been relatively close together. The closeness of their location is specified by a tenth century Arab geographer al-Idrisi who wrote: "There are four crossings from Kuyaba to Arsa and from Arsa to Slavia, four days."[3] A further reference to the location of

---

[1] Author's note: Ruma means Byzantium here.

[2] Новосельцев Анатолий. *Восточные источники о восточных славянах и Руси VI–IX вв.* Москва, 1965. p. 315.

[3] Новосельцев Анатолий. *Восточные источники о восточных славянах и Руси VI–IX вв.* Москва, 1965. p. 317.

Chapter 3: What Languages Tell Us

the Ruses inhabitation is given by a ninth century Arab geographer and author, ibn Rustah who wrote in his *Book of Precious Treasures*: "As for the ar-Rusiia, they live on an island surrounded by a lake ... that takes three days of road and it is covered with forests and swamps. They have a king called the Khakan of the Ruses."[1] Such a large island, whose length would have been greater than 100 kilometres and was also covered in swamps and forests has long been unknown in Ukraine. Subsequently, however, it was established that in the mists of antiquity, during the intensive thawing of the glaciers, the Dnipro separated into two mighty sub-rivers below Kanev, creating two arms splitting from the mouth of the modern River Irdyn. The right arm bore its waters to the lowlands where the Irdyn and Tiasmyn rivers now flow and where the present day Irdyn swamp, which is 44 kilometres long and lies between them, is situated. At present two rivers flow in opposite directions from both ends of this long swamp, the Irdyn and the Irdynka. The left arm, as it does now, bore its waters along the Dnipro's current course. The two sleeves converged far to the south, just before the modern day city of Kremenchuk, which create a huge island. Its approximate contours are delineated in a light colour on a map of Ukraine in the fifth decade of the twentieth century before the Kremenchuk reservoir was created (figure 3.12).

---

1   Ibid p. 302.

Figure 3.12: The Island of the Ruses

When the glaciers completely thawed and the flow of the Dnipro reduced, the right arm gradually shrank, became overgrown with trees and shrubs and was unfit for navigation. During the period when the Ruses lived on its banks it would certainly have been navigable, as is illustrated by the remains of ships, anchors and oars which have been excavated from the Irdyn swamp.[1] The modern city of Cherkassy is situated on this island, which is still called The Island of the Ruses.

The location of The Island of the Ruses and the state of Kuyaba can therefore be established. The two were not distant from one another on the central Dnipro. There was also a short distance, four daily marches between the capitals of the states, as recorded by the Arab geographer al-Idrisi. This demonstrates that all three of the Ruses'

---

1 Знойко Олександр. *Міфи Київської землі та події стародавні*, Київ : Молодь, 1989. p. 40.

Chapter 3: What Languages Tell Us

states, Kuyabia, Slavia and Arsania were located nowhere else but on the territory of modern Ukraine. However, Russian historians, stubbornly clinging to the fabrication regarding the summons to the Varangians, do not recognise these facts and try to prove that the Ruses' state of al-Slavia was in the north on the land near Lake Ilmen. However, the distances from any of these capitals to the Ilmen area far exceed those indicated by al-Idrisi. The Russians cast his account aside and try to prove that the Varangians, advancing to the south-east from Stara Ladoga, first conquered the Volga river route in the eastern countries and only subsequently the Dnipro river route to Byzantium, known from the chronicle as the "path from the Varangians to the Greeks". We see that, yet again, the Russians are pursuing the same goal, to position Stara Ladoga and Novgorod ahead of Kyiv. They justify their version of history by referring to the discovery along the Volga route of a large number of treasure hoards of oriental coins and note the absence of similar finds on the Dnipro route. This justification is the kind of deception which involves speaking part, but not the whole, of the truth. The whole of the truth is that the Normans mastered the Dnipro route at the beginning of the AD era, half of millennia before they conquered the Volga route, when the Dnipro and its tributaries supplied "solar stone" (sonâčnij kamìn′) or amber, burštin (also known as elektron, ântar, alatir and by other names) from the Baltic region. In those days the only known amber deposits were in the Baltic regions where it was found on the surface. Subsequently, during our era, it was discovered that amber occurs elsewhere, particularly in Ukraine, but it lies deeper underground than in the Baltics and our ancestors were not aware of its deposits on their territory. Therefore, they supplied amber from the Baltics along the so called "amber paths" which ran not only to the Mediterranean, where the chief consumers of unprocessed amber were situated, but also in the direction of Scythia and later Sarmatia along the Neman, Daugava, Pripyat and Dnipro rivers. This is evidenced by the amber jewellery which was widespread among the Sarmatians and many examples of which are found in the burials of not only noble but also ordinary Sarmatians in the form of necklaces, weights for spindles and other items.[1] Subsequently, the "amber paths" that ran in the direction of Sarmatia transferred to the well-known "paths from the Varangian to the Greek" and conversely from "the Greek to the Varangian". The fact that at the boundary of the new era there already existed trade routes along the Dnipro, Neman, Daugava and Pripyat rivers and their tributaries is illustrated by the discovery of coins. However, trade at that time existed in the form of natural exchange or barter, with limited money in circulation. Roman and Greek coins had not, as yet, acquired as wide a distribution as they would later during the period of the Kyivan state. Nevertheless,

---

1 Клочко Л. *Бурштинові шляхи за скіфських часів*. Геолог України. Київ, 2011. № 3–4. pp. 173–180.

coins dating from that period were found. In the Belarusian city of Druya, Vitebsk oblast, for example, Roman money dating from the first century has been found. Similarly, in Klimovichi, in Mogilev oblast, Belarus, a treasure trove of 1,815 coins from the first Roman emperors was discovered.[1] Two caches of second century Roman coins were discovered in Sosnytsia, 90 kilometres north of Chernihiv, Ukraine near the Desna river.[2] Roman money dating from the Antonin period was found near the town of Chornobyl in the nineteenth century.[3] However, it transpired that the oldest find on the "amber path" was coinage of the Bosporus minted in the third century BC in Crimea. It was discovered in the Belarusian city of Pinsk on the Pripyat river and came from Crimea, perhaps from the Ancient Greek city of Olbia, located near the modern city of Ochakiv. It could have been transported from Olbia along the Ingul, Dnipro and Pripyat rivers to where it was found in modern Pinsk. According to research by V. Antonovych and Yu. Kulakovsky, the Olbian Greeks knew of the impossibility of the Dnipro rapids so they bypassed them, opting for a more accessible route along the Ingul river. They then dragged the boats to the middle Dnipro where its right arm

---

1 Мельникова А. А. *Находки монет античного мира в Беларуси* // Крыніцаз-наўство і спецыяльныя гістарычныя дысцыпліны: навук. зб. Мінск: БДУ, 2008. Вып. 4. p. 72.

2 See: https://uk.wikipedia.org/wiki/%D0%A1%D0%BE%D1%81%D0%B-D%D0%B8%D1%86%D1%8F.

3 Антонович В. *Археологическая карта Киевской губернии*. Москва: Тип. М. Г. Волчанинова, 1895. p. 5.

flowed past the Island of the Ruses of which we already know. The Dnipro's waters then rose to Kyiv, thence to Pripyat and other rivers. It is not surprising that in the Tyasmin Basin, which was then part of the right Dnipro arm, so many Roman coins were found.

It is precisely because the Greeks chose a direct route along the Ingul river, bypassing the rapids, that Claudius Ptolemy knew only of cities along the central and upper Dnipro, from Kyiv to Orsha. He did not name a single city on the lower reaches of the river where the rapids were because, obviously, he lacked any information about them. On the banks of the Daugava, which is the nearest of all the Baltic rivers to Orsha, several hundred Roman copper coins were discovered.[1] All these discoveries confirm the existence of an ancient "amber path" at the beginning of the AD period. It passed along the Ingul, the middle and higher Dnipro, then overland and subsequently along the River Daugava to the Baltic locations where amber was discovered. Therefore, Kyiv (termed Metropolis by Ptolemy) was known to the Normans at the beginning of the AD period and the efforts of Russian historians to position it behind Stara Ladoga and Novgorod have no basis. It is from Kyiv, not Stara Ladoga, that the temporary rule of the immigrant Varangians over our land began. The name of one of them, King Askold, has been passed down to us and

---

1 История Латвии. I – IV век до н.э. https://travelkap.club/latvija1/histori-02/index.html

he was followed by Rurik. The Kagan of the Ruses might have preceded Askold, he who, according to the Bertinian annals, sent the embassy to the Frankish empire of Louis (see section 3.18). However, the name of the Kagan has not been preserved. The mythical Kyi should not be taken into account because we have demonstrated that the name of Kyiv was not taken from this mythical personage. On the contrary, the name of the city evoked the name of its mythical creator. The chronicle says that Prince Kyi went to Tsaregrad (Constantinople Byzantium) and was greatly honoured by the emperor. However, the Greek chronicles do not say anything about his visit there. Presumably the chronicler ascribed to the mythical Kyi the real actions of Prince Askold who indeed went on a campaign against the Greeks in AD 860, during the time of the Byzantine Emperor Michael I.[1]

3.21 The Ruses - The Cossacks - The Ukrainians

The ancestors of Ukrainians, from the ninth century onwards and after the arrival of the Scandinavians, began to call themselves Ruses, Rusy, Rus', Rusiny, Rusichy. These names remained commonly accepted for internal use among Ukrainians, like self designations, for a few centuries and externally in relations with neighbouring states and peoples. This is confirmed by numerous

---

[1] Котляр М. Ф., Плахонін А. Г. *Походи русі на Візантію.* // Енциклопедія історії України у 10 т., Т.8: Па–Прик. Київ: Наукова думка, 2011.

facts. The chronicle, for example, says that in 1188 the Suzdal Prince Vsevolod sent his eight years old daughter Verkhuslava to Rus' to marry the 16 year old Rostyslav, the Prince of Bilhorod (which is now Bilohorodka village near Kyiv). The chronicle says that, "then Yakiv came from Rus' and having sent Verkhuslava..."[1] It was obvious, for the author who wrote about this event, that Suzdal was not Rus'. Similarly, during the thirteenth century, one of the largest states in Europe, the Grand Duchy of Lithuania, Rus' and Samogitia was formed on the terrain of Eastern Europe and would greatly expand in the fourteenth century. Its name is usually shortened to GDL (the Grand Duchy of Lithuania) in Russian sources because they prefer not to mention the word Rus' (in its adjectival for Rus'ke in the original) because it exposes its subsequent theft by Moscow. A further example can be given relating to the sixteenth century publication of Ptolemy's *Geography* in Venice in a Latin translation. The compiler of the work explains in the notes that the territory of the historic Sarmatia, to which Ptolemy referred, was divided between Polonia, Rossia, Prussia, Lithuania, Livonia, Podolia and Moskovia.[2] Therefore, during the time the book was published in 1548, Moskovia and Rossia as the author terms them were separate countries. A country which was

---

1 *Літопис руський* / пер. з давньорус. Л. Є. Махновця; відп. ред. О. В. Мишанич. Київ: Дніпро, 1989. pp. 345, 346.

2 Ptolemeo Cl. *La Geografia di Claudio Ptolemeo* Alessandrino. Venetia: Per Gioan Baptista Pedrezano, 1548. p. 85b.

Chapter 3: What Languages Tell Us

located on the edge of the central Dnipro river with its centre in Kyiv was called Rossia by Europeans in the Latin language, which is very close to the current name of Russia. In combination with Podolia, which lies at the interfluve of the Southern Bug and Dniester rivers, Rossia occupied the territory of present day Ukraine. Moscovia was situated to the north-east of Rossia. In official documents dating from the seventeenth century, Bohdan Khmelnytsky called his people Ruskyij, the adjectival form of Rus' and the northern neighbouring people Moskovs'skyj, or Muscovite.[1] However, over time, as Muscovy colonised Ukrainian territories, the concept of Rus' and Muscovy began artificially to converge. The Constantinople Patriarchate played an especially negative role in this convergence by being the first to introduce the term "Little Rossia" (or *Micra Rossia* in their Latin) for the six ecclesiastical dioceses of the separate Halychyna Metropolitan and Great Rossia (*Megale Rossia*) for the nineteen under the Kyiv Metropolitan. So, with Constantinople's gentle touch, the church and state figures of Moscovia caught this initiative and began actively to develop it, especially after the Pereyslav Council of 1654 and the non-canonical accession of the Kyiv Metropolitan to the Moscow Patriarchate in 1686. It was via their efforts and not without the assistance of a "fifth column" of church officials and Cossack elders that

---

[1] *Універсали Богдана Хмельницького*. Київ: Вид. дім «Альтернатива»,1998. pp. 50, 137.

Muscovy was proclaimed Rossia or Great Rossia in 1721. The real Rus', which was called Rossia by foreigners, was give the name Little Rossia, Malorosiâ, and then not all of it but only the area on the Dnipro's left bank. The peoples were also named accordingly from these terms, the Great Rossians and the Little Rossians.

The transformation of the Ruses into the Little Rossians outraged their descendants who expressed their protest via the book *Istoriâ Rusovъ, ili Maloj Rossii* (*The History of the Ruses or Little Rossia*).[1] The unknown author of this book reminds the Great Rossians who is who and glorifies the deeds of the descendants of the true Ruses who, in his opinion, were the Cossacks. So for a time the name Cossacks, rather than Little Rossians, became the name of our people. However, when Russia first liquidated the Zaporozhian Sich and then the Cossack Hetmanate, the descendants of the Ruses were forced to return to their old name, Ukrainians. That name originates, as we have discussed, from the Scythian Ou-kraina, which was recorded by the Byzantine historian Jordanes in his work *Getica*.

---

1   *Історія Русів* / пер. І. Драча; вступ. ст. В. Шевчука. Київ: Рад. Письменник, 1991. p. 22.

Chapter 4: What the Artefacts Confirm

At every stage of their history, as defined by each subsequent name, Ukrainians left traces of their activity in the form of material remains which archaeologists term artefacts. They attribute the artefacts to certain historical cultures which are ascribed names according to various conditions. These name are, as a rule, determined by the name of the settlement where a given culture was first discovered (Chornoliska, Zarubynetska, Chernyakhivska etc.). The time period when these cultures existed is usually determined by isotopic methods. The artefacts discovered are extremely valuable and significant as witnesses to the historical path of a people, but they have a significant disadvantage of, unfortunately, being "mute". The information obtained by archaeologists from them resembles the movement of shadows on an illuminated cloth. It shows us how people moved, what utensils they used, what they were able to do and in what order they came into this world and departed into non-being. However, it does not tell us who they were, what language they spoke, what they called themselves and what they were called by neighbouring peoples. There are no artefacts that can answer these questions. In order to compel the answers to the questions to "speak" we need to use all the accessible acquisitions of modern science and position them in accord with the linguistic and genetic witnesses of the past. Then, with a suite of the testimonies of all three witnesses, a true picture of the past is sketched. The people behind that backlit cloth screen give us their voices and tell us something about themselves. Let us examine the most significant artefacts from the past life of ancient Ukrainians, which will supplement and confirm what the genetic and linguistic witnesses have told us in sections 2 and 3.

4.1 The Archaeological Heritage left by the People of Trypillia

A particular feature of Trypillian culture is its extraordinary prevalence in Ukraine where mementoes of its existence have been found in 19 of the country's 24 oblasts. The Cherkasy region is exceptionally richly endowed with these relics and its territory is a unique site for archaeologists. Indeed, at a depth of no greater than one metre lie the remains of a few massive proto-cities burned by the Trypillians. Each of these towns, it is estimated, were inhabited by several thousands and in some cases more than 10,000 people. The fact is that the people of Trypillia, according to the archaeologists, periodically changed their place of residence, relocated to new uninhabited territories, built new dwellings on their new location and burned their old ones. At that time they probably did not know how to consistently support the fertility of the soil, which

Chapter 4: What the Artefacts Confirm

was gradually depleted, they were therefore compelled to relocate to new areas with more fertile ground. A wooden frame served as the fundamental element of a Trypillian house and its walls, both externally and internally, were decorated with clay. In addition, the floor between the rooms and the attic, as well as the floors between the levels of two and three storey buildings, were also filled with clay. Indeed, it is thanks to this clay that we have managed to learn so much about the people of Trypillia and their life. When they burned their residences, the wood, grass and other organic materials were consumed by the fire but the clay only hardened and stored traces of human life for several millennia.

Figure 4.1 shows the appearance of an excavation on one of the incinerated buildings of the Trypillian settlement near Lehedzyne village in the Cherkasy region.

An attentive researcher can observe at the site of this fire, for example, crockery fragments with the imprint of human fingers and hands and can conclude that the Trypillian people did not have a potter's wheel at that point in time. The indentations of timber on the remnants of the fired clay allow the researchers to reproduce the design of the building and by reckoning the thickness of the clay covering that fell during the fire can determine the building's outer appearance and whether it was one, two or three storeys. The imprint of fabric on the exterior of a clay pot leads to the conclusion that the people of Trypillia already knew how to produce fabrics and sew clothes from them.

Figure 4.1: The remains of an incinerated Trypillian building

Therefore, they had some kind of weaving apparatus or loom and they sowed and cultivated fibrous plants such as flax or hemp. The fragments unearthed from these dwelling incinerations include the remnants of a large, multi-channel pottery kiln wherein there were Trypillians' fire clay jars of up to one metre in height which were designed for storing grain. Similar pottery kilns only appeared in Western Europe, on the island of Crete, almost 3,000 years later.[1]

The remnants of the incinerated house allow researchers to determine its size and internal arrangements. There

---

1 Відейко Михайло. *Гончарні горни трипільської культури: нові горизонти досліджень*. Познань: Archaeologia Bimares, 2019. Т. 5. p. 858.

Chapter 4: What the Artefacts Confirm

was, for example, a stove in the corner of the dwelling and beds for sleep and rest by the wall on the right. On the opposite side there was a place for crockery and household utensils. The arrangement reminds me very strongly of the house of my grandfather, Karpo Mykytovych Dushko, my mother's father, who gave me refuge when I was four years old during the Nazi occupation, which was situated in the village of Dubovi Hryady in the Kharkiv region. My grandfather's dwelling was practically identical to a Trypillian residence, a house whose walls were plaited with branches and covered internally and externally with a mixture of clay and chaff. The floors in the house and in the attic were covered with a similar mixture. In winter the floor in the living room was covered with straw so that your bare feet felt the cold less. In summer it was covered in grass cuttings from which a pleasant aroma and a coolness emanated. A quarter of the room was occupied by a stove constructed from bricks fashioned out of raw, unfired clay. Millet was poured thickly on the stove and covered with a burlap. It would be impossible to conceive of a better mattress to sleep on: millet so gently fits itself to the body of the sleeper. However, most importantly, my grandfather had the same way of life as the people of Trypillia. The harsh wartime conditions compelled him and my grandmother to adjust to a completely natural way of farming because there was nothing anywhere to buy nor to exchange goods for, everything had to be made with their own hands: from a needle and a spoon to soap and matches. A horse's tail hair served as a needle, grandfather carved spoons from linden logs, added gunpowder, which was plentiful then, to a mixture for making matches and cooked up home made soap from waste fat and caustic soda which had miraculously remained. They, just like the Trypillians, grew hemp plants, which they soaked in the river in late autumn, then dried and crushed on a special apparatus to separate fibres from solid residues. Grandmother spun threads from the fibres during the long winter evenings in the light of an oil lamp despite the deficit of such fuel because there was no kerosene. They carried an old loom, passed down from great, great grandfather through the generations, down from the attic in spring. It occupied almost half the room and they wove cloth with it. Then the fabric was bleached in summer under the searing sun and, finally, sewed into clothing. They lived exactly like the people of Trypillia. These ancestral skills had been passed down through hundreds of generations of ancient Ukrainians over the millennia until the present day. It transpires that Ukrainians inherited not only their language and their genes from the Trypillians but also their way of life, their culture.

It is interesting that the discovery of a Trypillian proto-city in Cherkasy region was due also to clay whose impurities changed the colour of the soil, rendering it lighter in places where the Trypillian buildings had once stood. This was particularly noticeable in late autumn, after the harvest had been gathered and the ground cleared of vegetation. This allowed aerial photography of the area to provide a

Chapter 4: What the Artefacts Confirm

Figure 4.2: A recreated Trypillian dwelling in Legedzyne village

bird's eye view and record and map out the locations of groups of Trypillian buildings. It was subsequently possible to determine the precise coordinates of each building by utilising geomagnetic reconnaissance equipment. Eleven Trypillian settlements were identified and mapped as a result of this research in Cherkasy region. The territory where they are located was granted the status of a State Historical and Cultural Reserve entitled "Tripìl's′ka kul′tura" (Trypillian Culture). The reserve now occupies an area of approximately 2,000 hectares and the largest Trypillian settlement, situated between the villages of Legedzyne and Talianki, has an area of over 450 hectares. The tireless populariser of Trypillian culture and film director Vladislav Chabanyuk and his colleagues have, by their tireless efforts, gathered a rich collection of Trypillian antiquities. These have provided the basis for a museum in the village of Legedzyne and the adjacent full-size reconstruction of a two storey Trypillian dwelling (figure 4.2).

It is assumed that people lived on the second floor while the first was used for household needs and, possibly, livestock/cattle was kept there.

4.2 An Aryan God on the Oril River

A stone stele, which resembles a human being and was discovered on the left bank of the Oril river near Kernosivka village in 1973, tells us about the Steppe-Folk who lived in the third millennium BC in the Dnipro area (figure 4.3).

The site is on the boundary of the Kharkiv and Dnipropetrovsk regions and was found by chance when an excavator was digging a silo trench near the village. The excavation team would probably have buried the idol in the ground again were it not for the ubiquitous schoolchildren. They examined the object carefully and realised it was more than just a stone. The statue, the sculpture, was then transported back to the village by a cart, the soil was washed from it and it was placed in a yard. When archaeologists were summoned from Dnipro to the site they were shocked at the idol's unique appearance. None of them had ever seen such a marvellous artefact: an imposing man cast his severe gaze upon them from deep-set eyes. He was armed with a bow, axes, a mace

Chapter 4: What the Artefacts Confirm

and a dagger. There were drawings on all four sides and a depiction of a vertical tail, perhaps an imitation of a horse's tail. The stele was transported to the city of Dnipro and is now stored in the Dmytro Yavornytsky National Historical Museum of Dnipro where it was named the Kernosivsky Idol and it was established that it was created at the cusp of the second and third millenniums BC. Ukrainians should be grateful to those school pupils, who were not indifferent to the statue's possible significance, and the director

Figure 4.3:
The Kernosivsky Idol

of the Dnipro Museum, Horpina Vatchenko, who was able to protect this priceless discovery of global significance when an attempt was made to transfer it to the Hermitage. The statue is fashioned from sandstone, formed as grains of sand cement to each other. It is obvious that the statue once stood

249

partially dug into the ground as evidenced by the lower third of the object which has not been carved. There are several theories attempting to explain the inner nature and purpose of this stele. The most logical explanation in my view is one which relies on Indian and Greek mythology provided by the Russian archaeologist Leonid Klein.[1] He believes that it was not an accident that the sculpture painted the back of the idol's torso with exposed internal organs (spine, shoulders, ribs, pelvic bones) as if the figure had its skin removed. These "skinless" deities are described in Indian myths, particularly the *Rigveda,* where they are demigods called the *Gandharvas* and in Iranian mythology where they are the *Gandareva*. The ancestors of humanity are born from these gods according to Indo-Iranian mythology. The absence of skin on the Kernosivsky Idol says that the sculptor depicted on the stone a god, rather than a person or Shaman, whom the Steppe-Folk worshipped. The "skinlessness" of the *Gandharvas* and the Kernosivsky Idol testifies that they were created by the same tribe of Steppe-Folk who migrated to India from the banks of the Oril. That tribe, as we have previously discussed, were the Aryans (see section 2.15).

During their journey to India the Aryans left, in Central Asia, another type of deity in the form of an imaginary "skinless" horse called *Bargush* who, according to Tajik beliefs, is found in lakes. At a later period when the

---

[1] Клейн Л. С. *Древние миграции и происхождение индоевропейских народов.* Санкт-Петербург, 2007. pp. 101–103.

Chapter 4: What the Artefacts Confirm

descendants of the Aryans came to Greece (Leonid Klein terms them "Greco-Aryans") the image of the water horse, *Bargush* in the mythology of the local Greeks, assumed the form of a centaur, a mythical creature with a horse's body and a human torso. Two characteristic features can be traced in all three of these mythical creatures. The first is the equine connection, the horse tail of the Kernosivsky Idol with a pair of horses on its foreground, the horse's body of the Greek centaur, and finally a whole horse, albeit an aquatic one, among the Tajiks. This peculiarity can be explained by the fact that, for the Aryans, the horse was of primary importance, providing them with transport, military power, meat, clothing and footwear.

The second interesting feature is the power these mythical creatures exercised over women. The Indians considered the *Gandharvas* to be the owners of unmarried maidens and guardians of their innocence. They told of how the *Gandharvas* tried to exercise the rights of gods on these unmarried maidens before marriage and do that with them which really the groom must do. The water horse, *Bargush,* according to the Tajiks, had a similar interest: he fascinated women with music and song and they flocked to him like moths to a light. The Grecian centaurs did not lag behind their related deities in this area and seduced women with their athleticism and strength. It is probably this particular interesting feature of these mythical characters that was reproduced by the ancient sculptor in a drawing on the side of the Kernosivsky Idol. It portrays a sexual scene between a man with a tail and a woman with her hands raised in prayer. This sex scene probably signified the god's sacred blessing on the existence and continuation of that human race which the god himself had conceived. At a much later point in history, 2,000 and 3,000 years after the Aryans, the authors of the bible utilised and slightly modified this idea of the Aryan sculptor. They write that God's will was fulfilled by the Holy Spirit and God's blessing, which is depicted on the stone graphically, will be given by the creators of the Bible in the words of the Angel Gabriel, as addressed to the Virgin Mary: "Hail, thou that art highly favoured, the Lord is with thee: blessed art thou among women... And, behold, thou shalt conceive in thy womb."[1]

The man with the horse's tail depicted in this drawing is the Kernosivsky Idol, the Aryan god in a reduced form because there was not much room left on the stone. This is the god-patriarch who, according to the Aryans, gave birth to them. His mace symbolises the supreme power which, according to the sculpture, stands above that of the mother goddess and arises from the triumph of the patriarchy of the Steppe-Folk over the matriarchy of Trypillia (see 2.18). This is, obviously, the origin of the second peculiarity of these mythical creatures, the power over women as a result of the triumph of patriarchy over matriarchy. The male sex of the god is shown by the naked front part of the idol. The sculptor only left him with a belt on which to hang

---

1 Luke, 1:28-31, King James Version.

Chapter 4: What the Artefacts Confirm

weapons from his wardrobe in order to vividly depict the masculine likeness of this god. The mace that the Aryan god holds in his hand will later become a symbol of supreme power among all the descendants of the Aryans, including Ukrainians. It will be handed over both to Cossack hetmans and Ukrainian presidents in a tradition that stretches back to the Kernosivsky Idol.

In addition to this drawing, which, in the sculptor's view, shows the origin of the Aryans from the god he portrayed, there is another symbolic illustration on the stele which shows the omnipotent will of the god. It depicts a man with a tail, obviously the god again, setting two dogs upon someone (figure 4.4).

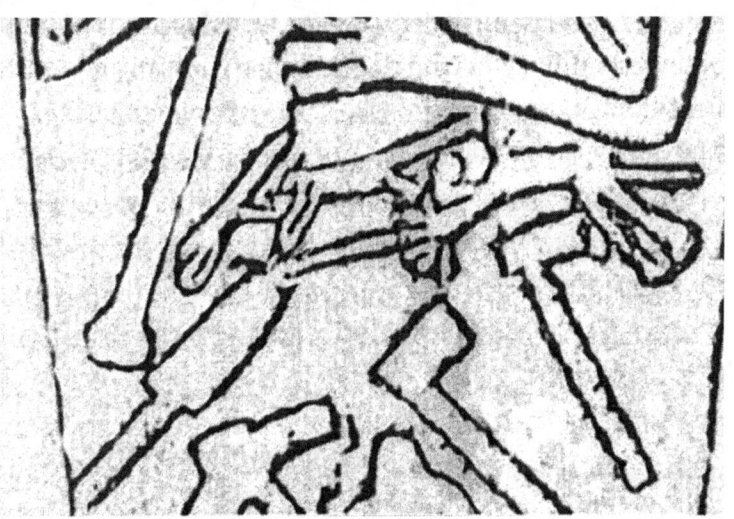

Figure 4.4: Part of an image on the Kersonivsky Idol

Dogs are symbols of the afterlife (e.g. the Cerberus dogs) which direct the Aryan god to the one who deserves to be punished with death for his sins. You can only marvel at how expressively the Aryan sculptor has conveyed by his drawings that verbal phrase that we often repeat after our Aryan ancestors: "Everything is in the hand of God!"

However, let us take a closer look at the hand of this god. It is six fingered and disproportionately large in proportion to the head. Such individuals are called *Rukastyj* or large handed in English. Indeed, in Indian mythology, one of the *Gandharvas* is named *Hasta* which translates as hand and in Greek mythology there is a centaur called Chiron whose name means large handed. By the way, the name Chiron is the origin of such common and often heard words such as Chirurge (surgeon in German) and chiromancy, the practice of divination using the lines on the palm of one's hand. Other similar terms include chirotony, the initiation of a spiritual individual such as a priest by the laying on of hands in blessing, and chiropractic, medical treatment by the manual manipulation of the spine. In the ancient world people who were depicted as having six-fingered hands were regarded as sages, spiritual healers, seers. They were in effect viewed as having extraordinary abilities and being omnipotent. The Aryan sculpture depicted his god as just such an omnipotent and omniscient being and endowed him with a sixth finger and a large hand. This conception of an omniscient god lives on in the proverbs

Chapter 4: What the Artefacts Confirm

of many nations: "God knows it," the Ukrainians say, and the English agree when they say "God knows, I don't". The tradition of depicting gods with large hands and broad palms is also observed in Indian mythology: this is how the main god Savitar is glorified in the texts of the *Rigveda*. He has golden, broad and beautiful hands with which he blesses and vivifies all of the world's processes. The laws of Savitar are such that neither Varun nor Indra, neither Mitra, nor Rudra, nor any other Gods of Indian mythology dare violate them.[1]

The decryption of the inner essence of the sculptural image of the Aryan god demonstrates that the ideas initiated by the Aryans were seized on, developed and disseminated both by subsequent generations of this people and other peoples. These conceptions became the foundation of the world view of the people of those times. They were reflected in other religions, particularly Christianity, Islam and Buddhism and certain of them have survived at the everyday level as we have just discussed. The Aryan god Varuna, for example, became the Greek deity Uranus and Indra became Zeus etc.

The discovery of the Kernosivsky Idol is like a flash of lightning, clearly illuminating the millennial path of our ancestors, beginning with the Aryans. It brings the remote, ancient past closer and unites it with the present.

---

[1] The Rig Veda / trans. by R. T. H. Griffith. Book 2. Himn XXXVIII. Savitar, 1896.

The village of Dubovi Hryadi is very near, only 14 kilometres from where it was found and was the setting for my childhood as described. In addition, a crystallographic analysis of the composition of the sandstone from which the sculpture was produced showed that the probable location of the site where the Aryans extracted blocks thereof was a quarry near Dubovi Hryadi.[1] The coordinates of the quarry's location are recorded in the cadastral register of natural building materials in Kharkiv oblast.[2] The depth of the sandstone layer there, according to geologists, was about two metres. However, the quarry is no longer utilised and the location where it was sited was levelled during work to lay a canal in the Oril river valley which now supplies Dnipro water to the Donbas. There are Scythian burial mounds on both sides of the Oril river between Kernosivka and Dubovi Hryady. They bear witness to how, 1,500 to 2,000 years after the Aryans were there, the Oril tribe of Scythians pastured herds of horses, flocks of sheep and herds of cows on the Oril grasslands. Then, 1,500 to 2,000 years after that point, in the middle and the second half of the twelfth century there were battles on the Oril river on more than one

---

1 Нікітенко Ігор та ін. *Мінералого-петрографічне дослідження керносівського ідола*. Форум гірників-2014: мат. міжнарод. конференц. Нац. гірничий ун-т. Дніпропетровськ, 2014. Т. 3. pp. 92–96.

2 Строительные материалы Харьковской области / сост. С. Р. Барская, И. Н. Ремизов, Д. Г. Сергеев и др. Киев: «Будівельник», 1965. p. 22.

Chapter 4: What the Artefacts Confirm

occasion between the Ruses princes and the Polovtsians, however, the river was then known as the *Êrel'* or *Ugol*.¹ A few centuries later, the Oril *palanka* of the Zaporozhian Cossacks was established there with its centre in Kozyrshchyna village, which is the present day village of Pereshchepyne on the Oril river.²,³ The spirit is captivated by thoughts of how, on the trails and meadows of the Oril valley, where we played our childhood games, the lives of our ancient and recent ancestors seethed unceasingly over the millennia: the Aryans, Scythians, Ruses and the Cossacks. Five thousand years ago on high ground over the left bank of the Oril river this stone Aryan god stood. People went to him with their prayers and requests as children go to their father, genuinely hoping that what they asked for would be granted. It was from this place, from the Oril river, from the Kernosivsky Idol, that the routes for the Aryan migration spread to distant Eurasian lands when climatic conditions deteriorated (see figure 3.7). The name of the Oril river perhaps derives from the word Aryans whom their neighbours, the Finno-Ugric peoples, termed *Oriia* in their language (so the Oril river would be the river of the O*riia* people). Three to three and

---

1 Літопис руський / пер. з давньорус. Л. Є. Махновця; відп. ред. О. В. Мишанич. Київ: Дніпро, 1989. S. 257, pp. 293, 333.

2 Translator's note: a *palanka* was a settlement with a small fortification and a Cossack garrison during the era of the Zaporozhian Cossacks.

3 Яворницький Дмитро. *Історія запорозьких козаків*: у 3 т. Київ: Наукова думка, 1990. Т. 1. pp. 60, 62, 160, 161.

a half thousand years after the Kernosivsky Idol appeared, his double, the god Perun, was reared on the banks of the Dnipro in Kyiv, albeit he was fashioned from wood rather than stone. The ancient Ukrainians went to him with their prayers but in 988 Perun and the pantheon of pagan gods were displaced by the Christian God in its three guises: the Father, the Son and the Holy Spirit. The position of the god-patriarch in the Aryan religion and also that of the god Perun within paganism was now occupied by the Christian God the Father. He delegated part of his power to God the Holy Spirit who impregnated the Virgin Mary, and his son, Jesus Christ, who atoned for the sins of humanity to achieve their salvation.

The stone Aryan god had yet another double, the Zbruchansky Idol, who was about the same age as the god Perun but with a different, happier fate, for it survived to the present day. The idol was buried on the bed of the Zbruch river for several centuries, probably by the pagans at that time when Christianity was forcefully implanted on Rus' and everything pagan was destroyed as "mementoes of paganism". In the summer of 1848 when the river became very shallow, the idol's cap protruded from the water, it was spotted and dragged ashore by oxen. The Zbruchansky Idol is now preserved in Poland in the Krakow Archaeological Museum (figure 4.5).

The idol previously stood not far from where it was found on Mount Bogit where the remains of an Eastern Slavonic pagan temple were discovered. The name of

Chapter 4: What the Artefacts Confirm

Figure 4.5: The Zbruchansky Idol in a Krakow museum and its copy on Sophia Square in Kyiv

the mount probably derives from the word for God, *Boh*, and it is located within Medobory Nature Reserve in the Ternopil region. The Zbruchansky Idol, by contrast with the Kernosivsky Idol, which represents the Aryan God as a single personage and with Christianity, which embodies God in the trinity of his guises, depicts the Eastern Slavonic god in four people: two of male and two of female gender. Each one of the four figures is responsible for their side of the world. The Zbruchansky Idol is therefore also called the World-Seer, who sees all four sides of the world simultaneously, symbolising the all-encompassing deity of the universe. The Western Slavs created a similar image of the four-faced god in the Middle Ages. There is, for example, the noted wooden four-faced statue of Svitovyt (Sviatovyt, Svantevit) that stands at Cape Arkona in the Jaromarsburg on Rügen Island in Germany.[1] However, that idol repeated the fate of the wooden image of the god Perun and was destroyed by the Christians of neighbouring Denmark in the twelfth century.

There is now a copy of the Zbruchansky Idol in Kyiv on the alley which connects Sophia Square with Mykhailivska Square. It serves as material confirmation of the ancient history of Ukrainians which lasts from pagan, pre Christian times. However, its double, the Kernosivsky Idol which is older by 3,000 years, should stand next to the Zbruchansky Idol. This renowned monument of global significance that is the Kernosivsky Idol should be as important to Ukrainians as the Scythian Golden Pectoral or the symbols of Svarga (swastikas) in Saint Sophia Cathedral in Kyiv, or the Tryzub on Sarmatian coins. A copy of the Aryan god, erected in the capital of Ukraine, would be visible confirmation that the history of Ukrainians dates back to a much older period and at least since their Aryan ancestors dwelled there. The history of the preservation of the Zbruchansky Idol in the river bed suggests that the Kernosivsky Idol was also once hidden only under the earth rather than the water. This is certainly not the only image of a god which the Aryans had in their era. There is hope, therefore, in new,

---

1 Святовит // *Енциклопедія українознавства*: в 11 т. / ред. В. Кубійович; Наукове товариство ім. Т. Шевченка у Львові. Львів, 1998. Т. 7. p. 2731.

similar discoveries of the Aryan legacy which remain on Ukrainian terrain.

4.3 The Weird Mare Milkers

The lives and the activities of the Cimmerians on Ukrainian territory are testified to not only by the toponyms derived from their names: the city of Novgorod-Siversky, the river Siversky Donets, the Cimmerian (Siversky) Bosphorus (now the Kerch Strait), the ancient city of Kimmerik in the Crimea, etc. They are also evidenced by the numerous burials found in the southern and central regions of Ukraine: the *Vysoka Mohyla* (Tall Grave) in Zaporizhzhia, where the Cimmerian martial nobility was buried,[1] the elite burials of Cimmerian Warriors with their combat chariots near the villages of Nosachiv and Kvitka in Cherkasy oblast, a tomb near Vilshana village in the same area and many other on the territory of Crimea, Dnipropetrovsk, Luhansk, Donetsk, Mykolayiv, Kirovohrad, Poltava and other Ukrainian regions.[2] The burial mound (Kurgan) near Vilshana village was found to contain the burial of a youth of approximately fifteen years of age who was interned with a gold bracelet signifying that the son of a chief of the

---

1 Бідзіля В. І. *Висока Могила*. УРЕ: у 12 т. / гол. ред. М. П. Бажан. 2-ге вид. Київ: Головна редакція УРЕ, 1978. Т. 2. p. 244.

2 Махортих Сергій. *Військова справа кіммерійців*. Записки товариства ім.Шевченка. T CCXLIV: Праці археологічної комісії. Львів, 2002. pp. 195–203.

Cimmerians was buried there.[1] By the way, this is the same Vilshana village Taras Shevchenko wrote of in his poem Haidamaki, where he had to undergo humiliating service as a "Cossachok" in the service of Lord Engelhardt, and which he visited many years later as a renowned poet. Vilshana is also where the forebears of the globally renowned boxers Vitaly and Volodymyr Klitschko lived.[2]

However, the most brilliant and impressive event associated with the Cimmerians was the discovers on the territory of modern Mykolaiv of a "city of the Cimmerian people" whose existence had been recorded by the ancient Greek poet Homer in his poem *The Odyssey*. The indicative name given to the city by Homer 3,000 years ago "the city of the Cimmerian people" became the oldest written name of any of Ukraine's renowned cities. Archaeological research shows that it was a port city located on the Ingul river at its confluence with the Southern Bug river. The city occupied an area of approximately six to seven hectares and existed in the thirteenth to the ninth centuries BC. The city was created five centuries earlier than neighbouring Olbia, which was founded by Greek colonists and is the same age as late Troy and a witness to the Trojan wars. This archaeological monument has been ascribed the indicative name *Dykyj Sad* (The Wild Orchard) because it appeared

---

[1] Ковпаненко Г. Т., Скорый С. А. Ольшана: *погребение предскифского времени в Украинской Правобережной Лесостепи*. Stratum plus. Кишинев, 2003–2004. № 3. pp. 265–288.

[2] Вільшана. http://uk.m.wikipedia.og.

Chapter 4: What the Artefacts Confirm

in a park of barren "wild" trees planted in the nineteenth century. The port city was structured in a fashion typical of that era. It consisted of a fortified citadel surrounded by ditches and ramparts wherein lived the elite, rich artisans who fashioned goods from bronze, and then the suburbs and settlements beyond the moats where the "middle class" and the common folk lived. Only one fifth of the site has been excavated to date. However, a rich collection of bronze artefacts has been unearthed: a studded cauldron with a 37 litre capacity, over one dozen Celtic axes and other bronze items. Similarly, a unique collection of fragments of ceramic crockery from the Cimmerian era, which is far more diverse than similar finds in Cimmerian burial sites, was collected.[1]

The *Dykyj Sad* archaeological site would ideally see the creation in Mykolaiv of a museum complex of global significance entitled "Cimmeria" which would be as enticing for tourists as England's Stonehenge or Turkey's Troy.

Cimmerian culture, in the opinion of an authoritative archaeologist Oleksij Terenozhkin, merged with early Scythian culture. Indeed Scythian and Cimmerian warriors were identically equipped. Their burial sites also differed little apart from the "animal" style of ornamentation found in Scythian burials but absent from Cimmerian graves.

---

1 Черняков І. Т. *«Дикий Сад», Гомер, Геродот, Троя, ахейці та кіммерійці* (коментар одного археологічного відкриття в Україні). Праці Центру пам'яткознавства. 2010. Вип. 17.pp. 116–122.

Herodotus confirms that these two peoples coexisted alongside each other for a period when he writes, "even in the Scythian land there still exist Cimmerian fortifications and river crossings, there is also an area called Cimmeria and the so called Cimmerian Bosphorus".[1] Furthermore, according to ancient historians, the Cimmerians, Scythians and Sarmatians had a shared, unofficial name of the "strange milkers of mares". So, in the poem *The Iliad,* which was created in the ninth to the eighth centuries BC by several generations of Greeks but ascribed to a single author, Homer, there is a reference to the so called Galactophages: "the strange people the Hippomolgs who eat only milk" in the translation of Mykola Gniedych.[2] In another translation by Boris Ten we read of the "Hippomolgs who drink only milk from under mares".[3] The word Hippomolg when translated from Ancient Greek means "milkers of mares", Galactophages, those who consume only milk. The exact name of this people is not given in *The Iliad*, however, in *The Odyssey*, which was created at a later date in the eighth century BC, this people were referred to specifically as the Cimmerians. The notable Roman historian and geographer of Greek origin, Strabo, who lived at the cusp of the BC and AD periods, summarised information on the peoples

---

1 Геродот. *Історії в дев'яти книгах* / пер. А. Білецького. Київ: Наукова думка, 1993. Кн. IV, 4, 12.4, 12.

2 Гомер. *Илиада* / пер. Н. И. Гнедича. Москва: Наука, 1990. Песня XIII, 5, 6.

3 Гомер. *Іліада* / пер. Б. Тена. Харків: Фоліо, 2006. Пісня XIII, 5, 6.

Chapter 4: What the Artefacts Confirm

of the northern Black Sea coast left by the works of his predecessors such as Hesiod, Aeschylus, Eratosthenes etc. He noted that Homer "united the Mysians with the Hippomolgs, Galactophages and Abians who are Scythians and Sarmatians and who are nomadic with caravans... and Hesiod testifies to this".[1] Why did these Hippomolgs and Galactophages seem strange to the historians of antiquity? It was probably because they saw that the Cimmerians, Scythians and Sarmatians had a robust facility for consuming raw milk without being troubled by digestive disorders. This trait indicates the common origin of these people from the Steppe-Folk whose bodies had, over the millennia, developed the appropriate enzymes for digesting raw milk. This was a weird trait indeed for people accustomed to the Mediterranean food of the day.

Another common tradition observed alike by the Cimmerians, Scythians and Sarmatians was the burial of the dead in existing or newly constructed grave mounds. They regarded the mound as the home of the deceased in the afterlife. The tradition of building a mound on the graves of the dead was begun by Steppe tribes as early as the fourth millennia BC. There were already numerous grave mounds prior to the Cimmerian period. According to the archaeologists there are approximately 150,000 burial mounds in Steppe Ukraine. Between 70% to 80%

---

1 Страбон. *География* / пер. Г. А. Стратановского. Москва: Наука, 1964. Кн. VII. III, 3, 7.

of these were constructed by tribes from the Yamna culture before the Cimmerian time and only 2% to 3% by the Scythians.[1] However, the Scythian mounds stand out from the others due to their large scale, particularly those in which Scythian kings were interred with their wives, servants, horses, weapons and other miscellaneous items. According to Scythian beliefs, these may all have been required by the deceased in the afterlife. These kingly burial mounds reach up to 20 metres in height and the diameter of their bases can reach hundreds of metres. The lower ranking dead were interred in smaller grave mounds and the common people were buried in family grave mounds whose height did not exceed one metre. The higher the mound then, as a rule, the deeper the burial pit. The whole structure resembled a Steppe pyramid sunk into the earth, similar to the Egyptian pyramids which, by the way, appeared later than the Kurgan burials of the Scythians. It is unsurprising that there was a dispute between the Egyptians and the Scythians, as the Roman historian Gnaeus Pompeius Trogus wrote, concerning which of them was the older people. The antique world, as the historian observed, recognised the Scythians as the older of the two peoples.[2]

---

1 Скорий С. А., Кислий О. Є. *Курган. Надмогильний пагорб*. Енциклопедія історії України. Київ: Наукова думка, Т. 5. http://history.org.ua/?termin=Kurgan.

2 *Justini in historias Trogi Pompeii epitomarum*. Lubecae; Lipsiae: Widemeyerus, 1702. Lib. 1–2.

Chapter 4: What the Artefacts Confirm

There is a particular location on Ukrainian territory where a large concentration of Scythian graves, with large monarchical ones among them, has been observed. It is an area on both sides of the Dnipro river near the city of Nikopol on the right bank and the city of Kamyanka-Dniprovska on the left bank. It was here that, in ancient times, a trade path lay from Crimea to the right bank through shallow waterways with a depth of about one metre along the Dnipro. Scythian trading caravans moved south along this route which bore grain they grew to sell. They were met by waves of foreign merchants bearing Mediterranean goods into Scythia. Three millennia later this, the shortest and most convenient route, was used by so-called Chumaky or salt merchants who went to Crimea for their product. It was possible to ride on horseback across the Dnipro here without even getting your feet wet. It was here too that the remains of two large Scythian cities were discovered, Kapulivske on the right bank of the river and Kamyanske on its left bank. Archaeologists are inclined to think that the Kapulivske settlement was the political and administrative centre of the Scythian state under King Ateas, who ruled in the fifth to the fourth centuries BC, and his successors.[1] The *Velykyj Luh* or "Great Meadow", with its rich flora and fauna, stretched for 100 kilometres above the crossing as far as Khortytsia. Herodotus wrote of its rich pastures saying

---

[1] Болтрик Ю. В. *До питання про політичний центр Скіфії.* Старожитності степового Причорномор'я і Криму : зб. наук. праць. Запоріжжя, 2004. Т. XI. pp. 38–41.

that "among other rivers the Borysfen is the most useful to people because the best and most nourishing pastures lay around it, it has many fish pleasant to the taste, and its water is very pure... and the fields around it are wondrous and where the land is not sown tall grass grows there".[1] The Scythians manage to save many herds of horses and cattle from dying even in years of severe drought thanks to the fertility of the Great Meadow. In the Cossack Era the Great Meadow, which was sung of then (The *Sich* is our Mother and the Great Meadow our Father), became the birthplace of the Zaporozhian Cossacks.[2] The creation of the Kakhovka Reservoir in the late nineteen fifties destroyed this unique natural habitat, the only one of its kind in Europe, and engulfed many Scythian monuments under the water.

The Scythian royalty were fittingly appreciative of the fertile quality of the Great Meadow, the nutritious pastures it was surrounded by and the impossibility of connecting trade routes from the right and left bank across the Dnipro and they chose this area as their central residence, their metropolis. This explains why such a large quantity of Scythian burial mounds were found here, in a chain which stretched from the north to the south on both sides of the Dnipro. They created, in the picturesque language of

---

1 *Геродот. Історії в дев'яти книгах* / пер. А. Білецького. Київ : Наукова думка, 1993. Кн. IV, 53.

2 Translator's note: a Sich was an administrative and military centre of the Zaporozhian Cossacks.

Chapter 4: What the Artefacts Confirm

archaeologists, the Golden Belt of Scythia. On the right bank this belt consists of the Chortomlyk, Tovsta Mohyla (in which the globally renowned Golden Pectoral was found), the Oleksandropol and Tomakivka grave mounds and many others. On the left bank it includes the Mamai-gora, the Solokha (in which a unique golden crest now stored in the Hermitage was found), the Chmyreva Mohyla, the Oghuz Kurgan and other burial mounds. It was in this area where, after the prolonged mourning of the whole people Scythian kings were buried, which Herodotus called the land of the Gerrhi[1], the Kinska or Konka river together with the Dnipro and its other tributaries once created the Great Meadow, which he referred to as the River Gerr.[2]

Each Kurgan is like a separate page or a separate phrase in humanity's history prior to written records. Those mounds which are destroyed are sheets torn from that unwritten book. The excavation of these mounds, even by professionals, damages and often destroys them. Therefore, more and more archaeologists in the recent past are inclined to think that the intact mounds need recording and leaving untouched for future generations, in whose time as yet unknown means and methods of reading the information in these mounds without destroying them will be found. The most significant mounds have already been excavated but renewing them

---

1 *Геродот. Історії в дев'яти книгах* / пер. А. Білецького. Київ: Наукова думка, 1993. Кн. IV, p 71.

2 Ibid, 56

by giving them their original appearance is now an issue. How, for example, can the Oghuz, the largest Scythian burial mound in Ukraine, be restored after archaeological research; the mound is over 21 metres high and was built in the late fourth century BC as the tomb of a Scythian monarch who was, possibly, the heir of Ateas.[1] Although the mound was looted in ancient times, archaeologists have nevertheless found many valuable artefacts therein which tell us of the life of the Scythians.

The enormous wealth, luxurious household artefacts and valuable gold items found in the burial mounds of Scythian kings are the results of the labours of many tribes ruled by these kings. These tribes included those who formed the proto-Ukrainians: the Scythian-ploughers and Scythian-farmers, the Budini and Neuri and others listed by Herodotus. There are traces of their residence discernible in the remains of Scythian settlements which are strewn over almost all the territory of modern Ukraine: from the Scythian city of Neapolis in Crimea to the northernmost example, Khotivsky on the outskirts of Kyiv, from Lyubotynsky near Kharkiv to Nemirivsky in the Vinnytsa region. They include gigantic settlements such as Bilsk in the Poltava region, Khodosivske in the Kyiv region and some others. The Bilsk settlement, for

---

[1] Болтрик Ю. В., Фіалко О. Є. *Огуз – курган скіфського царя кінця IV ст. ло н.е. Золото степу.* Археологія України / авт.-упоряд. П. П. Толочко, В.Ю. Мурзін. Акад. наук України, Ін-т археології. Київ; Шлезвіг, 1991. С. 178. p. 178.

example, covered an area of four thousand hectares, enough to accommodate 40 ancient cities of a similar size to Troy. The settlement consisted of a residential area protected from its foes by a circular fortified wall and, as a rule, a deep moat filled with water which was then surrounded by an earthen embankment. The military nobility were continuous inhabitants of these settlements along with artisans engaged in blacksmithing, working foundries and producing bronze and iron items. During periods when foes assailed the settlements from outside their walls, the surrounding population, who were engaged in crop farming and animal husbandry in peaceful times, would be saved by residing temporarily within the fortifications.

There was, as we have noted, little difference between the Cimmerians and the Scythians and, similarly, little distinction between the Scythians and the Sarmatians. Each of these three peoples was a separate Steppe tribe but related to the other two. The ancient historians noted this characteristic feature and unified them with a joint name, "the strange milkers of mares". Herodotus says that, "When the Scythian King Idanthyrsus gathered an army against the Persian Emperor Darius, one of the first groups to respond to his summons were the Sarmatians who joined the army of King Scopasis."[1] It

---

1 Геродот. *Історії в дев'яти книгах* / пер. А. Білецького. Київ: Наукова думка, 1993. Кн. IV, 120.

follows from this account that the Sarmatians lived near the Scythians and did not come from beyond the Don to drive the Scythians from their lands as our historians traditionally claim. What happened was simply this, over time the Sarmatians gradually supplanted the Scythians in the ruling tiers of their land and the Scythian state was eventually ruled by Sarmatian kings. History has left the names of some of them on coins from the Greek city of Olbia, which they conquered. You can see, on the reverse side of the coinage, portraits of the Sarmatian King Forzo, his successor Inismei and, corresponding, Ancient Greek inscriptions. Furthermore, as recently as 1984, archaeologists found the burial of one of the Sarmatian kings of the first century AD in a small Kurgan no higher than one metre near the village of Porohy in the Vinnytsia region. All the indications are that this was the grave of King Inismei. The personal symbol of the king found at the site is a particularly convincing argument that he was interred here; it is a *tamga* depicted on the coinage with an inscription of his name and repeated a number of times on artefacts from the Porohy burial. The word *tamga* means brand and, initially, the *tamga* was used on domestic livestock or property belonging to a certain owner. However, over time, the status of the *tamga* increased and eventually it became the personal symbol of a state ruler, his royal seal. Each Sarmatian king had their own *tamga* which reflected his connection with his forebears and was his own personal seal. One of the Sarmatian *tamgas*

Chapter 4: What the Artefacts Confirm

Fig. 4.6. Tamga from the Sarmatian burial, which is repeated on coins with the image and name of King Inismei

is a Tryzub, a trident, an image of which remained on Sarmatian coinage (see figure 3.4) which was inherited by their descendants, the Kyivan princes, who in turn passed this symbol to their descendants, Ukrainians.[1] The image of the Sarmatian trident occurs, inter-alia, among all the descendants of the Aryans. However, it only became the main state emblem for Ukrainians, thereby affirming the direct link of this Ukrainian symbol with the Aryan sign of the *trisuttâ*, the trident, via the intermediate ancestors of the Ukrainians, the Sarmatians.

4.4 From the Antes and the Huns, to the Ruses and the Cossacks

In section 3.14 we saw that over time our ancestors, after they had been called Cimmerians, Scythians and Sarmatians, obtained a whole bouquet of names from various sources: the Antes, Huns, Kuny, Kuiavy, Saviry etc. All of these referred to the same indigenous people,

---

[1] Translator's note: a Tryzub is also the state emblem of Ukraine and was the seal of the Kyivan princes.

the proto-Ukrainians. However, since the term proto-Ukrainians is not used by modern archaeology it is necessary within our research to deploy the concept of "populations of archaeological cultures". Archaeologists have, for example, discovered antiquities relating to the Antes which belong to the Penkivska archaeological culture. The Penkivka covered the boundaries of steppe and forested steppe regions stretching from the Siversky Donets area to the lower Danube. Hundreds of Antes settlements dating from the fifth to the seventh centuries have been discovered in Ukraine. They were usually located in river valleys, including those of the Tyasmin, Southern Bug and Dnipro among others. A metal workshop, where the Antes smelted iron, was found on an island in the Southern Bug.[1]

However, with regard to the Hun burials of Attila's era, few of them have been discovered in Ukraine, perhaps because they are most often individual, collective burials, which are rare, and there are, in some cases, no mounds over the grave. Odesa archaeologists reported that in 2006 a man showed them photographs of antique jewellery which, he said, he "found" on the shores of Lake Yalpug near the border with Romania. The archaeologists determined from the photographs that these items were amazingly valuable, delicately worked jewellery

---

1 *Археологія України: курс лекцій: навч. посіб.* / за ред. Л. Л. Залізняка. Київ: Либідь, 2005. p. 389.

Chapter 4: What the Artefacts Confirm

in the Polychrome style and that there were such a large number they must have originated in the burial of a noble Hun leader from the end of the fifth century, possibly one of Attila's sons. Unfortunately, all of this jewellery is in the private collection of an unknown owner and further study to

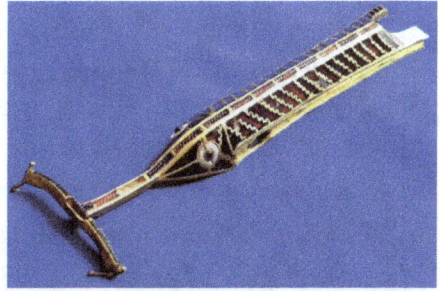

Figure 4.7: Hun Jewellery

establish to whom it belonged is impossible. The archaeologists only obtained photos of the items that were for sale and certain of these are displayed in figure 4.7.[1]

After the decline of the Hun kingdom, the indigenous Hun population did not, of course, go elsewhere. The northern group of Huns, whom the Byzantine historian Jordanes called the Saviry and Nestor the Chronicler the Sivery (see 3.14), left traces of their habitation in the form of archaeological relics of the Romenskaya culture of

---

1 *Прикраси гунів знайшли під Одесою.* Газета по-українськи, 12 February 2010.

the seventh to tenth centuries. This culture was identified by the talented archaeologist Mykola Omelyanovich Makarenko after excavations near the city of Romny. (Makarenko was destroyed by the Soviet authorities after he wrote a well-grounded protest against the dismantling of St. Michael's Golden Domed Monastery in Kyiv on behalf of the Academy of Sciences in 1934.) Archaeological sites linked to Romenskaya culture confirm that descendants of the northern Huns settled on the Desna, Seym, Vorskla and Sula rivers among others, just where the chronicler Nestor indicated they resided. Their settlements, which include Donets on the territory of the present Kharkiv, Ltava on Ivanova Gora (which is named after the Ukrainian author Ivan Kotlyarevsky) in the centre of Poltava, Opishnyanske near Opishnya village and others, were surrounded by a number of smaller settlements. The residents of the latter were able to take refuge in the larger settlement in the event of a hostile attack.

Similarly, traces of the residence of the early Ruses on the territory of Ukraine have been discovered, including those of the inhabitants of Slavia, Artania or Kuyavia of whom the Arab geographer Al-Istakhri wrote (see 3.20).[1] The remains of one such settlement dating from the seventh to the eighth century were found on Kniazha Hora near Kaniv where the River Ros' once flowed into the Dnipro

---

[1] Новосельцев Анатолий. *Восточные источники о восточных славянах и Руси VI–IX вв.* Москва, 1965. p. 315.

(the river mouth has moved several kilometres down the river as a consequence of land reclamation work).[1] Subsequently, in the tenth to eleventh centuries, during the era of the Kyivan state, the Ruses rebuilt this settlement and surrounded it with a fortification wall, a rampart and a ditch. They transformed it into a fortified town and it became an important centre for craft, trade and customs processing. Some archaeologists believe it was the city referred to as Roden' in the chronicles where Prince Yaropolk of Kyiv hid in 978 followed by his younger brother Volodymyr. This did not save Yaropolk, Volodymyr the Baptiser lured him from the town and had him executed.[2] The city and its inhabitants were destroyed by the Mongols in the thirteenth century and it was never renewed.

Archaeologists have found a cemetery of a kind unusual for Ukrainian territory not too far from where the leader of the Antes, Bozh, died in 380, near Ostriv village in the Rokytnyansky district of Kyiv region. The graveyard was not the burial site of locals but of emigrants from the southeastern Baltic region, the forebears of modern Lithuanians and Latvians. Archaeologists had never observed anything like it before. Scholars suggest that the Baltic population was moved there in the eleventh century by the Kyivan Prince Yaroslav Mudryi (also known as Yaroslav the Wise)

---

1 Мезенцева Г. Г. *Древньоруське місто Родень*. Княжа Гора. Київ, 1968. р. 11; Бондар М. М. *р* Київ: Вид-во Київського ун-ту, 1971. р. 82.

2 *Літопис руський* / пер. з давньорус. Л. Є. Махновця; відп. ред. О. В. Мишанич. Київ: Дніпро, 1989. р. 46.

to strengthen the southern borders of Rus' against nomadic raiders. The chronicle reports that, for example, a similar settlement of captive Polish was established by Yaroslav on the River Ros', "and Yarolslav sat them by the Ros' and they live there to this day".[1] In addition to the cemetery above, which has been conditionally designated *Ostriv* (The Island), there are many other archaeological sites concentrated in this area: burials from the Scythian period of the seventh to eighth centuries BC, a gigantic settlement linked to the Chernyakhov culture of the third and fourth centuries and linked to the Prague-Korchak and Penkivka cultures of the sixth to seventh centuries. There have also been finds linked to two large settlements of the Kyiv state era near the Sukholisy and Busheve villages and there are also archaeological relics linked to the Cossack period of the seventeenth to eighteenth centuries.[2] Therefore, all archaeological cultures from the Scythian to Cossack eras are represented in one location and that has given rise to the idea of creating a nationally significant museum complex called *Ostriv*. Scientists from Poland, Lithuania and Germany who participated in the research of archaeological relics for the complex are also interested in the findings in this area.[3]

---

1 *Повість врем'яних літ*: літопис (за Іпатським списком) / пер. з давньоруської, післяслово, комент. В. В. Яременка. Київ : Рад. Письменник, 1990. p. 236.

2 Прокопенко Марія. *Таємничий острів балтів*. День, 26 квітня 2019.

3 *Проєкт «Острів»*. Інститут археології НАНУ.

Chapter 5: A System Analysis of the Witness Testimonies

The indicative materials obtained from genetic, linguistic, anthropological and archaeological witnesses shed an objective light on the historic path of Ukrainians from different angles. They allow us to undertake a comprehensive system analysis of their indicators in order to obtain robust answers to a number of questions that are up for discussion: the historical age of the Ukrainian nation, Ukrainian statehood, the age of Ukraine's capital Kyiv etc.

5.1 The Antiquity of the Ukrainian Nation

According to the Byzantine historian Jordanes (sixth century AD), the Scythians called the land where they lived *Oj* or *Oj-kraïna,* which subsequently became the chronicle name *Oukraïna*. This fact, in the first instance, completely cancels all the fabrications of modern and recent ideologues who assert that the name Ukraine means a periphery of Poland or Russia or some other state that was not even in embryo during Scythian times. Ukraine could not of course be peripheral to an entity that did not exist then. Secondly, if the name *Oj-kraïna* existed, apart from the self designation of Scythians, S*koloty*, there must have been a common name of the peoples who were included in the Scythian state union entitled

Oj-kraïna. This general name must, logically, have been "Ojkrainians" a term which, since Scythian times, has been preserved in the collective memory of many generations of the ancestors of Ukrainians. It lasted until Cossack times when, due to historical circumstances discussed in 3.21, it did not come to the fore but became transformed into the name Ukrainians. So, in spite of its ancient Scythian origins, the name Ukrainians became the last in a number of previous names recorded in historical documents in reverse order: Cossacks, Ruses, Antes, Huns, Sarmatians, Scythians, Cimmerians, Steppe-Folk (including Aryans) and Trypillians. The total duration of the existence of these names, if we count from the oldest, Trypillians, is over seven thousand years, from the fifty-fourth century BC to the present. Let us analyse what portion of these seven millennia corresponds to the existence of Ukrainians.

In 2.21 this question was formulated as follows: from what time and from what name in the chain of designations of our forebears should they be regarded as Ukrainians? In other words, how old is the Ukrainian nation? As stated in the foreword, Ukrainian historians allocate only one to one and a half thousand years to the existence of the Ukrainian nation. Let us use the objective criteria proposed in 2.21 to solve this difficult issue, which are as follows: in the event of a correspondence (or a discrepancy) during the time covered by the testimonies of the genetic, linguistic, anthropological and archaeological witnesses to the lives of ancestral Ukrainians, where and when these testimonies

Chapter 5: A System Analysis of the Witness Testimonies

converge without contradicting one another for the first time is the time the reckoning of the historical age of the Ukrainian people must commence.

The first group of witnesses is the genetic. In subsection 2.9 it was shown that the dominant haplogroup of Ukrainians, R1a1a (EU19), has existed for 10,000 years, that is much longer than the existence of the two genetically related civilisations formed after the release of their common ancestors from the Ukrainian Ice-Age Refuge which existed in parallel for a period: the Trypillian and Steppe-Folk civilisations. It follows that the existence of haplogroup R1a1a completely covers, indeed overlaps, the time period of the existence of our ancestors who had the names above starting with the Trypillians and ending with the Cossacks and the present day Ukrainians.

The second group are the linguistic witnesses. The research using the Swadesh lists and the mathematical calculations based upon them (see 3.5) has shown that the Ukrainian language originates from the last centuries of Trypillia. It is a continuation of the Trypillian language and the basis for the formation of the Slavonic language group. The testimonies of the genetic and linguistic witnesses converges at a point beginning from the middle of the third millennium BC (during the last forty-five centuries).

The third group are the anthropological characteristics. These features of ancestral Ukrainians (skin colour, hair, eyes, external appearance) were determined by autosomal studies of the genes of the Steppe-Folk who lived in the second millennium BC (see 2.13) and the reconstructions of their appearance from the fragments of the Tarim Mummies including, for example, the reconstructed portrait of the "Loulan Beauty" (figure 2.7). The physical characteristics of the Steppe-Folk clearly correspond to the European appearance of modern Ukrainians. The Aryan depicted on the tomb of Pharaoh Horemheb (figure 3.6) corresponds anthropologically to the image of Cossack Mamay on numerous folk paintings despite the gap of over three thousand years between these images. Furthermore, genomic studies of the remains of Europeans show that forty-five centuries ago there was a mass invasion of Central, Eastern and Northern Europe from the Steppes. This event had a significant influence on the anthropological characteristics of Europeans: their genomes are composed primarily from the contribution of the Steppe-Folk (see 2.16).

The facts presented here demonstrate that over the last forty-five centuries the testimony of the genetic, linguistic and anthropological witnesses corresponds. During these centuries the dominant haplogroup, R1a1a, was extant along with the Ukrainian language which diverged from the Lithuanian language in the same period. Simultaneously, the European anthropological characteristics of the forebears of Ukrainians remained unchanged in this period.

The fourth group of witnesses that testify to the continuity of Ukrainian history are the archaeological ones. The most renowned artefacts from the life of our Ukrainian

Chapter 5: A System Analysis of the Witness Testimonies

ancestors are given in the sixth column of table 5.1 below. Each of the ancestral peoples of Ukrainians left traces of their residence on the territory of modern Ukrainians. They include the remnants of Trypillian settlements and the Aryan stone stele, which symbolises their deity. There are also the toponyms with which the Cimmerians left the name they called themselves on the map and the Golden Pectoral of the Scythians. There are, similarly, the Sarmatian trident which became the prototype of Ukraine's state emblem and the treasures from the burial of the Hun chief. The medieval traces are the cathedrals and churches of the Ruses and finally there is the Cossack written memorial, the prototypical constitution, the first of its kind in the world: *The Constitution of the Rights and Freedoms of the Zaporozhian Army.*

There is, therefore, a correspondence in the testimonies of the genetic, linguistic, anthropological and archaeological witnesses to the life of Ukrainian ancestors throughout the historical path of Ukrainians, from the present to the Trypillian era. The people of Trypillia are, therefore, first named as the ancestors from whom the Ukrainian nation commenced. The nation's historical age extends for at least four and a half millennia rather than the one and a half millennia claimed by Ukrainian historians. If they estimate the historical age of the Greeks as being 3,500 years (and this does not contradict the historical facts) then it must be acknowledged that the historical age of Ukrainian as substantiated here at 4,500 years looks

Table 5.1: Consolidated information about the ancestors of Ukrainians

No	Sequential name of group of Ukrainian forebears	The names of their states	The period of existence of their states	The most renowned kings, rulers, chiefs, hetmans	The most renowned material witnesses to the lives of ancestral Ukrainians
1	The Trypillians	?	Sixth to third millennium BC	?	1. Proto-cities in Cherkasy region (fourth millennium BC) 2. Trypillian settlement in Kyiv (third millennium BC)
2	The Steppe-Folk (The Aryans)	1. Aratta? 2. Aryavarta in India	Third to second millennium BC	1. Ardjuna 2. Krishna 3. Trita (the heroes of the Rigveda	1. The Kernosivsky Idol in the Dnipro region. (third millennium BC) 2. The Aryan symbols of the *Svarga* and the Trisuttâ.
3	The Cimmerians	Cimmeria	Ninth to seventh centuries BC	1. Dugdammi 2. Teushpa 3. Sandakshatru	1. Toponyms with the words Siversky and Kimmerijskyj (Cimmerian) 2. The city in Mykolaiv (tenth century BC)
4	The Scythians	1. Scythia 2. Tavro-Scythia	Seventh to first century BC	1. Idanthyrsus 2. Taxasis 3. Madij 4. Ateas 5. Skilur 6. Palak	1. The Scythian Golden Ring (seventh to fourth century BC) 2. Neapolis, the Scythian city in Crimea (second century BC)
5	The Sarmatians	1. Sarmatia 2 Roxolania 3 Alania	Third century BC Third century AD	1 Skopasis 2 Forzoj 3 Inismei 4 Amaga	1. The Tryzub Tamga - the main emblem of Ukraine 2. The burial of the Sarmatian chief Inismei in the Vynnitsia region

Chapter 5: A System Analysis of the Witness Testimonies

No	Sequential name of group of Ukrainian forebears	The names of their states	The period of existence of their states	The most renowned kings, rulers, chiefs, hetmans	The most renowned material witnesses to the lives of ancestral Ukrainians
6	The Antes	The Antes Kingdom (Antes Union)	Fourth to seventh century AD	1. Bozh 2. Ardagast	Archaeological finds relating to the Penkivska culture extending from the Don to the Dnister
7	The Huns	The Hun Kingdom	Fourth to seventh century AD	1. Bolemyr (Balamber) 2. Rugilla 3. Attila 4. Odoacer (Odovacar)	Jewellery from the burial of a Hun chief near lake Yalpug in the Odesa region (the end of the fifth century)
8	The Ruses	1. Kuyavia 2. Rus' 3. The Grand Duchy of Lithuania, Rus' and Samogitia	Eighth to fifteenth centuries AD	1. Bravlin 2. Svyatoslav (III) 3. Volodymyr (IV) 4. Yaroslav (V) 5. Danylo (XII) 6. Vitovt	The cultural and historic legacy of the middle ages on Ukrainian territory from the Carpathians and Volhynia to the Donbas and Crimea.
9	The Cossacks	1. The Hetmanate 2. The Zaporozhian Army	Fifteenth to eighteenth centuries	1. Vyshnevetsky 2. Sahaidachny 3 Khmelnytsky 4. Mazepa 5. Vyhovsky 6. Orlyk 7. Kalnyshevsky	1. Exhibits in the Khortytsia Museum on Khortytsia Island 2. Exhibits in the Yavornytsky Museum in Dnipro City 3. Treaties and the Constitution of the Rights and Freedoms of the Zaporozhian Army

Note: In order to consolidate the information in the table the names of the Kyivan princes are given in accord with their position in their line of succession: Svytoslav III is Svytoslav the Brave, Volodymyr IV is Volodymyr the Baptist, Yaroslav V is Yaroslav the Wise and Danylo XII is Danylo Halytsky.[1]

---

1 *Літопис руський* / пер. з давньорус. Л. Є. Махновця; відп. Ред. О. В. Мишанич. Київ: Дніпро, 1989. pp. 474–519.

quite legitimate. The Ancient Greek language should, logically, have developed later than Ancient Ukrainian, when the Dnipro natives left their fellow tribes and gradually reached the Southern Balkans Peninsula where they created the Ancient Greek language (figure 3.2).

A study of the historical path of Ukrainians has shown that its main phenomenon is the durability of the haplogroup R1a1a (or R-M17, EU19) initiated and tempered in the harsh conditions of the Ukrainian Ice-Age Refuge. This haplogroup has not only remained extant in Ukraine for the 10,000 years it has existed and become dominant among modern Ukrainians, but was also distributed far from Ukraine by the Steppe-Folk across the vast spaces of Europe and Asia. This phenomenon secured the core of Ukrainians, the bearers of their dominant haplogroup, whose continuous territory of habitation has changed little from Scythian times to the present. According to the testimony of Herodotus, this area includes a "rocky peninsula that extends into the sea", i.e. Crimea is original and eternal Ukrainian territory.[1]

We Ukrainians have no reason to consider our nation as unique. However, that area of the planet, the Ukrainian Ice-Age Refuge where our ancestry found themselves in the Last Glacial Maximum, is indeed very special. Mother nature has tempered and formed us as we are. We have

---

[1] Геродот. *Історії в дев'яти книгах* / пер. А. Білецького. Київ: Наукова думка, 1993. Кн. IV, 99, 101.

inherited a peaceful disposition as creators and farmers from our Trypillian ancestors, while our Steppe-Folk forebears have bequeathed us the character of unbreakable warriors-defenders of their land. One social media user express this very aptly: "I believe that being a Ukrainian is synonymous with pride. Even without arms and legs I will crawl snake-like, I will tear at the foe with my teeth, but I will not surrender!" The selfless determination to defend one's own land from foreign invaders is powerfully illustrated by the descendants of the Steppe-Folk, the Ukrainian nationalists and soldiers of the Ukrainian Insurgent Army. They had no chance of victory but fought against the foreign invaders to the end, to the last breath; they were forced to battle with both the Hitlerite and Stalinist occupiers. This characteristic attribute of our ancestors has been vividly demonstrated by the new generation of Ukrainians: the courageous defenders of Donetsk Airport who earned the nickname Cyborgs for their unbreakable resolve in the face of the Russian occupiers. Ukrainians, like every nation, have their own unique historical path and we are obliged to know the true path our people have taken and guard it from contrived, generally accepted, and false narratives which not only foreign but also our own historians try to impose upon us.

5.2 What Language did the Scythians Speak?

The vast majority of scholars regard the Scythians as having spoken an Iranian language on the basis of the many

Scythian words preserved in Ancient Greek and Assyrian-Babylonian texts, having found equivalents in Iranian languages. However, this does not take into account the fact that these words were transported into Iran (which was then Persia) from the Dnipro region by the Aryans, who are the ancestors of both Iranians and Ukrainians. If Scythian texts had been preserved it would be possible to find equivalents for Iranian words in Scythian and regard the Iranians as Scythian speaking. This would indeed be true, taking into account the fact that the Aryans, Scythians and Iranians share an ancestral homeland in Ukraine's Dnipro region. It is from there that the flow of Indo-European languages began (figure 3.2). The direction of the flow of Indo-Iranian languages depicted in figure 3.2 indicates that the Scythians were not Iranian speaking but, on the contrary, the Iranians were Scythian speakers.

In a multi-ethnic union such as Scythia was, people spoke various languages including proto-Ukrainian which at that time, according to the calculations undertaken in 3.5, already existed. Furthermore, given the origin of proto-Ukrainian and the Aryan language from a single Trypillian source we reach the conclusion that the Scythian language was most probably proto-Ukrainian, which later became dominant in the area where Scythia had been situated. This hypothesis is sustained by the fact that the Slavs constituted the majority in Scythia and their language, obviously, was the language of the first Slavs, proto-Ukrainian. The other Slavonic languages branched off from that language when their bearers moved from the Central Dnipro Basin at the end of the first millennium BC (see 2.20). The theory historians promote, that Scythians were Iranian speakers, is not backed up by any convincing evidence. This also applies to the Sarmatians who, according to Herodotus, successfully mastered the Scythian language thanks to the Amazons. There are words from the Scythian language (proto-Ukrainian) which sometimes penetrate the Greek and Latin language: *med* and *kvas* in Priscus of Panium; *strava* and *Oj-kraïna* (Ukraine) in Jordanes; *neaset* (the equivalent of the modern Ukrainian n*enasitec'* meaning insatiable), *veruči* (the equivalent of the modern Ukrainian *viruûčij* meaning seething) in *Constantine VII* Flavius *Porphyrogenitu*; *bulani* (the equivalent of the modern Ukrainian *volinâni* people from Volhynia); *koûni* (the equivalent of the modern Ukrainian *kiâni*) in Claudius Ptolemy and many others.

5.3 When was Ukrainian Statehood Born?

Nineteenth century Muscovite historians invented a number of non-existent names for Rus' in order to disguise their country's misappropriation of the "foreign to them" name of Rus' (or *Rossia* in Greek and Roman sources). These fabricated terms included Kievan-Rus', Muscovite Rus', North-Eastern Rus', South-Western Rus' and a host of others ending in the word Rus'. This compelled Mykhailo Hrushevsky to develop a new term, Ukraine-Rus' in order to renew and protect the significance of the name Rus' and simultaneously the name of its people, Ukrainians. The analysis contained in table 5.1 shows that, beginning with Cimmerians, the predecessors of Ukrainians under different successive names had their own states. Otherwise, if they were stateless they would never have been able to preserve their millennia-old language, whose origin dates back to Trypillian culture. It would also have been unable to conserve its dominant haplogroup, R1a1a, which was initiated approximately 10,000 years ago on the territory of modern Ukraine and, over the millennia, was passed from generation to generation by Ukraine's indigenous people. Its generic passport is carried by about half of Ukraine's male population at present. These two factors, the preservation of the language and the haplogroup over several millennia, testify to the very ancient nature of Ukrainian statehood.

It is thanks to the robustness of haplogroup R1a1a that the statehood of our Ukrainian ancestors recovered time after time over the millennia after defeats by external foes. The durability of Ukrainian statehood was also assisted by the desire of those Ukrainian forebears for freedom and democracy whose forms were embodied in mass gatherings, the Narodne Viče (people's chamber), Kozac'kij Kiš (Supreme Assembly of Zaporizhzhya Cossacks) and Ukraīns'kij Majdan (Ukrainian Resistance Square).

The characteristic features of statehood on the historical path of Ukrainians are particularly noticeable from the period when the ancestors of Ukrainians became known as Scythians. These include elements such at the presence

Chapter 5: A System Analysis of the Witness Testimonies

of a head of state (king), international treaties, a diplomatic service, a regular trained army, a census undertaken by counting arrowheads, the national celebration in honour of the god Areus etc. It is thanks to the "Father of History", Herodotus, that we have sufficient information about Scythia: this includes the name of the Scythian king, Idanthyrsus, who led resistance against the Persian Emperor Darius I during what is known as the Year of the Scythian-Persian War (most researchers believe this was 512 BC) and, ultimately, the final outcome of the war which was unsuccessful for the Persians. Scythia survived this conflict and strengthened its statehood. Almost 200 years later, the Scythian army repeated its success by defeating the army of Zopyrion, one of the military commanders in Alexander the Great's army. Ukraine has every ground for announcing officially, at state level, that 512 BC is the year its statehood was born and celebrating its 2,550th anniversary in 2038 (unfortunately the 2,500th anniversary passed unnoticed in 1988). Such a step by Ukraine would evoke shock and rejection, not only from Ukraine's neighbouring state but among a portion of Ukraine's citizenry, schooled in that long-implanted anti-Ukrainian ideology. However, there is no point in being afraid of that because, regarding Ukrainians, there are irrefutable facts recorded in historic documents and scientific works by the world's scholars from every era. Ukrainians should not engage in a contest with Russians over which people has the most ancient roots for their statehood. Ukrainians and Russians are, figuratively speaking in different weight categories, like those which govern boxing. Even the artificially invented 1,150th anniversary of Russian statehood, which they observed in 2012, in no wise compares to the 2,500th anniversary of Ukraine's statehood.

It is known that the earlier ancestry of Ukrainians, the Aryans and Cimmerians, also had statehood. There is, however, a dearth of specific information regarding these phenomena by contrast with the data we possess about the Scythians. The name Scythian is, furthermore, the one which was extant for the longest period of all the Ukrainian ancestral designations we know. Let us recollect how the Byzantine Priscus, in his work *The History of Byzantium* (Ἱστορία Βυζαντιακή in Ancient Greek), one thousand years after Herodotus alternately called the ancestors of Ukrainians the Scythians or the Huns. Then 500 years later than him, in the tenth century, the Greeks called the Kyivan prince, Svytoslav the Brave, a Scythian. So the name of Scythian was spoken for 1,500 years from King Idanthyrsus to Prince Svyatoslav. The origin of Ukrainians, from the Scythians and their descendants the Ruses, was probably known to Mykhailo Hrushevsky. However, within the conditions of political and punitive Soviet oppression, he was compelled to halt halfway and make a compromise when he introduced the term Ukraine-Rus' into historiography rather than Ukraine-Scythia. He therefore cut off a part of the ancient history of Ukraine as written by Herodotus. It is time to supplement Ukraine's history with the extremely significant information which Mykhailo Hrushevsky was not permitted to convey to his people and in our historic works use the more accurate name for our state of Ukraine-Scythia. This has long been discussed but it will not move forward without government support.[1] It is necessary to prepare, at parliamentary level, an appropriate legislative bill entitled "On the Celebration of Ukrainian Statehood" with a convincingly evidenced justification and adopt it at a session of the Ukrainian Parliament.

Ukrainians and Scythians have a common territory, a common proto-Ukrainian language, that commenced in Scythian times. The name Ukraine came from Scythia and Ukrainian statehood and should be commemorated in accord with its Scythian origins.

5.4 How Old is Kyiv?

The history of Ukrainians is very closely linked with its country's capital Kyiv. The city enjoys an extremely favourable geographical and physical situation at the intersection of Eastern European water and land trade routes. Kyiv has always, therefore, played a role in unifying Ukrainians and defending them from hostile attacks. In subsection 3.11 we substantiated the origin of the name Kyiv from the ancient proto-Finnish word for stone. However, from what point in time did the name initiated by

---

1 Петрук В. *Велика Скіфія переможе. Стабільна територіальна модель Великої Скіфії-України* : монографія. Київ: ДП «Інформаційно-аналітичне агенство», 2011. pp. 280–283.

the proto-Finns for their settlement become the name of the city of Kyiv?

When researching the territory of Kyiv and its environs, the Kyivan archaeologist Ilya Samoilovsky concluded that the city had existed from at least the second century BC, so it is over two thousand years old. Samoilovsky's theory is evidenced by approximately one dozen settlements dating from that era on Kyiv's territory and two large cemeteries found in the area of the Korchuvatyi and Karavajev Dachas.[1] However, his theory was not supported for a number of reasons, primarily because it was not supported by written confirmation of the city's name in those ancient times. It is global practice to recognise the age of a city according to the chronological correspondence of two signs. The first sign is archaeological, the presence of the traces of the existence of a city, village, fortress or settlement, in the exact place where the present city is located. The second sign is the written trace of a record of the city's name in any information recorded no later than the date of the archaeological traces of its existence. This second sign was lacking in support of Samoilovsky's theory. The name Kyiv, or an earlier variant thereof, was not discovered to be recorded anywhere earlier than the second century BC. Other capital cities were more fortunate in this regard.

---

[1] Самойловський Ілля. Коли виник Київ (До 1100-річчя першої літописної згадки про Київ). Науково-інформаційний бюлетень Архівного управління УРСР, № 4. С. 19–23.

Chapter 5: A System Analysis of the Witness Testimonies

Yerevan, for example, the Armenian capital's age was successfully established thanks to the discovery of a cuneiform text. It recorded that King Argishti I of Urartu founded the fortress of Erebuni in 782 BC. The remains of an ancient fortress whose age corresponded to the reign of Argishti I was indeed discovered on the outskirts of modern Yerevan. Therefore, in both the signs we have noted, the written and archaeological converged, the name Erebuni changed on several occasions by successive generations of the original population until it became Yerevan. In 1968, the Armenians celebrated the 2,750th anniversary of their capital and in 2018 its 2,800th anniversary.

The Italian capital Rome was also happily able to establish its age. The date of its foundation, 753 BC, was determined by the Roman scientist, encyclopedist and author Marcus Terentius Varro (116 BC-27 BC). He carefully researched the historical works of his predecessors and on that basis left the date of the founding of the "Eternal City" for posterity. The core of Ancient Rome was the Palatine Hill, one of seven hills upon which modern Rome stands. Traces of habitation have been discovered there which are even older than the founding date determined by Varro, which it transpires is only 29 years after the establishment of Yerevan. The Romans now celebrate the anniversary of their city's founding annually by arranging a festive procession along the streets with people wearing the costumes of their predecessors from all eras.

The Parisians were assisted in this matter by the Roman general and author Julius Caesar who, in his notes dating from 53 BC, left a record of the name of a small fishing village, Lutetia (or Lukotekia), situated on an island in the River Seine. The village of Lutetia swelled incredibly and sprawled onto both banks of the river. The Parisians, with gratitude to Julius Caesar, solemnly celebrated the 2,000th anniversary of their city in June 1952 with a short, five year delay caused by the harsh post-war conditions.

The Kyivans also celebrated the anniversary of their city's founding in 1982. However, the city's age was not determined in accord with global practice and the correspondence of the two signs, archaeological and written, that we have discussed, it was instead determined by a resolution of the Communist Party and the Soviet government which allocated 1,500 years to the city. Kyivans have subsequently been celebrating the day of their city's founding on the last Saturday and Sunday of May, obediently adding another unit to the baseless and contrived date imposed on them by Moscow every year.

However, we have at hand another, earlier date that Claudius Ptolemy helped to set. In the book *The Dawn of Kyiv*, it is mathematically proved that the geographical location of Metropolis, reported by Ptolemy and taking into account errors found in his coordinates, places it exactly on the site of modern Kyiv.[1] Ptolemy's Metropolis is therefore

---

1 Чорний Георгій. *Київ досвітній*. Київ: Гамазин,. pp. 124–127.

Chapter 5: A System Analysis of the Witness Testimonies

Kyiv, just as Julius Caesar's Lutetia is Paris, Erebuni in the cuneiform text is Yerevan and Varro's settlement on the Palatine Hill is Rome. In other word we have found the written sign we need to determine the age of Kyiv and which was lacking in support of Ilya Samoilovsky's theory, although it does not have the antiquity of his account. However, there is now the possibility to review the anniversary of Kyiv imposed by Moscow.

Ptolemy wrote his work *Geography*, in the estimation of scholars, in approximately AD 150.[1] This date should be considered the date of the very first written mention of Kyiv and gives Kyivans the grounds to celebrate the 1,875th anniversary of their city's founding in May 2025 and its 1,900th anniversary in 2050. That is, of course, unless some earlier record of the city's existence emerges before then which brings its age closer to that of the "Eternal Cities" Rome and Yerevan. Indeed, Kyiv preserves in its underground recesses, the area of Lvivska Square and Stritenska and Velyka Zhytomyrska streets, traces of a Trypillian settlement dating from the third millennia BC, which is far older than the Roman and Yerevan settlements.[2] Kyivans, playing martial games while wearing the armour of their ancestors will not be limited to princely and Cossack era weaponry, they will also be able to legitimately wear the

---

[1] Бронштэн В. А. *Клавдий Птолемей*: II век н. э. Москва: Наука, 1988. p 15.

[2] Климовский С. И. *Замковая гора в Киеве: пять тысяч лет истории* / предисл. М. В. Поповича. Киев: Стилос, 2005.p. 11.

armour and bear the weapons of the Scythian, Sarmatian and Hun periods and that relating to other events dating back to the Trypillian period.

In addition to Kyiv, there are other ancient Ukrainian cities which have grounds for believing the anniversary outlined above also relates to them and for celebrating it with Kyiv. These include Chernihiv (Chernihov) and Lyubech, and there is also the Belarusian city of Orsha. Ptolemy, however, provides information about these cities under other names but these can be deciphered.

Chernihiv is referred to by Ptolemy as Serimon (Σέριμον). Serimon's latitude, adjusted for the substantial systematic errors uncovered in Ptolemy, is only half a degree away from corresponding with Chernihiv's true latitude.[1] Indeed, the similarity between the names of Chernihiv and Serimon is obvious. It should be noted that the sound *ch* is absent in Ancient Greek. Therefore, it is possible that the name Serimon in Ancient Greek conceals the actual name Cherimon with the accent on the *i* or some other proto-Ukrainian name. However, the vowel sounds in the ancient and the modern names coincide. The presence of a written indication of the city's existence in Ptolemy's work is obvious and Chernihiv does not lack an archaeological indication of its existence at the time he was writing. The remains of a city, conditionally named Yalivshchyna, and adjacent settlements, which date back to the second and

---

1 Чорний Георгій. *Київ досвітній*. Київ: Гамазин, 2014. p. 124.

Chapter 5: A System Analysis of the Witness Testimonies

the first millenniums BC, have been detected there. These remnants, when combined with Ptolemy's written account of the city of Serimov, give Chernihiv residents grounds to celebrate the anniversary we have described.

The latitude of the current urban village of Lyubech completely corresponds to the corrected coordinates of the settlement of Azagarion ('Αζαγάριον) recorded by Ptolemy. Lyubech too is one of the unique, strategically significant locations where people settled in antiquity. The monotonous lowland of the Dnipro valley in this area suddenly gives way to a significant ascent on the left bank, which creates ideal conditions for the development of a city fortress. It is hard to say how correctly Ptolemy renders the proto-Ukrainian name of the city, but the characteristic word *hora* (mountain) combined with the preposition *za* (possibly by the mountain) is apparent in the name Azaharion. The area of higher ground does not resemble a mountain but there is nowhere within a distance of 50 kilometres of Lyubech in both directions along the Dnipro worthy of that term so the locals may have referred to this higher ground as a mountain; then this is additional confirmation linking Azaharion to the location of modern Lyubech. The ancient settlement of people in the area of Lyubech in Ptolemy's time may be evidenced by the presence in the village of a huge man-made burial mound.

The latitude of the city of Saron (Σάρον), as reported by Claudius Ptolemy, if we adjust it for the systematic error we have detected in his work, almost coincides with the latitude of the modern Belarusian city of Orsha. The name Saron could mask the name Sharon because the *sh* sound is also absent in Ancient Greek which instead utilises the *s* which is the closest variant in that language. Orsha is a 'less similar' name than we see in the pairing of Cherimon and Chernihov but let us recollect how the Slavonic word v*ručij* (that is the equivalent of the modern Ukrainian *viruûčij, meaning* seething or boiling) later became the city of Ovruch. So there is nothing surprising in the fact that over two millennia Sharon could become Orsha. However, let us leave this issue for the Belarusians. Ukraine needs to adopt an appropriate government decree to celebrate the anniversaries shown here, the 1,875th and 1,900th birthdays of the cities of Kyiv, Chernihiv and Lyubech.

Epilogue

I am far from believing that everything that is written here is absolutely true. Each subsequent researcher standing, figuratively speaking, on the shoulders of his predecessors as a rule sees further and deeper than them and has the right and the possibility to criticise their work. However, I have no doubt about the need to adhere to two important principles in the illumination of historical processes.

The first principle is that historical science should be based on reliable facts verified by the corroborative testimony of the past's objective witnesses, which are genes, language and artefacts. A one-dimensional approach towards the coverage of historical processes in which archaeology prevails must be consigned to the past. Only a comprehensive analysis of the testimonies of all three witnesses, with the inclusion of scientific acquisitions and methods from different spheres, is capable of reproducing a true picture of past historical processes.

The second principle is that the history of Ukrainians and Ukraine has above all been written under the diktat of colonisers and needs to be rethought and supported by robust facts obtained from research undertaken in compliance with the first principle. There is no need to be fearful and pay heed to the racket raised by the former colonisers and their supporters in Ukraine regarding "rewriting history". It really needs to be rethought and rewritten by taking into account the latest discoveries and discarding the fictitious myths of the colonisers, which are not confirmed by the facts.

Ukrainians are not a unique people but their historical path has its own special differences from the courses taken by other nations. A deep and true knowledge about their history, about their own recent and ancient ancestors, must become the guarantee of a dignified life for Ukraine now and in the future in this complicated world. It is no wonder that our renowned philosopher Hrihoriy Skovoroda, conscious of the enormous influence of the knowledge of past events on the future fate of his people, wrote that "Everyone must know his people and himself within his people".

Works Cited

1. Антонович В. Археологическая карта Киевской губернии [Antonovich, V. (1895). *Archaeological map of the Kiev province*]. Moscow: Typography of Volchaninov M.G. (in Russian).

2. Археологія України : курс лекцій : навч. посіб. [Zalizniak, L.L. (ed.) (2005). *The Archaeology of Ukraine: a course of lectures: tutorial textbook*]. Kyiv: Lybid (in Ukrainian)

3. Бідзіля В.І. Висока Могила. [Bidzilya, V.I. (1978). *High Grave*]. In Ukrainian Soviet Encyclopedia (USE) in 12 volumes, 2nd ed., (Vol. 2). Kyiv: Main Edition of USE (in Ukrainian).

4. Біленька-Свистович Л., Рибак Н. Церковнослов'янська мова : підруч. зі словником для духов. навч. закл. [Bilenka-Svystovych, L. & Rybak, N. (2000) *Church Slavonic language: textbook with a dictionary for Theological Seminaries*]. Kyiv: Krynytsia (in Ukrainian).

5. Болтрик Ю. В., Фіалко О. Є. Огуз – курган скіфського царя кінця IV ст. до н. е. // Золото степу. Археологія України [Boltryk, Yu. V. & Fialko, O.E. (1991). Oguz - The Burial mound of a Scythian king of the end of IV century BC]. In *The gold of the Steppe. The Archaeology of Ukraine.* Kiyv, Schleswig: Inst. of Archaeology (in Ukrainian).

6. Болтрик Ю.В. До питання про політичний центр Скіфії // Старожитності степового Причорномор'я і Криму : зб. наук. праць. Т.11 [Boltryk, Y.V. (2004). On the question of the political centre of Scythia]. In *The Antiquities of the Steppe Black Sea coast and Crimea: Coll. Science Works*, (Vol. XI). Zaporizhzhya: Inst. of Archaeology (in Ukrainian).

7. Бондар М. М. Минуле Канева та його околиць [Bondar, M. M. (1971). *The History of the Kanev and its environs*]. Kyiv: Kyiv University (in Ukrainian).

8. Боргардт А. А. Бич Божий (Аттила – 5-й каган гуннов и его время) [Borgardt, A. A. (1998). *The Scourge of God (Attila - the 5th kagan of the Huns and his time)*]. Donetsk: Donetsk Physics and Technical Institute of Galkin A.A. (in Russian).

9. Боргардт О.О. Дві культури [Borgardt, O.O. (1999). Two cultures] Donetsk: Donetsk Physics and Technical Institute of Galkin O.O. (in Ukrainian).

10. Боргардт Олександр. Дві культури. 5-те вид.[Borgardt, Alexander (2016). *Two cultures*. (5th ed.]. Kyiv: Prostir (in Ukrainian).

11. Брайчевский М.Ю. Когда и как возник Киев [Braychevsky, M.Yu. (1964). *When and how Kiyv arose*]. Kiyv: Naukova dumka (in Russian).

12. Бронштэн В.А. Клавдий Птолемей: II век н.э. [Bronshten, V.A. (1983). *Claudius Ptolemy: II century AD*]. Moscow: Nauka (in Russian).

13. Бурячок Андрій. Мовна ситуація в Київській Русі // Мова державна – мова офіційна: мат. наукової конференції. [Buryachok, Andrij (1995). The language situation in Kyivan Rus']. In *State language - official language: Proceedings of a Scientific Conference*. Kyiv: All-Ukrainian Society "Prosvita" (in Ukrainian).

14. Вакулишин Сергій. Кінець світу. [Vakulishin, Sergiy. (2001, August 09). The End of the World]. Kyiv: *Stolytsya* (in Ukrainian).

15. Васильева Н. И. «Великая Скифия». Новый взгляд на историю Древнего Мира. [Vasilieva, N.I. (2000). *"The Great Scythia". A new look at the history of the Ancient World*]. Moscow: Metagalactica (in Russian).

16. Велика ілюстрована енциклопедія України. [*The large illustrated encyclopedia of Ukraine*]. Kyiv: Mahaon-Ukraine, 2008 (in Ukrainian).

17. Великий потоп і виникнення Чорного моря [*The Great Flood and the emergence of the Black Sea*]. In the site Aratta – Ukraine. URL: http://aratta-ukraine.com/text_ua.php?id=26 (in Ukrainian).

18. Величко Самійло. Літопис. Т.1 [Velychko, Samijlo (1999). *The Chronicle*, (Vol 1)]. Kyiv: Dnipro (in Ukrainian).

19. Вельтман А. Аттила и Русь IV–V веков. Свод исторических и народных преданий. [Veltman, A. (1858). *Attila and Rus' IV-V centuries. A collection of historical and folk legends*]. Moscow: Typography of the University (in Russian).

20. Вельтман Олександр. Аттіла і Русь IV та V століть. [Veltman, Alexander (1996). Attila and Rus' IV and V centuries]. Kyiv: *Osnova*, 30 (8) (in Ukrainian).

21. Відейко М. Ю. Трипільська цивілізація. [Videjko, M.Yu. (2002). *The Trypillian civilization*]. Kyiv: Akademperiodika (in Ukrainian).

22. Відейко Михайло. Гончарні горни трипільської культури: нові горизонти досліджень. [Videjko, Mykhailo (2019). The Pottery kilns of Trypillian culture: new horizons of research]. Poznan: *Archaeologia Bimaris*, Vol 5 (in Ukrainian).

23. Гаврилюк Н. Гіміррі // Енциклопедія історії України. Т. 2. [Gavrilyuk, N. (2004). Gimirri. In *Encyclopedia of the History of Ukraine. Vol.2*]. Kyiv: Naukova dumka (in Ukrainian).

24. Гаплогруппы. *Haplogroups* URL: https://ru.wikipedia.org/wiki/Гаплогруппы (in Russian).

25. Геродот. Історія в дев'яти книгах, книга IV / пер. А. Білецького, [Herodotus, (1993). *The Histories in Nine Books, Book IV* / trans. A. Biletsky]. Kyiv: Naukova Dumka (in Ukrainian).

26. Гомер. Илиада / пер. Н.И. Гнедича. [Homer (1990). *The Iliad* / trans. N.I. Gnedich]. Moscow: Nauka (in Russian).

27. Гомер. Іліада / пер. Б. Тена. [Homer (2006). *The Iliad* / trans. B. Ten]. Kharkiv: Folio (in Ukrainian).

28. Гомер. Одіссея / пер. Б. Тена. [Homer (2001). *The Odyssey* / trans. B. Ten]. Kharkiv: Folio (in Ukrainian).

29. Григорий Турский. История франков / пер., примеч. В.Д. Савуковой. [Gregory of Tours (1987). *A History of the Franks* / translation and annotations by
V. D. Savukova]. Moscow: Nauka (in Russian).

30. Диба Юрій. Географія початкової русі за східними джерелами // Княжа доба: історія і культура. Вип. 10 [Dyba, Yuri (2016). Geography of the initial Rus' according to eastern sources. In *Princely era: history and culture*. Issue. 10]. Lviv (in Ukrainian).

31. Древнегреческо-русский словарь / сост. И. Х. Дворецкий. [*Ancient Greek-Russian dictionary* / comp. I.H. Dvoretsky]. Moscow: State publisher of foreign and national dictionaries, 1958.

32. Євангеліє від Іоанна. [*The Gospel According to John*].

33. Євангеліє від Луки. [*The Gospel According to Luke*]

34. Заморка А. Новий льодовиковий період – уже чекаємо. [Zamorka, A. *We are already awaiting the new Ice Age*]. URL: http://naturalist.if.ua/?p= 307 (in Ukrainian).

35. Знойко Олександр. Міфи Київської землі та події стародавні. [Znojko, Oleksandr (1989). *Myths of the Kyivan land and ancient events*]. Kyiv: Molod (in Ukrainian).

36. Иордан. О происхождении и деяниях гетов. Getica / вступ. статья ; пер.; коммент. Е.Ч. Скржинской. [Jordanes (1960). *Concerning the origin and actions of the Goths. Getica* / introduction. article; translation.and commentary. E. Ch. Skrzhinskaya]. Moscow: Eastern Literature (in Russian).

37. История Латвии. I–IV век н. э. [*The History of Latvia. The First to the Fourth Centuries A.D.*]. URL: https://travelkap.club/latvija1/histori-02/index.html (in Russian).

38. История Украинской ССР. Том1 [*The History of the Ukrainian SSR*. Vol.1]. Kyiv: Naukova Dumka, 1981 (in Russian).

39. Ілля Валерій. Сварга: поезії. [Ilya, Valeriy (1996). *Svarga: poetry*]. Kharkiv: The "Maidan" Firm (in Ukrainian).

40. Історія Русів / пер. І. Драча; вступ. ст. В. Шевчука.
[*A History of the Ruses / trans. I. Drach; introductory article V. Shevchuk*]. Kyiv: Radyanskyj Pysmennyk, 1991 (in Ukrainian).

41. Каганець Ігор. Свастика і таємниці імені «Україна». [Kahanets, Ihor (2007). *The Swastika and the secrets of the name "Ukraine"*]. URL: https://www.ar25.org/article/svastyka-i-tayemnycya-imeni-ukrayina.html (in Ukrainian).

42. Калевала: фін. нар. епос / пер. Є. Тимченка ; передм. Д. Павличка ; іл. О.-Й. Аланена. [*The Kalevala: The Finnish Folk Epic / trans. E. Tymchenko; foreword D. Pavlychko; ill. O.-J. Alanen*]. Kyiv: Osnovy, 1995 (in Ukrainian).

43. Київ. Енциклопедичний довідник / за редакцією А. В. Кудрицького. [*Kyiv. The Encyclopedic reference book / edited by A.V. Kudrytskyj*]. Kyiv: Chief Editorial URE, 1981 (in Ukrainian).

44. Клейн Л. От Днепра до Инда. [Klein, L. (1984). From the Dnieper to the Ind. *Znanie-syla*, № 7. Moscow (in Russian).

45. Клейн Л. С. Древние миграции и происхождение индоевропейских народов. [Klein, L.S. (2007). *Ancient migrations and the origin of the Indo-European peoples*]. St. Petersburg (in Russian).

46. Климовский С. И. Замковая гора в Киеве: пять тысяч лет истории / предисл. М. В. Поповича. [Klymovskyj S.I. (2005). *Zamkova Hora in Kyiv: five thousand years of history / preface. M.V. Popovich*]. Kyiv: Stilos (in Ukrainian).

47. Клочко Л. Бурштинові шляхи за скіфських часів. *Геолог України*, 2011, № 3–4. [Klochko L., (2011). Amber ways in Scythian times. *Geologist of Ukraine*, 3-4]. Kyiv (in Ukrainian).

48. Книга Буття. [*Book of Genesis*]. X: 2, 3.

49. Книга пророка Єремії. [*Book of the Prophet Jeremiah*]. IV, 13.

50. Кобычев А.М. В поисках прародины славян. [Kobychev, A.M. (1973). *In search of the ancestral homeland of the Slavs*]. Moscow: Nauka (in Russian).

51. Ковпаненко Г.Т., Скорый С.А. Ольшана: погребение предскифского времени в Украинской Правобережной Лесостепи. *Stratum plus*, 2003–2004, № 3. [Kovpanenko, G.T. & Skoryj S.A. (2003-2004). Olshana: a burial of the pre-Scythian time in the Ukrainian Right-Bank Forest-Steppe. *Stratum plus*, № 3]. Chisinau (in Russian).

52. Котляр М.Ф. Бравлін // Енциклопедія історії України у 10 т., Т.1 : А–В. Київ: Наукова думка, 2003. [Kotlyar, M.F. (2003). *Bravlin*. In The Encyclopedia of the History of Ukraine in 10 volumes, Vol.1: А-В]. Kyiv: Nauk. Dumka (in Ukrainian).

53. Котляр М.Ф., Плахонін А.Г. Походи русі на Візантію // Енциклопедія історії України у 10 т., Т.8: Па–Прик. Київ: Наукова думка, 2011. [Kotlyar M.F. & Plakhonin A.G. (2011). *The Campaigns of the Rus' in Byzantium*. In The Encyclopedia of the History of Ukraine in 10 volumes, Vol.8: Па-Прик]. Kyiv: Nauk. Dumka (in Ukrainian).

54. Красуский Михаил. Древность малороссийского языка. Індо-Європа, ч.1. Київ, 1991 [Krasuskyi, Mykhailo (1991). *The Antiquity of the Little Russian language*, part 1]. Kyiv: Indo-Europe (in Russian).

55. Латышев В.В. Известия древних писателей греческих и латинских о Скифии и Кавказе. Т.1. Греческие писатели. [Latyshev, V.V. (1890). *Reports by the ancient Greek and Latin writers about Scythia and the Caucasus. Vol.1, Greek writers*] St. Petersburg: Imperial Academy of Science (in Russian).

56. Литовська мова. *The Lithuanian Language*. URL: uk.wikipedia.org/wiki/Литовська_мова (in Ukrainian).

57. Літопис руський / пер. з давньорус. Л.Є. Махновця ; відп. ред. О.В. Мишанич. [*The Rus' Chronicle* / trans. from the Ancient Rus' language by L.Ye. Makhnovets; edited O.V. Myshanych]. Kyiv: Dnipro, 1989 (in Ukrainian).

58. Ломоносов М.В. Краткой российской летописец с родословием. Сочинение Михаила Ломоносова. [Lomonosov, M.V.(1760). *A brief Russian chronicler with their genealogy. Composition by Mikhail Lomonosov*]. St. Petersburg: at the Imperial Academy of Science (in Russian).

59. Махортих Сергій. Військова справа кіммерійців // Записки наукового товариства ім. Шевченка. Т. CCXLIV: Праці археологічної комісії. [Makhortykh, Serhij (2002). Cimmerian military affairs. In *Notes of the Shevchenko Scientific Society*. Vol. CCXLIV: Proceedings of the Archaeological Commission]. Lviv (in Ukrainian).

60. Мезенцева Г.Г. Древньоруське місто Родень. Княжа Гора. [Mezentseva, G.G. (1968). *The ancient Rus' city of Roden'. Prince Mountain*]. Kyiv: Kyiv University (in Ukrainian).

61. Мельникова А.А. Находки монет античного мира в Беларуси // Крыніцазнаўство і спецыяльныя гістарычныя дысцыпліны : навук. зб., вып. 4. [Melnikova A.A. (2008). Finds of coins of the ancient world in Belarus. In *Krinytsaznavsto i spetsialniya discipliny*: scientific collection, issue 4] Minsk: Belarusian State University (in Russian).

62. Місто людей кіммерійських. [*The City of the Cimmerians*]. URL: uk.wikipedia.org/wiki/Місто_людей_кімерійських (in Ukrainian).

63. Мови Європи. Календар на 2001 рік.
 (За матеріалами Лінгвістичного навчального музею Київського національного університету імені Тараса Шевченка) / уклад. К. Тищенко. [*The Languages of Europe. Calendar for 2001*. (Based on the materials of the Linguistic Educational Museum of the Taras Shevchenko National University of Kyiv) / ed. K. Tishchenko]. Kyiv: Calvary, 2001 (in Ukrainian).

64. Наливайко Степан. Таємниці розкриває санскрит. [Nalyvajko, Stepan (2000). *Sanskrit reveals Secrets*]. Kyiv: Publishing centre "Prosvita" (in Ukrainian).

65. Наливайко Степан. Давньоіндійські імена, назви, терміни: проекція на Україну: Довідник. [Nalyvajko, Stepan (2009). *Ancient Indian nomenclature, names, terms: projection onto Ukraine: A Reference Book*]. Kyiv (in Ukrainian).

66. Никитин А.Г. Генетические корни трипольцев: что мы узнали после восьми лет исследований. [Nikitin, A.G. (2014). *The Genetic roots of the Trypillians: what we learned after eight years of research*]. *In Stratum Plus*, № 2 (in Russian).

67. Нікітенко Ігор та ін. Мінералого-петрографічне дослідження Керносівського ідола // Науковий вісник Національного гірничого університету. [Nikitenko, Ihor et al. (2014). *Mineralogical and petrographic study of the Kernosivsky idol*]. In *The Scientific Bulletin of the National Mining University*, Dnipro (in Ukrainian).

68. Новосельцев Анатолий. Восточные источники о восточных славянах и Руси VI–IX вв. [Novoseltsev, Anatoly (1965). *Eastern sources on the Eastern Slavs and Rus' in the Sixth to the Ninth Centuries*]. Moscow (in Russian).

69. Новый энциклопедический словарь / под ред. К.К. Арсеньева. Т. 26. АО «Издательское дело бывшее Брокгауз-Ефрон» [*New encyclopedic dictionary / ed. K.K. Arsenyev, Vol. 26*]. Petrograd: JSC "Izdatelskoe delo byvshee Brokgauz-Efron", 1915 (in Russian).

70. Партицький Омелян. Скандинавщина в давній Руси. [Partytskyj, Omelyan (1887). *Scandinava in ancient Rus'*]. Lviv (in Ukrainian).

71. Петрук Володимир. Екзампай. Сакральний центр Великої Скіфії. [Petruk, Volodymyr (2006). *Exampai. The sacred center of Greater Scythia*]. Kyiv: Taras Shevchenko National University (in Ukrainian).

72. Петрук В. Велика Скіфія переможе. Стабільна територіальна модель Великої Скіфії-України : монографія. [Petruk, V. (2011). *Great Scythia will win. The Stable territorial model of Great Scythia-Ukraine: monograph*]. Kyiv: State Enterprise "Information and Analytical Agency" (in Ukrainian).

73. Повість врем'яних літ : літопис (за Іпатським списком) / пер. з давньоруської, післяслово, комент. В.В. Яременка. [*The Tale of the Bygone Years*: The Chronicle (According to the Ipatian list) / translation from the Old Rus' Language, afterword and commentary by V.V. Yaremenko] Kyiv: Radyanskyj Pysmennyk, 1990 (in Ukrainian).

74. Полное собрание русских летописей (ПСРЛ) / под ред. А. А. Шахматова. 2-е изд. Т.2. Ипатьевская летопись. [*The Complete Collection of Rus' Chronicles (CCRC)* / ed. A.A. Shakhmatov. 2nd ed. Vol. 2. *Ipatiev Chronicle*]. St. Petersburg: Typography of M.A. Alexandrov, 1908 (in Russian).

75. Прикраси гунів знайшли під Одесою. *Газета по-українськи*. 2010. 12 лютого. [(2010, February 12). Hun Jewellery Found Near Odesa. *Gazeta po-ukrainsky* (in Ukrainian).

76. Проєкт «Острів». [*The "Ostriv" (Island) Project*]. Kyiv: The Institute of Archaeology of the NASU (in Ukrainian).

77. Прокопенко Марія. Таємничий острів балтів. *День*. 2019. 26 квітня. [Prokopenko, Mariya (2019, April 26) The Secret island of the Baltic People]. *Den* (in Ukrainian).

78. Романюк Ніна. Слідами волинських амазонок. *Україна молода*. 1999. 08 вересня [Romanyuk, Nina. (1999, September 08) In the footsteps of the Volhynian Amazons]. *Ukraina moloda* (in Ukrainian).

79. Рыбаков Б. А. Город Кия // *Вопросы истории*, № 5. [Rybakov, B.A. (1980). The City of Kiev. *Some Questions of history*, № 5]. Moscow (in Russian).

80. Самойловський Ілля. Коли виник Київ (До 1100-річчя першої літописної згадки про Київ). Науково-інформаційний бюлетень Архівного управління УРСР, № 4. [Samoilovsky, Ilua (1961). When Kyiv arose (To the 1100th anniversary of the first chronicle mention of Kyiv). In *Scientific information bulletin of the Archival Department of the USSR*, № 4]. Kyiv (in Ukrainian).

81. Святовит. Енциклопедія українознавства: [в 11 т.] / Наукове товариство імені Шевченка; гол. ред. проф., д-р Володимир Кубійович. [Svyatovyt. In *Encyclopedia of Ukrainian Studies*: [in 11 volumes] / Shevchenko Scientific Society; Chief Editor Prof., Dr. Vladimir Kubiyovych]. Kyiv: Globe. 1955–2003 (in Ukrainian).

82. Сегеда Сергій. У пошуках предків. Антропологія та етнічна історія України. Київ: Наш час, 2012. [Segeda, Serhij (2012). *In search of the ancestors. The Anthropology and Ethnic History of Ukraine*]. Kyiv: Nash Chas (in Ukrainian).

83. Силенко Лев. Святе вчення. Силенкова віра в Дажбога. Київ: АТ «Обереги». [Sylenko, Lev (1995). *The Holy teaching. Sylenko's faith in Dazhboh*]. Kyiv: JSC "Oberehy" (in Ukrainian).

84. Симоненко О. В. Амага. Енциклопедія історії України. Т.1: А–В. [Symonenko, O.V. (2003). *Amaga*. In The Encyclopedia of the History of Ukraine. Vol.1: A-B]. Kyiv: Naukova Dumka (in Ukrainian).

85. Сказания Приска Панийского / пер. Дестуниса. [*The Tales of Priscus of Panium* / translated by Destunys]. St. Petersburg, 1860 (in Russian).

86. Скляренко Віктор. Русь і варяги : іст.-етимол. дослідж. [Sklyarenko, Victor (2006). *Rus' and the Vikings: Historical and Etymological research*]. Kyiv: Dovira (in Ukrainian).

87. Скорий С. А., Кислий О. Є. Курган. Надмогильний пагорб // Енциклопедія історії України. Т.5. [Skoryj S.A.& Kislyj O.E. *The Kurgan. The Grave Mpund*. In The Encyclopedia of the history of Ukraine, Vol. 5]. Kyiv: Naukova Dumka (in Ukrainian).

88. Словник-довідник з археології / під ред. Н.О. Гаврилюк. [*A Dictionary-reference book on Archaeology* / ed. N.O. Gavrylyuk]. Kyiv: Naukova Dumka, 1996 (in Ukrainian).

89. Страбон. География. Кн. VII / пер. Г. А. Стратановского. [*Strabo. Geography. Book. VII.* / Translated G.A. Stratanovsky] Moscow: Nauka, 1964 (in Russian).

90. Стрижак О.С. Про що розповідають географічні назви. [Stryzhak O.S. (1967). *What geographical names tell us about*]. Kyiv: Naukova Dumka (in Ukrainian).

91. Строительные материалы Харьковской области / сост. С.Р. Барская, И.Н. Ремизов, Д.Г. Сергеев и др. [*Construction materials of the Kharkiv Oblast* / comp. S.R. Barskaya, I.N. Remizov, D.G. Sergeev, etc]. Kyiv: "The Budivelnyk", 1965 (in Russian).

92. Таримські мумії. [*The Tarym Mummies*] URL: https://uk.wikipedia.org/wiki/Таримські_мумії (in Ukrainian).

93. Тищенко К. Мовні контакти: свідки формування українців. [Tyshchenko, K. (2006). *Linguistic contacts: witnesses to the formation of Ukrainians*]. Kyiv: Akvilon-Plus (in Ukrainian).

94. Тищенко К. Етномовна історія прадавньої України. [Tyshchenko, K. (2008). Ethnolinguistic history of ancient Ukraine]. Kyiv: Akvilon-Plus (in Ukrainian).

95. Тищенко Костянтин. Всеслов'янськість мови українців // *Український тиждень*. 2012. 28 вересня – 4 жовтня, № 39 (256). [Tishchenko, Kostyantin (2012, September 28 – October 4) The All-Slavonic language of Ukrainians. In Ukrainskyj Tyzhden, № 39 (256) (in Ukrainian).

96. Універсали Богдана Хмельницького. [*The Universals of Bohdan Khmelnytsky*]. Kyiv: Publishing House "Alternatyva", 1998 (in Ukrainian).

97. Фараон Хоремхеб. Рельеф из саккарской гробницы Хоремхеба. [*Pharaoh Horemheb. Relief from the Sakkar tomb of Horemheb*]. The Netherlands: Leiden Museum.

98. Франко І.Я. Сотворення світу в світлі науки. [Franko, I.Ya. (1969). *The creation of the world in the light of science*]. New York: Oriana (in≈Ukrainian).

99. Черняков І.Т. «Дикий Сад», Гомер, Геродот, Троя, ахейці та кіммерійці (коментар одного археологічного відкриття в Україні). // Праці Центру пам'яткознавства. 2010. Вип. 17. [Chernyakov I.T. (2010). The "Wild Garden", Homer, Herodotus, Troy, Achaeans and Cimmerians (a commentary on an archaeological discovery in Ukraine). In *Proceedings of the Centre for Monument Studies*. Issue 17 (in Ukrainian).

100. Чорний Г.П. Нариси з історії конструкторського бюро. [Chornyi, G.P. (2011). *Essays on the history of the design bureau*]. Kyiv: Chetverta Khvylya (in Ukrainian).

101. Чорний Г. Де розташовувався дніпровський Самбатас X століття. *Українознавство*. 2013. №1 (46). С. 230–233. [Chornyi G.P. (2013). Where was the Dnipro Sambatas of the tenth century. *Ukrainoznavstvo*, 1 (46), 230–233]. Kyiv (in Ukrainian).

102. Чорний Георгій. Стародавня Україна і ранній Київ. [Chornyi, Georgii (2016). *Ancient Ukraine and Early Kyiv*]. London: Glagoslav Publications (in Ukrainian).

103. Чорний Георгій. Київ досвітній. [Chornyi, Georgii (2014). *Kyiv at Dawn*]. Kyiv: Hamazyn (in Ukrainian).

104. Шевченко Тарас. Кавказ. [Shevchenko Taras. *Caucasus*].

105. Шевченко Тарас. Сон (Комедія). [Shevchenko Taras. *The Vision* (A Comedy)].

106. Яворницький Дмитро. Історія запорозьких козаків: у 3 т. [Yavornytskyj, Dmitro (1990). *The History of the Zaporozhian Cossacks: in 3 volumes*] Kyiv: Naukova Dumka (in Ukrainian).

English and other Language Sources

107. Annales Bertiniani. Monumenta Germaniae historica / Ed. G.H. Pertz. Hannoverae: Bibliopolii Alvici Hahniani, 1826. Vol. 1.

108. Anthony, D.W. (2007). *The Horse, the Wheel, and Language: How Bronze-Age Riders from the Eurasian Steppe Shaped the Modern World*, Princeton University Press, Princeton; Oxford.

109. Appendix: Baltic Swadesh list. URL: http://en.wiktionary.org/wiki/Appendix:Baltic_Swadesh_lists

110. Appendix: Ukrainian Swadesh list. URL: http://en.wiktionary.org/wiki/Appendix:Ukrainian_Swadesh_lists

111. Basham, A.L. (2000). *The Wonder That Was India. 3rd revised edition.* Sidgwick & Jackson, New Delhi.

112. Cavalli-Sforza, L.L. et al. (1994). *The History and Geography of Human Genes*. Princeton University Press, Princeton.

113. Chunxiang, Li et al. (2010). Evidence that a West-East admixed population lived in the Tarim Basin as early as the early Bronze Age. *BMC Biology*, 8:15.

114. Claudii, Ptolemaei (1843). *Geographia*. Edidit Carolus Fridericus Augustus Nobbe. Lipsiae (in Latin).

115. Constantine, Porphyrogenetus. *De administrando imperio*.

116. Collins, N. (2018). Wars and clan structure may explain a strange biological event 7,000 years ago, Stanford researchers find. *Stanford News Service*, May 30.

117. Distribution of European mitochondrial DNA (mtDNA) haplogroups by region in percentage URL: http://eupedia/europe/european_mtdna_haplogroups_frequency

118. Eusebius, Pamphilus. *Chronicon*

119. France. *A Phaidon Cultural Guide*. Prentice-Hall, 1985, New Jersey.

120. Genetic data show mainly men migrated from the Pontic Steppe to Europe 5,000 years ago. *Science Daily*, 21 February 2017, Uppsala Universitet.

121. Gibons, A. (2000) Europeans Trace Ancestry To Palaeolithic People. *Science*, November. Vol. 290. No. 5494.

122. Glosbe – багатомовний онлайн-словник (multilingual online dictionary)

123. Gray, R. et al. (2011). Language evolution and human history: what a difference a date makes. *Philosophical Translations the Royal Society*, vol. 366.

124. Haak, W. et al. (2015). Massive Migration from the Steppe Was a Source for Indo-European Languages in Europe. *Nature*, vol. 522, no 7555, p. 207–211.

125. Haak, W. et al. (2008, November). Ancient DNA, Strontium isotopes, and osteological analyses shed light on social and kinship organization of the Later Stone Age. *Proceedings of the National Academy of Sciences of the United States of America*, vol. 105, no. 47.

126. Haber, M. et al. (2012). Afghanistan's Ethnic Groups Share a Y-Chromosomal Heritage Structured by Historical Events. *J. PLoS One*, vol. 7 (13).

127. Justini in historias Trogi Pompeii epitomarum. Lubecae; Lipsiae : Widemeyerus, 1702.

128. Karmin, M. et al. (2015, March). A resent bottleneck of Y chromosome diversity coincides with a global change in culture. *Genome Research*, 25 (4).

129. Keyser, C. et al. (2009, June). Ancient DNA provides new insights into the history of South Siberian Kurgan people. *Human Genetics*.

130. Khan, R. (2012, October 31). R1a1a conquers the world...in a few pulses. *Gene Expression*.

131. Kharkov, V.N. et al. (2004). Gene Pool Structure of Eastern Ukrainians as Inferred from the Y-Chromosome Haplogroups. *Russian Journal of Genetics*, vol. 40.

132. Loulan beauty closeup.jpg

133. McCrum, Robert. Cran, William. Mc Neil, Robert. *The Story of English*. Viking, 1986. New York.

134. Mendez, F.L. et al. (2013, March 7). An African American Paternal Lineage Adds an Extremely Ancient Root to the Human Y-Chromosome Phylogenetic Tree. *Am. J. Genet*, vol. 92 (3).

135. Mitochondrial Eve. URL: http://en.wikipedia.org/wiki/Mitochondrial_Eve

136. Parpola, A.(1995). The problem of the Aryans and the Soma: textual-linguistic and archaeological evidence. The Indo-Aryans of Ancient South Asia: Language, Material Culture and Ethnicity. Berlin – New York: Walter de Gruyter.

137. Passarino, G. et al. (2001). The 49a, f haplotype 11 is a new marker of the EU19 lineage that traces migrations from northern regions of the Black Sea. *Human Immunology*, vol. 62, p. 922–932.

138. Ptolemeo Cl. La Geografia di Claudio Ptolemeo Alessandrino. Venetia: Per Gioan Baptista Pedrezano, 1548 (in Italian).

139. Ptolemy's Geography. Book 3, chapter 5, § 25.

140. Rebala, K. et al. (2007). Y-STR variation among Slavs: evidence for the Slavic homeland in the middle Dnieper basin. *Journal of Human Genetics*, vol. 52, p. 406–414.

141. Reich D. (2018, March). Ancient DNA Suggests Steppe Migrations Spread Indo-European Languages. *Proceedings of the American Philosophical Society*, vol. 162, no.1.

142. The Rig Veda / trans. by R.T.H. Griffith. Book 2. Himn XXXVIII. Savitar, 1896.

143. Schenker, A.M. (1995). The Dawn of Slavic: An Introduction to Slavic Philology. *Yale University Press*, New Haven – London.

144. Scielstad, M.T. et al. (1998, November). Genetic evidence for a higher female migration rate in humans. *Nature Genetics*.

145. Semino, O. et al. (2000). The Genetic Legacy of Palaeolithic Homo sapiens sapiens in Extant Europeans: A Y-Chromosome Perspective. *Science*, vol. 98.

146. Shopov, Y. et al. (2010, September). Migrations caused by catastrophic flooding of the Black Sea during the Holocene. *Geologica Balcanica*, vol. 39.

147. Swadesh, M. (1952). Lexicostatistic Dating of Prehistoric Ethnic Contacts. *Proc. Am. Philos. Soc.*, vol. 96, p.p. 452–463.

148. Swadesh, M. (1955).Towards Greater Accuracy in Lexicostatistic Dating. *International Journal of American Linguist*, vol. XXI, p.p. 121–137.

149. Sykes, Bryan. *The Seven Daughters of Eve*. Transworld Publishers Ltd, 2001 London.

150. The Genomic Formation of South and Central Asia. URL: https://www.biorxiv.org/content/biorxiv/early/2018/03/31/292581.full.pdf

151. Torroni, A. et al. (1998, May). mtDNA analysis reveals a major late Paleolithic population expansion from south-western to north-eastern Europe. *American Journal of Human Genetic*, vol. 62 (5).

152. Willis, K. and Whittaker, R. (2000, February). The Refugial Debate. *Science*, vol. 287.

153. Y-DNA haplogroups in populations of Europe. URL: http://en.wikipedia.org/wiki/Y-DNA_haplogroups_in_populations_of_Europe

www.ingramcontent.com/pod-product-compliance
Lightning Source LLC
Chambersburg PA
CBHW070419010526
44118CB00014B/1820